I0795913

IMAGES
of America

NORTHFIELD

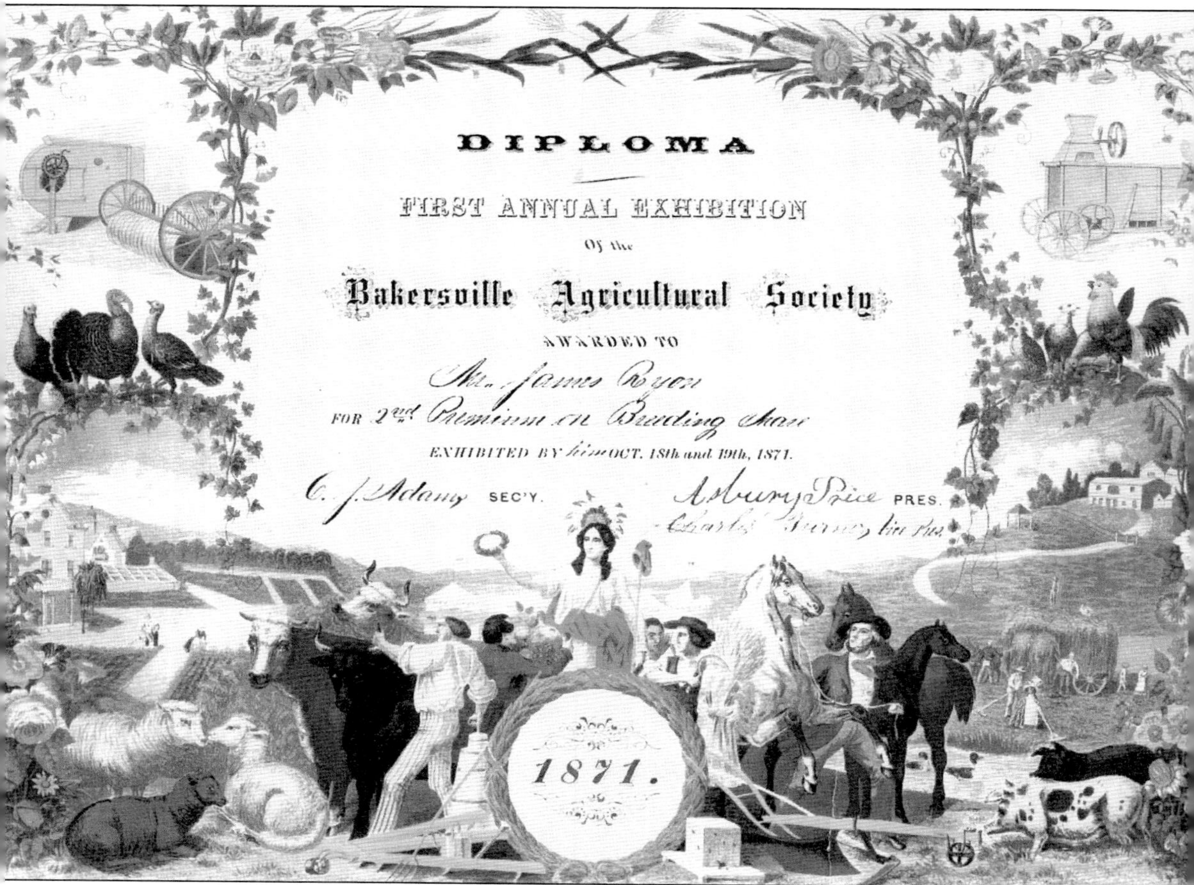

This certificate was awarded to James Ryon for "2nd Premium on Breeding Mare Exhibited by Him, October 18th and 19th, 1871" at the first annual exhibition of the Bakersville Agricultural Society. It is signed by C. J. Adams, secretary; Asbury Price, president; and Charles Turner, vice president. Asbury Price's granddaughter Lizzie Price, Northfield's first librarian, wrote that she remembered seeing Black Luce (or Lucy) at one of the Bakersville agricultural fairs. Black Luce, who was the last slave in Atlantic County, lived in Leedsville (now Linwood) and is said to have lived to be more than 100 years old.

IMAGES
of America

NORTHFIELD

Northfield Cultural Committee and Northfield Historical Society

ARCADIA
PUBLISHING

ISBN 978-0-7385-3657-6

Published by Arcadia Publishing
Charleston, South Carolina

Printed in the United States of America

Library of Congress Control Number: 2004107290

For all general information, please contact Arcadia Publishing:
Telephone 843-853-2070
Fax 843-853-0044
E-mail sales@arcadiapublishing.com
For customer service and orders:
Toll-Free 1-888-313-2665

Visit us on the Internet at www.arcadiapublishing.com

Contents

ACKNOWLEDGMENTS

We would like to express our sincere appreciation to the members of the Northfield Cultural Committee and the Northfield Historical Society, especially Tery Lever and Carol Patrick, for their tireless efforts to compile and research the photographs and information used in this publication. Thanks go to Roy Clark and Christopher Clark for contributing their expertise in processing the images, to Marge Milone for her typing efforts, and to all those who generously shared their memories, anecdotes, and photographs as we assembled the material used in this book. We especially thank Joyce Pullan for envisioning and then launching this project.

Information and photographs used in this publication came from the archives of the Northfield Museum and Casto House, family records and albums, newspapers and other published resources, and personal recollections of current and former residents. Where possible, data have been verified, but a great deal of the information has been handed down through family tradition, and in some instances documentation has been difficult to find. We have done our best to present an accurate and interesting history of Northfield. If any readers have additional information, we hope that they will contact us.

INTRODUCTION

Before Northfield, there was Bakersville. Before Bakersville, there was a loose settlement of farmers' and sea captains' homes built along the old Native American trail now known as Shore Road. Some of the names of the early settlers were Adams, Baker, Ireland, Lake, Price, Risley, Somers, Steelman, and Tilton—family names that are familiar to us even today.

Bakersville was named after Judge Daniel Baker, who, in turn, had named Atlantic County when an act was passed on February 7, 1837, creating a new county from Gloucester County. Gloucester County originally extended from the Delaware River to the Atlantic Ocean, encompassing what are currently Atlantic, Camden, and Gloucester Counties. Daniel Baker was the owner of one of the area's largest shipyards, which was located next to Warren Ryon's home, on the east side of Shore Road, between Mill Road and the first post office. From 1830 to 1880, shipbuilding and shipping flourished in Bakersville. A ditch large enough to accommodate two-masted oceangoing schooners went from Shore Road to a stream that enters the bay by Hackney's Boat Yard. One chief export was cordwood, which was shipped to New York. The cords of wood were stacked high from the present location of Surrey Avenue to Mill Road and an equal distance to the east. The wives of the sea captains watched for the return of their husbands' ships from the captain's watch on the housetop or the widow's walk on the second story of many Shore Road homes.

A general store, or "great store," stood at the corner of Mill and Shore Roads. It was founded in the 1820s by a New England peddler named Pardon Ryon. Wares were brought here from New York and Philadelphia, mainly by ship. The inland people bartered and traded for the goods brought from up and down the East Coast with herbs that their parents and grandparents had learned about from the Native Americans. From that corner one could look west up gravel-covered Tub Street (now the eastern section of Tilton Road), supposedly named because the women would take their washtubs from their front porches and walk west to the pumps at the tracks to do their wash.

A blacksmith shop and a mill were other signs of a flourishing town. The blacksmith shop, run by William Boice, was on Shore Road. The local mill, not surprisingly, was on Mill Road, at the pumping station by the tracks. Farmers who raised grain took it to the mill to be ground, and the miller took a "toll" of grain (described as about "two peck size"), which he could sell.

In 1817, the residents of Bakersville built the first public school, a brick building on the northwest corner of Tilton and Zion Roads, on about a quarter-acre of land donated by James Tilton. The teacher, Simon Lake, was paid according to the number of children attending the one-room schoolhouse. For example, one parent, Asbury Price, paid Lake $1.36 to cover fuel and tuition for his child for a period of three months. Later, Emaline D. Huntley of Connecticut was hired for $10 a month; she was expected to board with the parents of her students. Because shipping was so important to Bakersville, the children's courses included science and navigation. This first school was probably also the first church. It was called "Old Brick"—more properly, the Union Church and School House—and was used for public meetings as well as religious services. An 1858 record of Sunday school attendance included the names Daniel L. Adams, Japhet Adams, Jane Adams, Baker Doughty, Hester A. Doughty, Samuel B. Jerman, and Eliza Jerman. Later, in 1872, another school—a two-story wooden structure—was built on Mill Road, on land donated by Captain John Price. In its belfry was a bell that was rung to call the students to class.

On March 21, 1905, Bakersville was incorporated as Northfield, supposedly named because it was the "north field of the Ireland estate." Our book, in pictures and words, is presented for the 100th birthday of our city of Northfield, March 21, 2005.

And so the story continues. . . .

One
We, the People

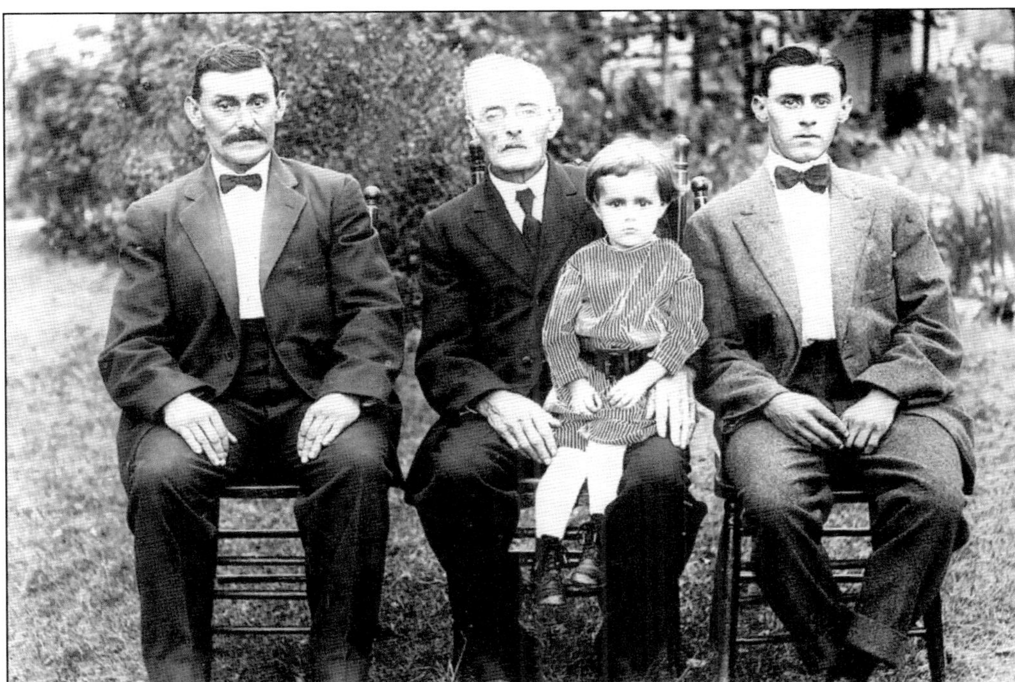

This photograph of four generations of the Risley family was taken on Edward P. Risley's 67th birthday, September 7, 1913. Pictured here are, from left to right, Allen Stout Risley, Edward P. Risley, Ernest Risley Jr., and Ernest Risley Sr.

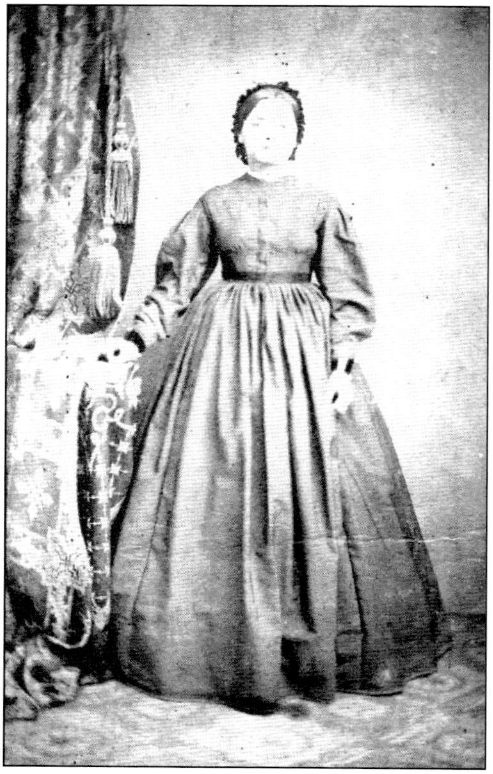

Two early residents of Bakersville were Margaret Risley and Daniel Risley.

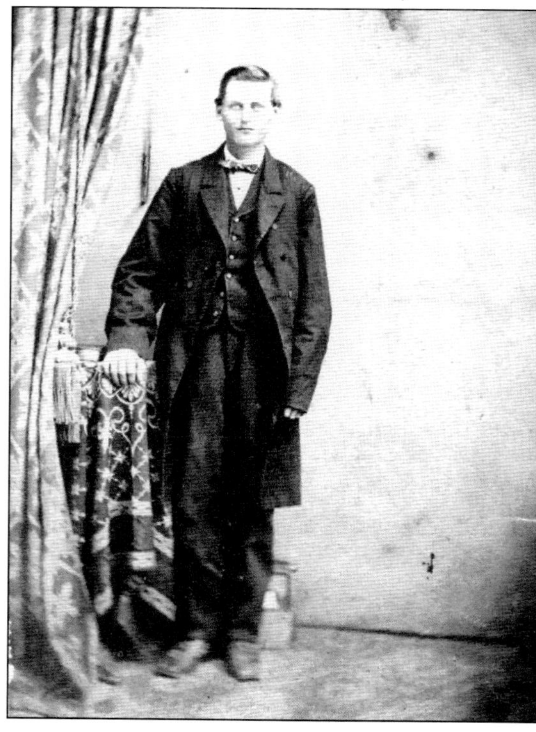

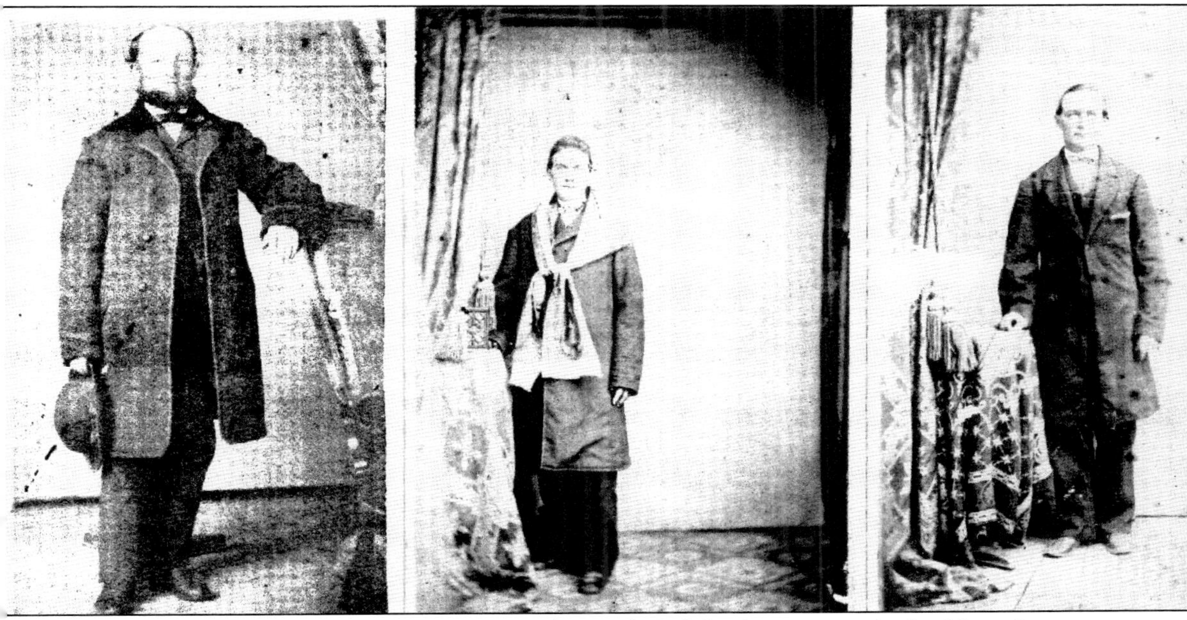

Bakersville grew into a diverse community that included ship's captains, shipbuilders, doctors, farmers, storekeepers, blacksmiths, and millers, among others. These photographs were found in old family files by Charles Sheppard, whose family has resided here for generations. Shown in the photographs above are, from left to right, Capt. Griffiths Ireland, William J. Clark, and Richard Somers.

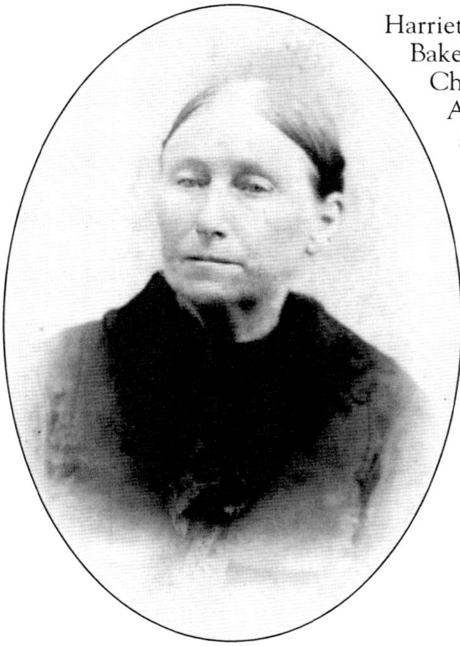

Harriet Matthews Lake Barrett (1813–1883) lived in Bakersville during the mid-1800s. With her first husband, Christopher Lake (1819–1846), she had two children. After his death, in 1852, she married Lewis Barrett, a sea captain and lay preacher. Their son Lewis H. Barrett was born in Bakersville, attended the one-room school there, and lived in the South Jersey area most of his life.

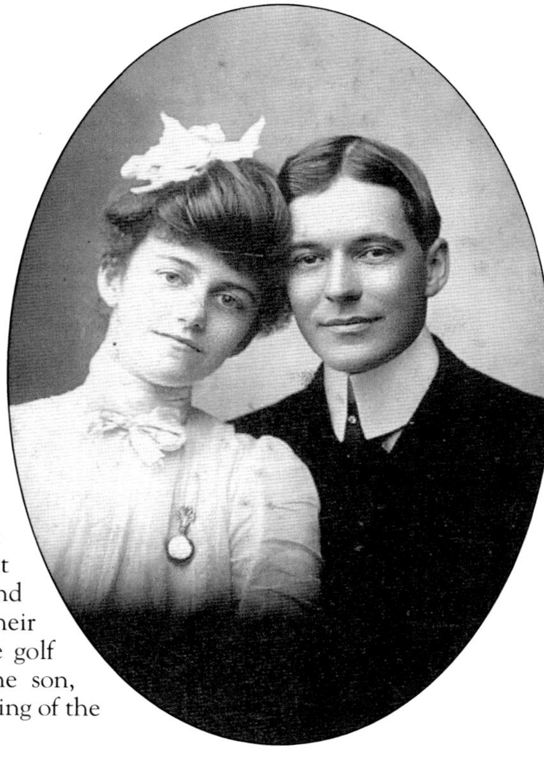

This photograph of Josephine and John Phineas "Phin" Wilson was taken in 1902. Wilson was Northfield's fourth police chief and brother-in-law to Mayor Eugene Swilkey. The family homestead at 26 East Oakcrest Avenue backed up to East Vernon Avenue, which was open and unfenced. The Wilson children, and later their grandchildren, would walk through to the golf links at the Linwood Country Club. One son, Joseph, was killed in the explosion and sinking of the yacht *Crystal*. (Courtesy of Pat Stephanik.)

Lewis Somers and Mary Ella Price, shown in this c. 1939 photograph, are descendants of some of the earliest settlers in this region. Price was a teacher in Bakersville for three years. For many years Somers was in the Coast Guard at the Great Egg Harbor Life Saving Station, in Longport. He later became a postman and, as the first rural free delivery mailman along the shore, delivered mail by horse and buggy as far as Scullville. (Courtesy of Linwood Historical Society.)

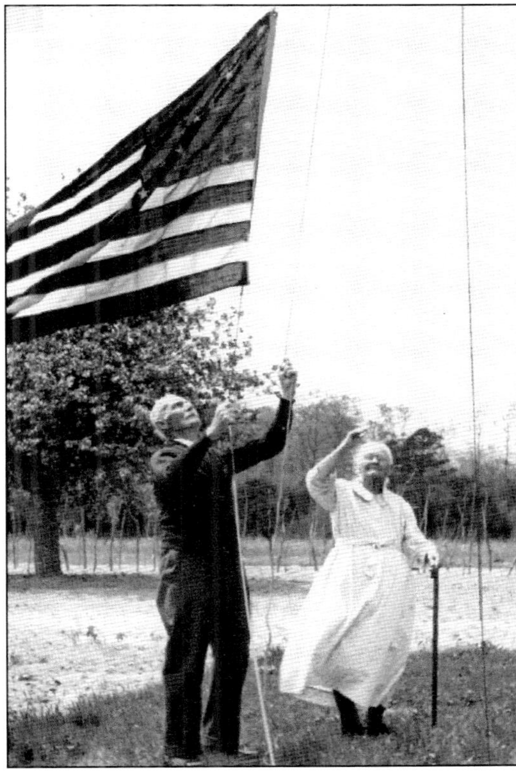

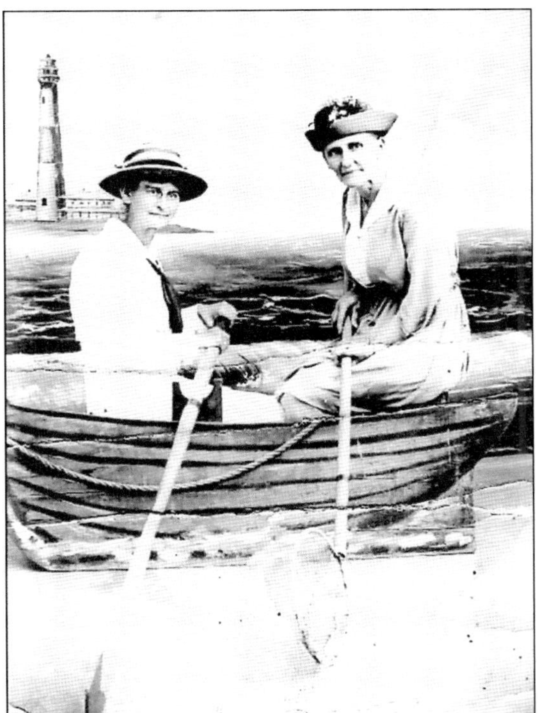

Lizzie Price (left) and Ina Smith posed for this photograph cn September 4, 1917.

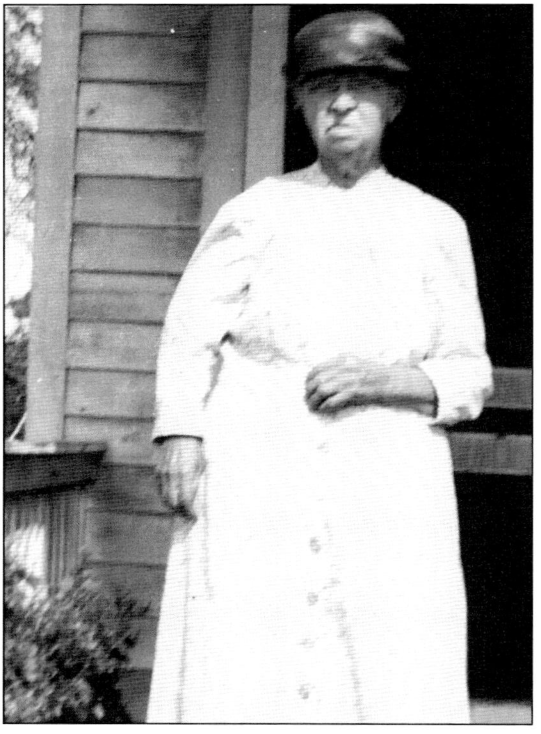

Carrie Price, whose family was one of the first to settle in Northfield, had a long career as a practical nurse. She was the sister of Henry, J. Martin, Susie, Eva, and Katie, and a first cousin to Lizzie Price. Her parents were Eliza Adams and J. Martin Price; her father was born in 1844 in Bakersville and lived here his entire life. According to his obituary, "His politics were Democratic, never voting for any other party during his life, of which he often boasted."

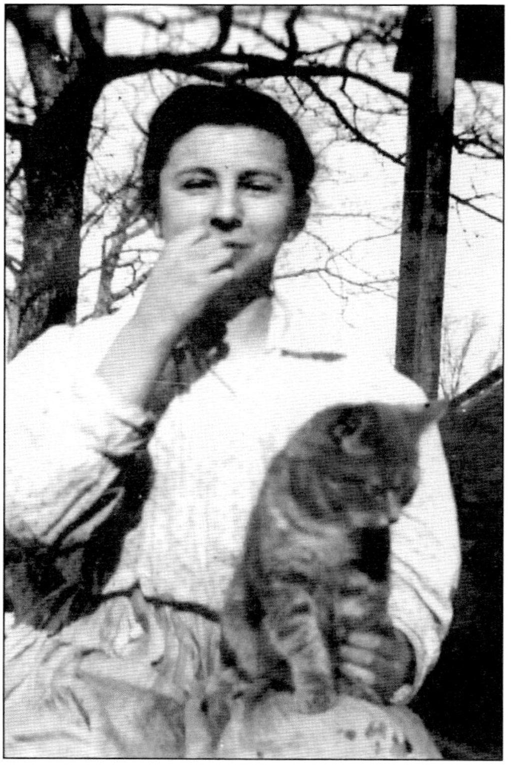

This photograph, identified as "Louisa and Stokes," is probably of Louisa Somers Stokes, wife of William Blood Stokes, the seventh mayor (1928–1929) of Northfield. The photograph was in an album donated to the museum by the estate of Sybilla Probst. Sybilla Probst grew up in Northfield and was the first curator of the Northfield Museum.

Lewis Lake is shown chopping wood next to his home, on West Mill Road, near the Mazza farm. Behind his home was an old barn, which he converted into a cockfighting ring, complete with spectator seats. After Birch Grove Park was established, Lake could always be found fishing or watching the ball games there. He was also known for his great knowledge of Atlantic County.

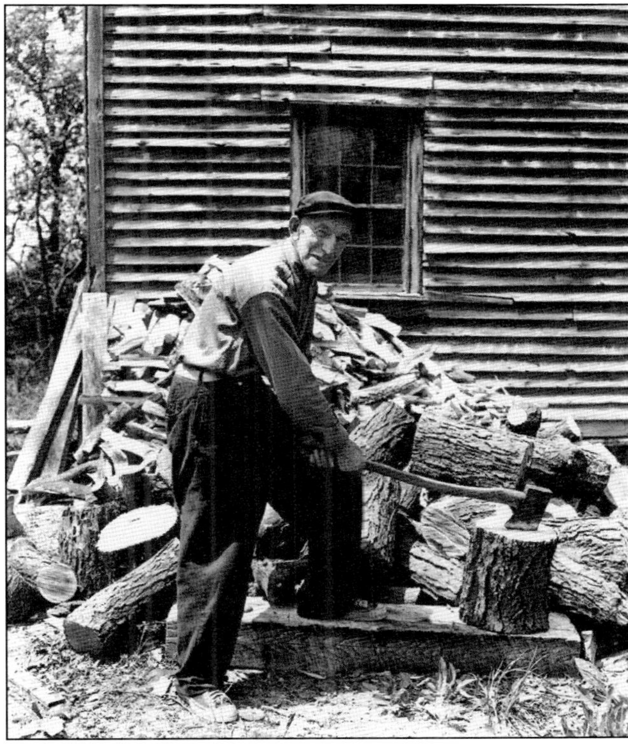

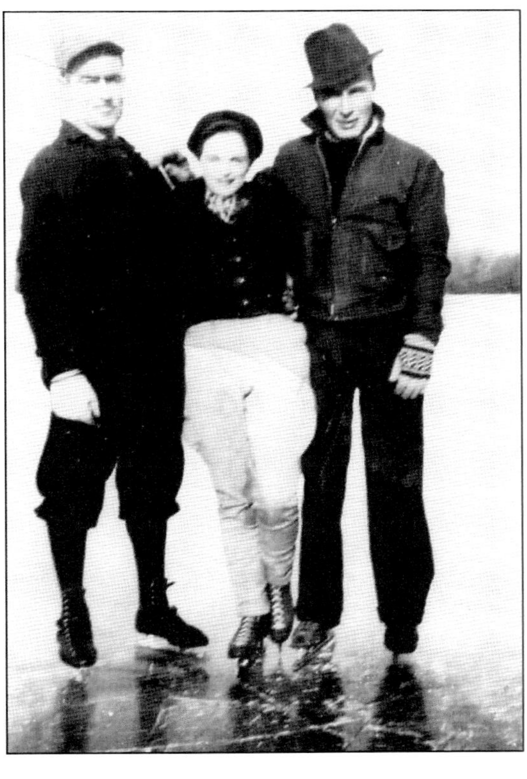

Bud Traynor (left), Dorothy Gannon Schmidt, and Capt. T. F. Schmidt pause for a moment while skating sometime during the 1940s. Both Traynor and T. F. Schmidt had admirable careers with the New Jersey State Police.

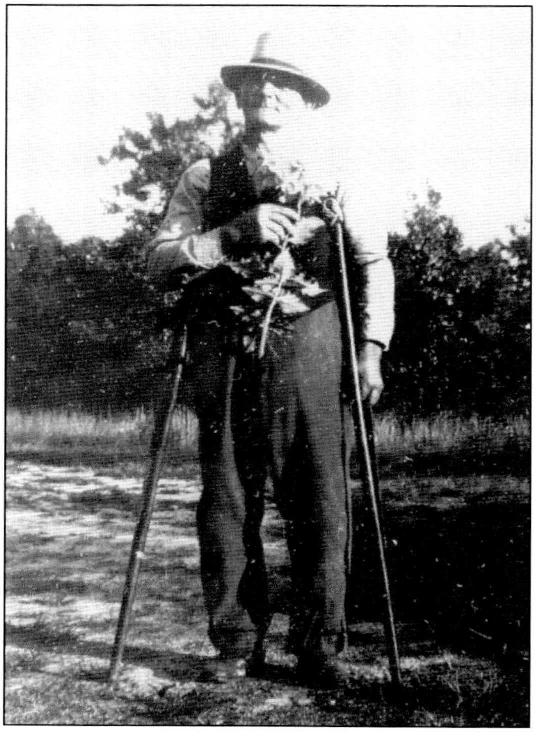

Peter W. Sutton, shown here in 1939, and his family were Northfield residents for many years. They lived on Shore Road and then on Cedarbridge Road. Sutton worked on the farm owned by Harry Collins, located just past Dolphin Avenue, and also raised pigeons to sell to Atlantic City hotels. He later became superintendent of Zion Cemetery Association. He and Lovinia Simpkins married in 1900; their children were Arthur, Harry, Sara (Lever), James, twins Horace and Louisa (Gaskill), and Anna (Pflegher).

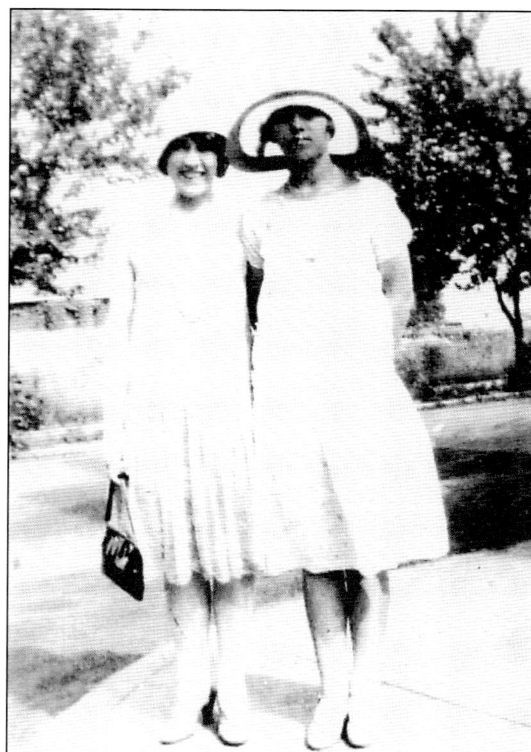

This photograph of Jennie Higbee (left) and Sara Sutton dates from c. 1930. In 1935, Sara Sutton married W. Everett "Bud" Lever, Northfield's chief of police.

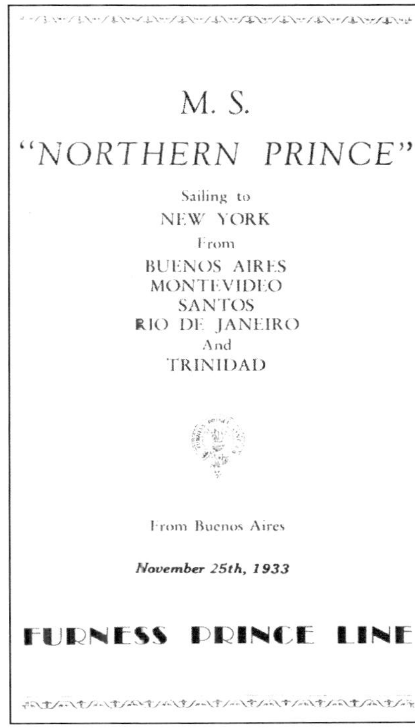

Victor Albert Plumbo and his wife, Margaret Santoro, emigrated separately from Italy, met and married in the United States, and eventually settled in Northfield Plaza. Their four sons and three daughters were born in the United States or in South America. The passenger brochure is from a 1933 voyage from Rio de Janeiro to New York. The photograph below, taken on that trip, shows Margaret Plumbo (left), with, from left to right, Helen, Mary, Victor, Robert, and Phyllis. Victor Plumbo, who gained a worldwide reputation as a specialty glass engineer, became chairman of the board of General Glass Equipment Company (GGEC) and General Glass International and, in 1954, purchased Friedrich & Dimmock. Three sons followed him into the industry. Louis Plumbo, who served in U.S. Air Force Military Intelligence during World War II, became chief executive officer of GGEC after his father's death. Robert Plumbo, a navy veteran of World War II, earned a bachelor of science degree in ceramic engineering and was considered a "glass genius." (Courtesy of the Plumbo family.)

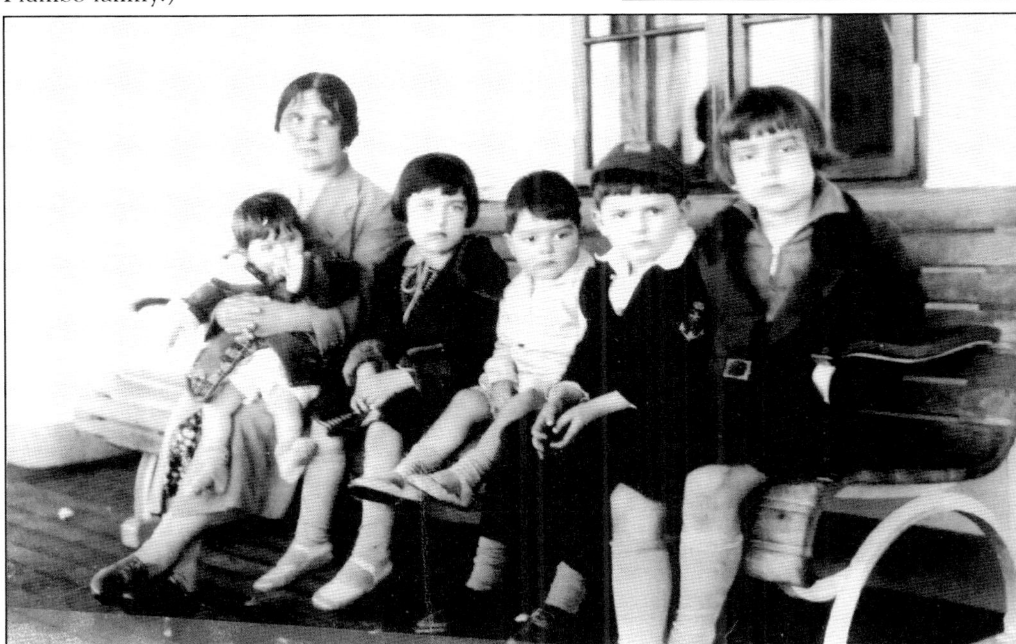

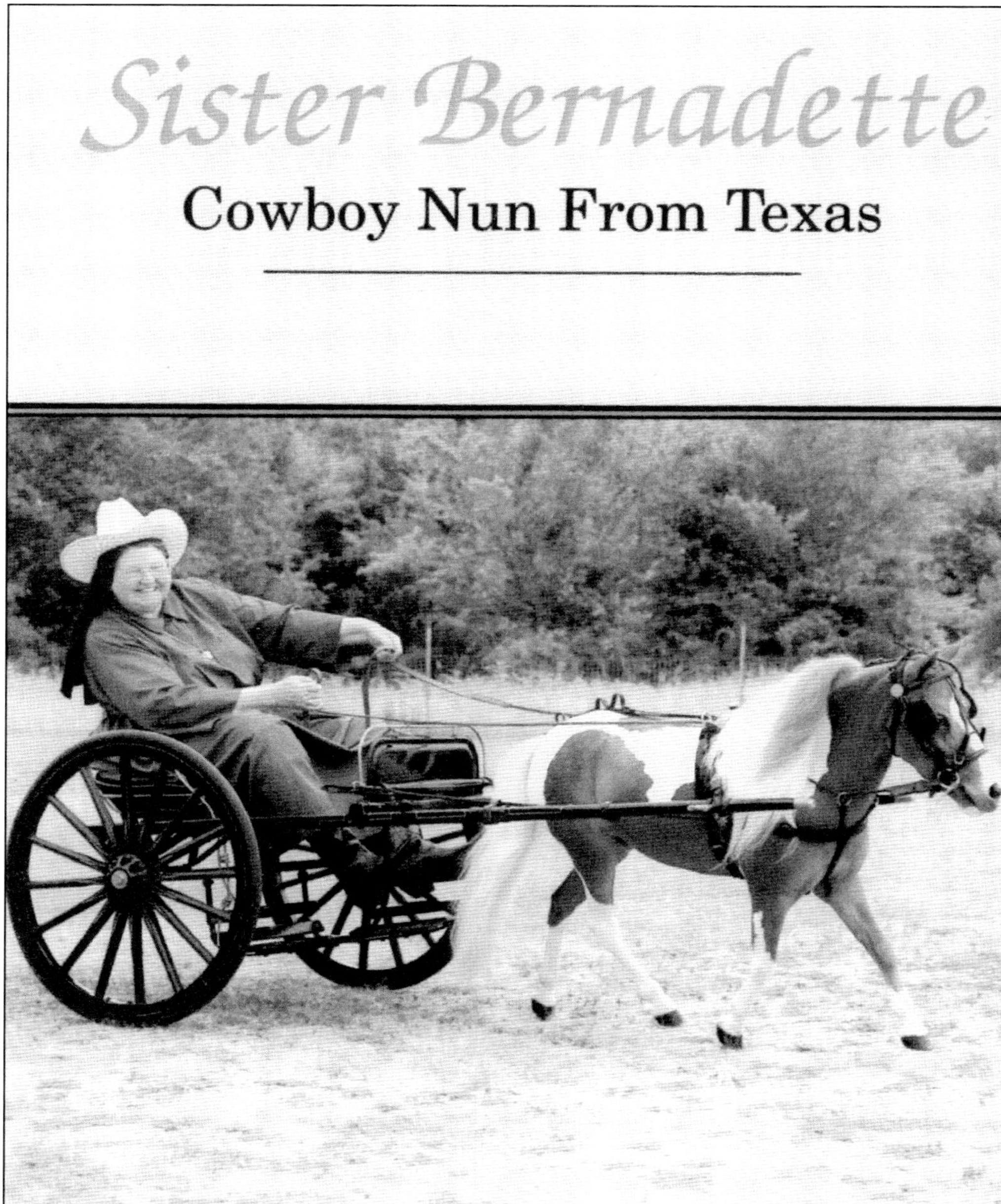

Rev. Mother Mary Bernadette, born Nina Henriette Muller on February 14, 1918, was the daughter of George Muller, Northfield city clerk from 1921 to 1960, and Nina Landis Muller. She attended Northfield schools and St. Peter's School in Pleasantville. She entered the Franciscan Order community in 1934 and later became a Poor Clare Sister, entering the cloistered community in 1951. She became famous as the "Cowboy Nun From Texas" and the "First Lady of the American Miniature Horse Industry." An artist and musician, she died in 1992. (*Sister Bernadette: Cowboy Nun From Texas* book cover permission granted by Centerpoint Press, www.centerpointpress.com, and Elizabeth Harper Neeld, Ph.D., www.elizabeth harperneeld.com.)

Coxswain Fred W. Gant enlisted in the submarine service in January 1943 and spent about 18 months in the Pacific theater of war. He was one of the first Northfield Museum volunteers. His father, Harry Gant, held life membership in the Northfield Volunteer Fire Company and served in Northfield's police department for 25 years.

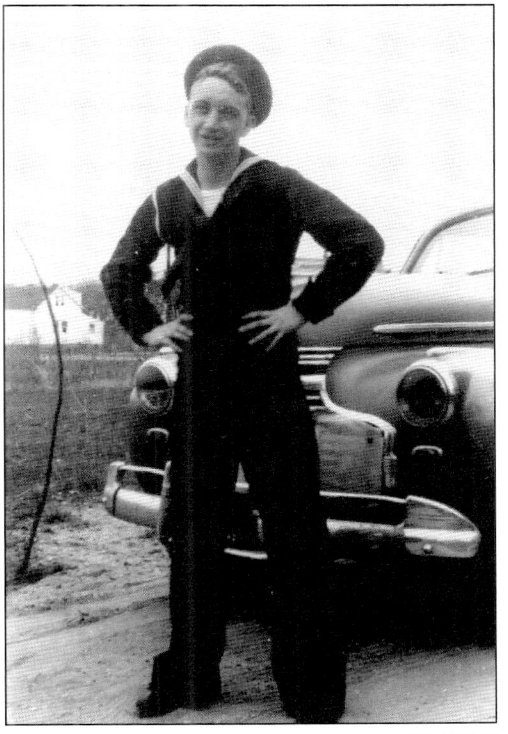

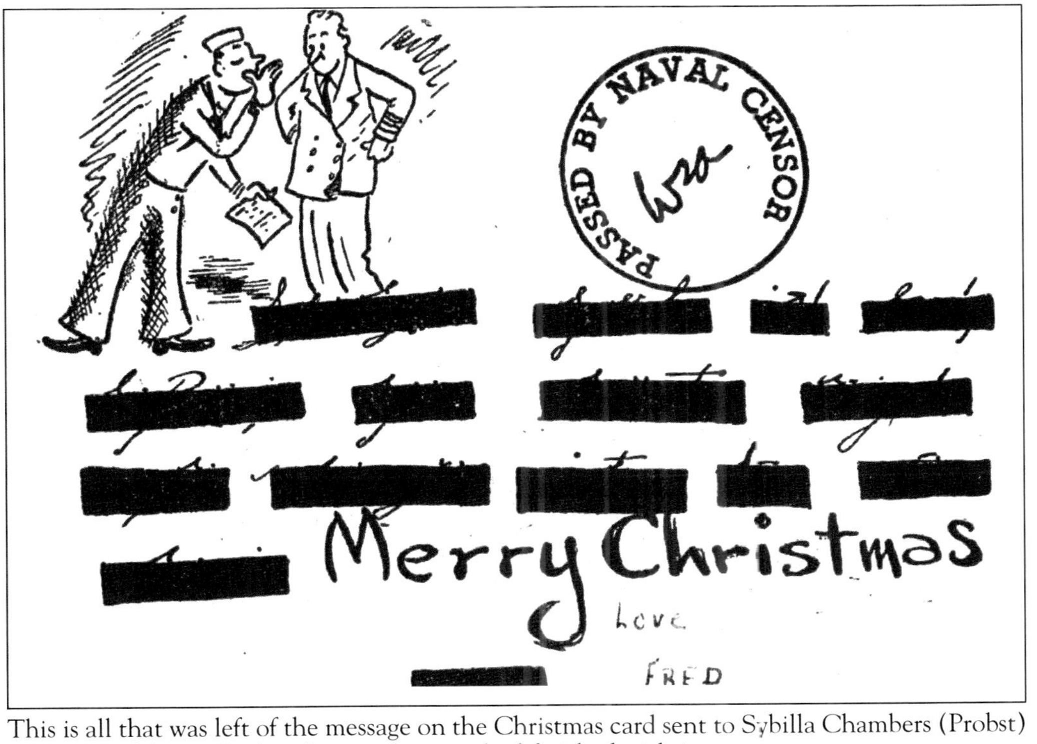

This is all that was left of the message on the Christmas card sent to Sybilla Chambers (Probst) during World War II after the naval censor had finished with it.

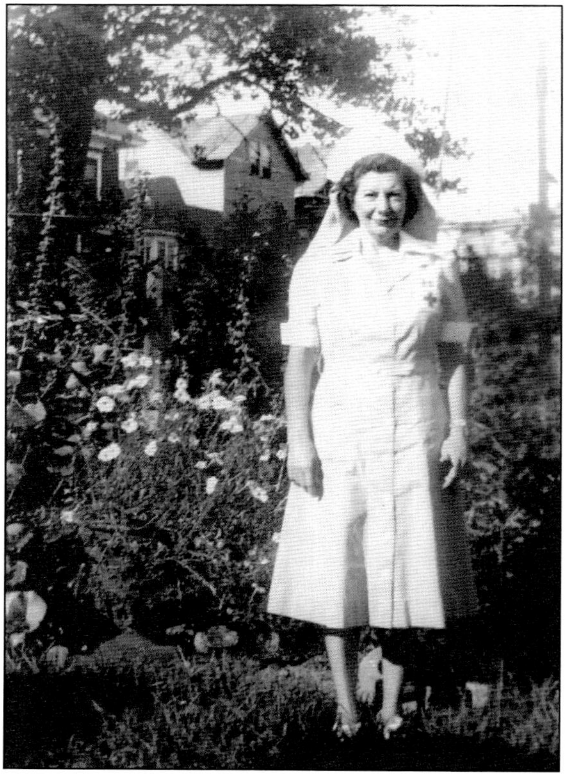

Margaret C. Hunt, a Northfield resident, worked at the Red Cross Center in Atlantic City. In this World War II–era photograph, she is shown in her Red Cross nurse's uniform.

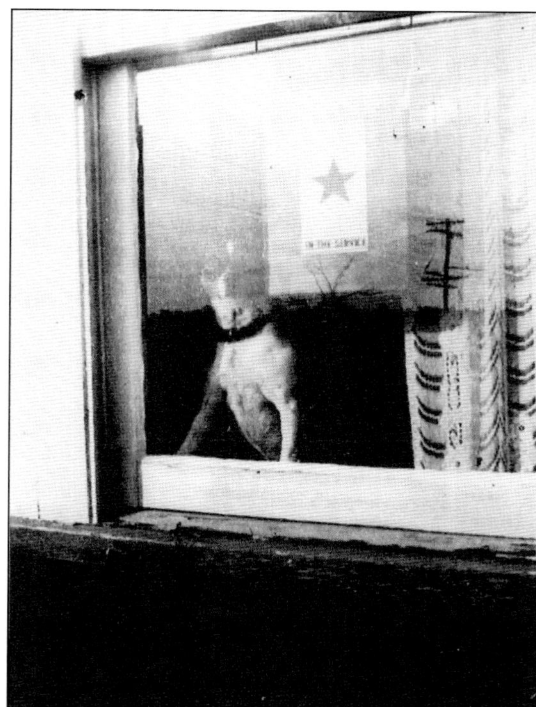

The Blue Star Flag, also known as the "Service Flag," was seen in many windows during World War II. Each blue star represented a service member on active duty. Here, Lucky looks longingly for her master, William D. Laughlin, who saw action on the USS *Rendova* in the South Pacific. After his discharge from the navy, he worked at Pleasantville Plumbing Supply for the next 35 years and then at the County Maintenance Building in Northfield.

Daniel Eugene "Gene" Quill, a member of the Mill Road School class of 1942, was voted best musician in Pleasantville High School's class of 1946. During his career, he played alto saxophone and clarinet with many famous bands. In its formative years, his orchestra was often heard at canteen dances, held at the Northfield Recreation Lodge. Orchestra members included Wally Roberts, Ronnie and Larry Palmisano, Bob Hoffman, Paul Porter, Fred Spangler, George Carey, Gene Boney, Phil Maxwell, and Jane Balestrieri (on piano).

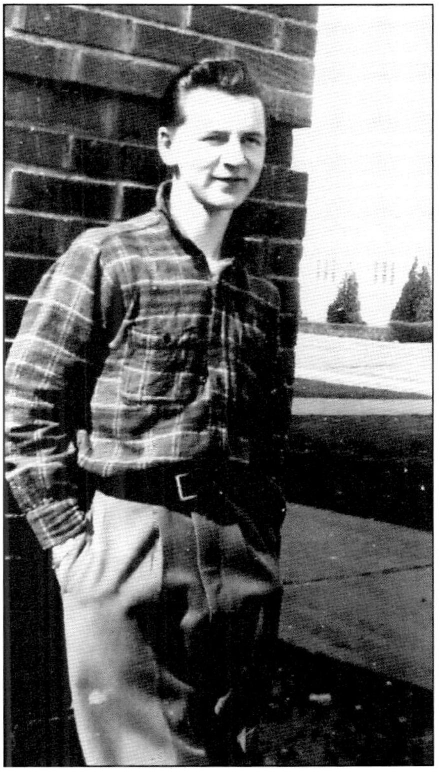

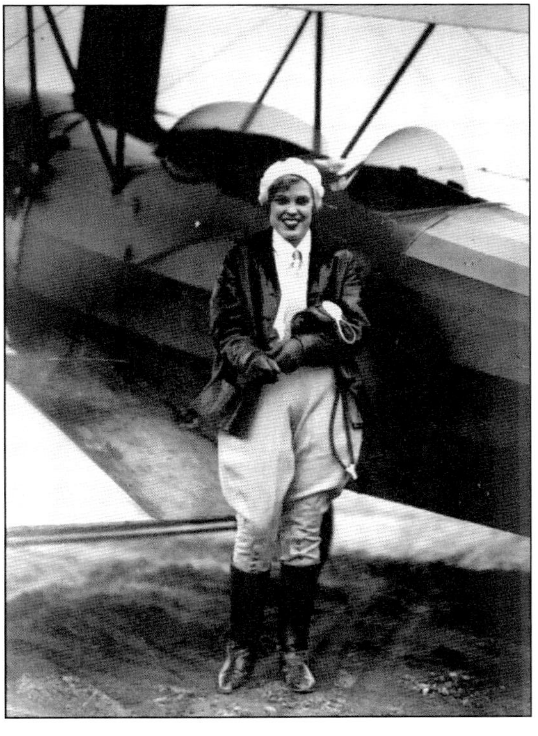

Ida Mae Hampton earned her pilot's license at Atlantic City's Bader Field at age 18 and was the first woman in South Jersey to earn her wings. At age 20, in September 1932, she was invited to copilot the ill-fated "American Nurse" nonstop flight to Rome, but she declined the invitation. During World War II, while living with her husband, William Wassell, in Philadelphia, she flew courier service between Philadelphia and Washington, D.C., for the Civil Air Patrol.

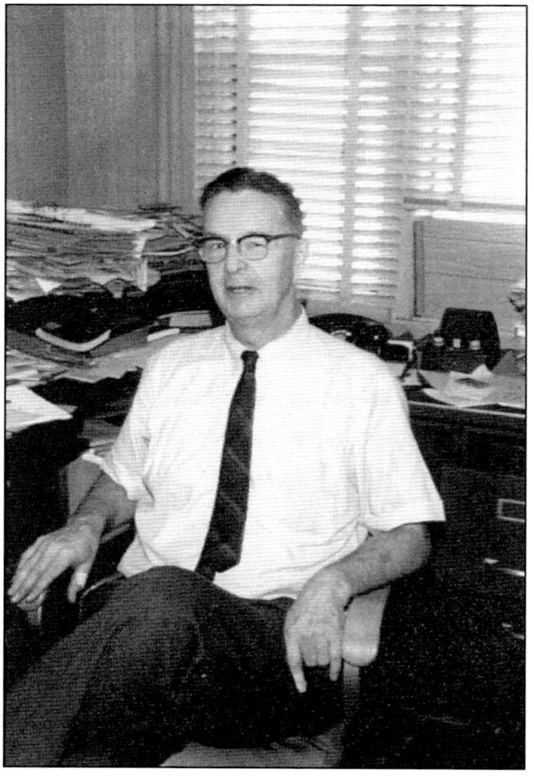

When John A. Hinman collapsed at his news desk on February 28, 1983, it signaled the end of an era. "A fair-minded American of the old school" was one of the many accolades that followed the demise of this longtime Northfield resident. Born in Ohio, Hinman earned a bachelor of science degree at Oregon State College. He was manager of the *Texas Daily Press League* in New York City until 1940, when he became owner-editor of the *Pleasantville Press*. During the 42 years he led the newspaper, he earned the respect of professional, business, and community leaders throughout the state. He was named Newsman of the Year in 1971. At his passing, this six-foot, two-inch-tall man with the booming voice was remembered as one who "gained professional stature through consistent, evenhanded, and thorough coverage of Mainland events and activities." Said one employee, "He would always take the time, no matter how busy, for just a 'Hello, this is Old Man Hinman!' " (Courtesy of the *Pleasantville Press* and the Hinman family.)

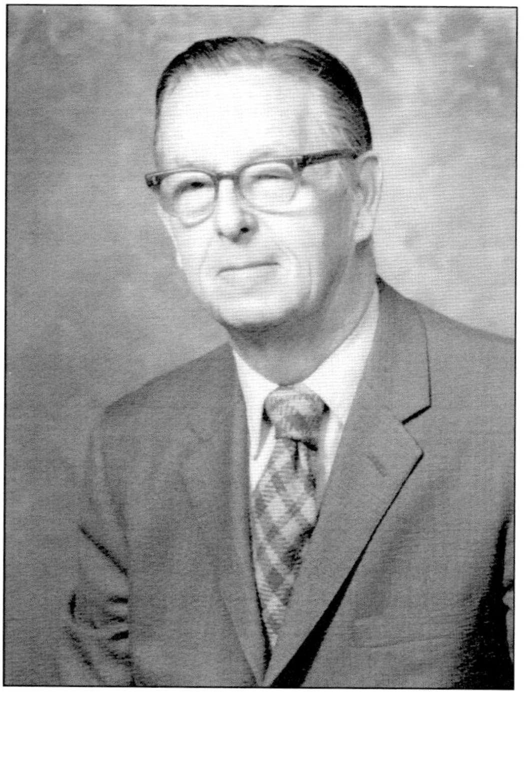

Two

WHERE WE LIVED

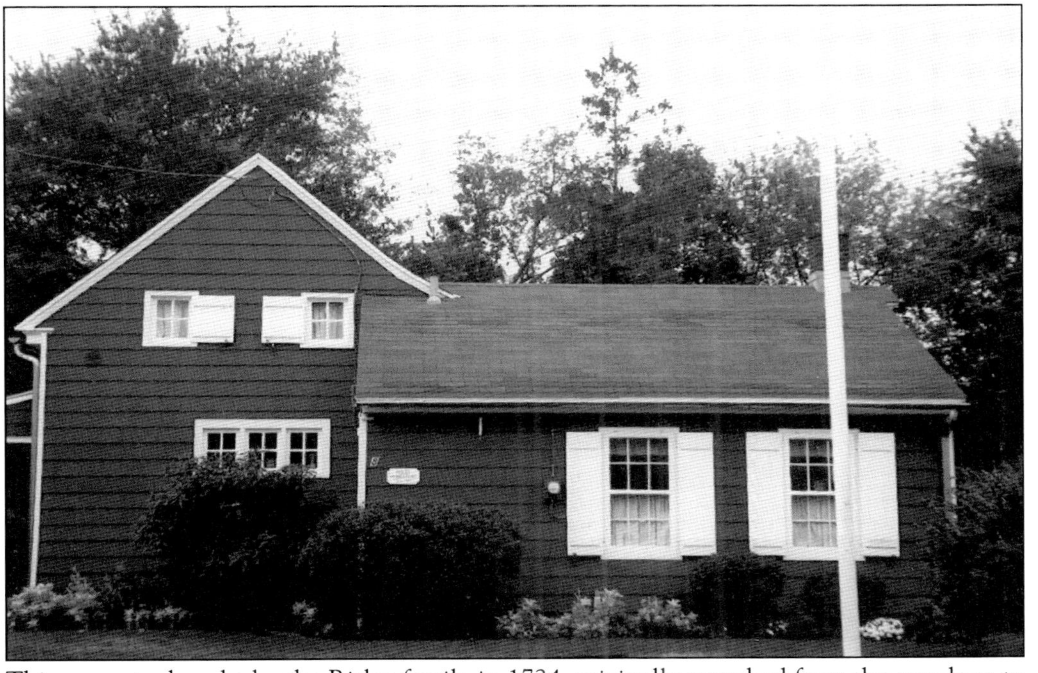

This property, bought by the Risley family in 1724, originally stretched from the meadows to New Road. The house, at 8 Virginia Avenue, was most likely built c. 1750. In the course of renovation and restoration after they moved in during the 1930s, Howard A. Stout Jr. and his wife, Virginia, discovered many interesting details about the original construction. Howard A. Stout Jr., an architect, designed many area buildings, including the bandstand at Birch Grove Park. In an interview, Virginia Stout related that the floor joists were put in with dovetail joints and no nails. Floorboards were finished only on the top side and were put together in tongue-and-groove fashion, using almost no nails. The Stouts did their best to preserve the oldest parts of the home: the living room, downstairs bedroom, narrow enclosed stairway, and upstairs bedroom loft. The greenhouse was built c. 1932. Virginia Risley Stout, the last of the direct Risley line, bequeathed the house to the Atlantic County Historical Society at her death in 1988.

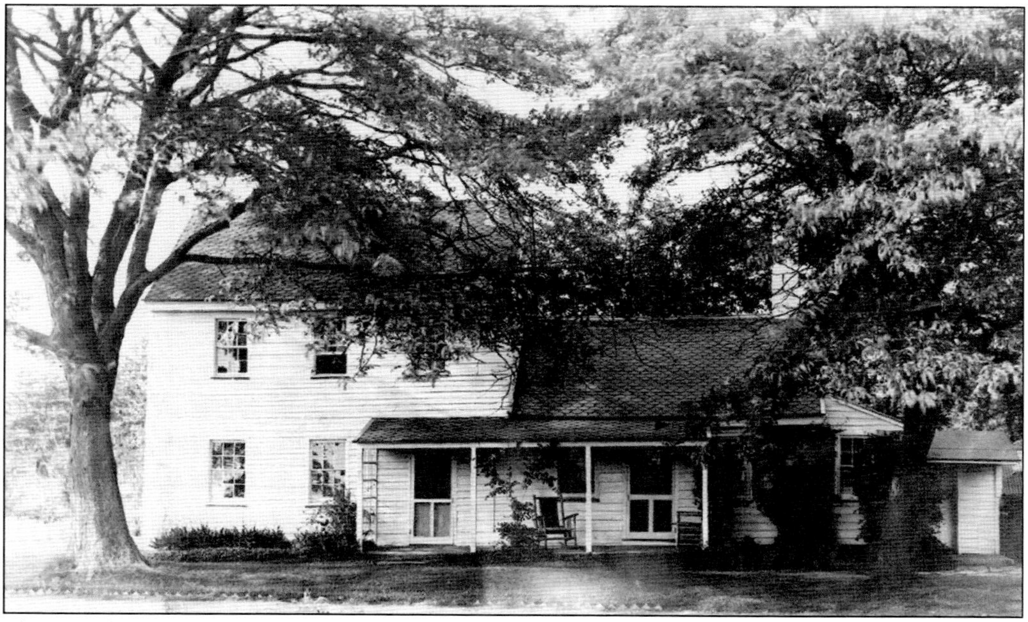

The Steelman-Weaver-Hampton house, at 15 Cove Avenue, is one of the oldest homes in Atlantic County. The original part of the house was built by James Steelman before the Revolutionary War. The living room and three upstairs bedrooms were added in 1800, and additional modifications have been made since then. This photograph shows the house as it looked in the summer of 1924.

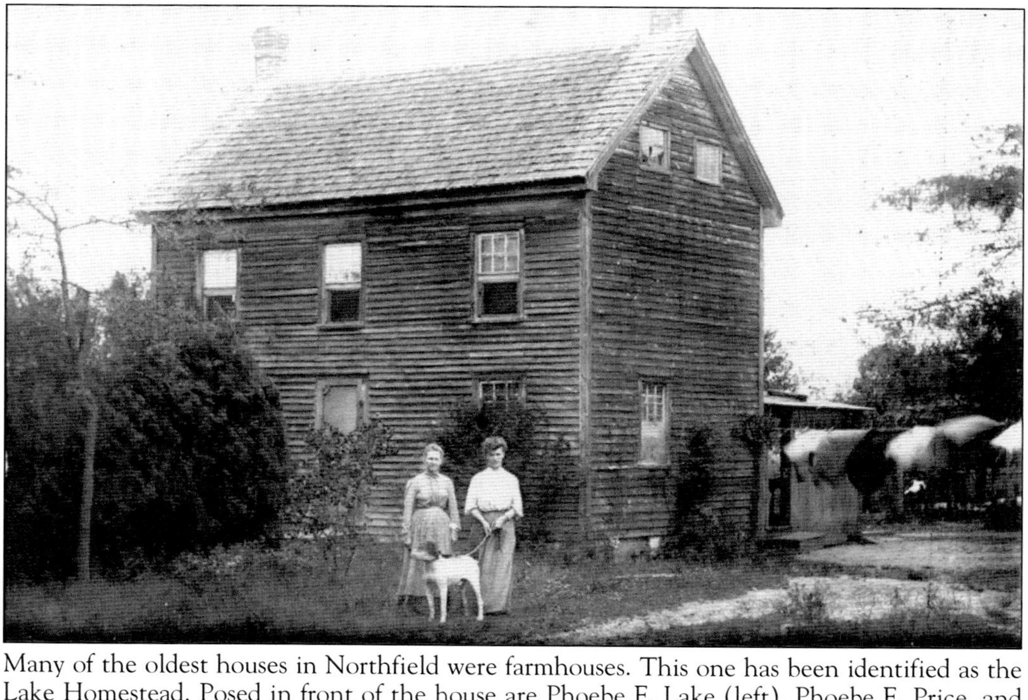

Many of the oldest houses in Northfield were farmhouses. This one has been identified as the Lake Homestead. Posed in front of the house are Phoebe E. Lake (left), Phoebe E. Price, and Trimer, the dog.

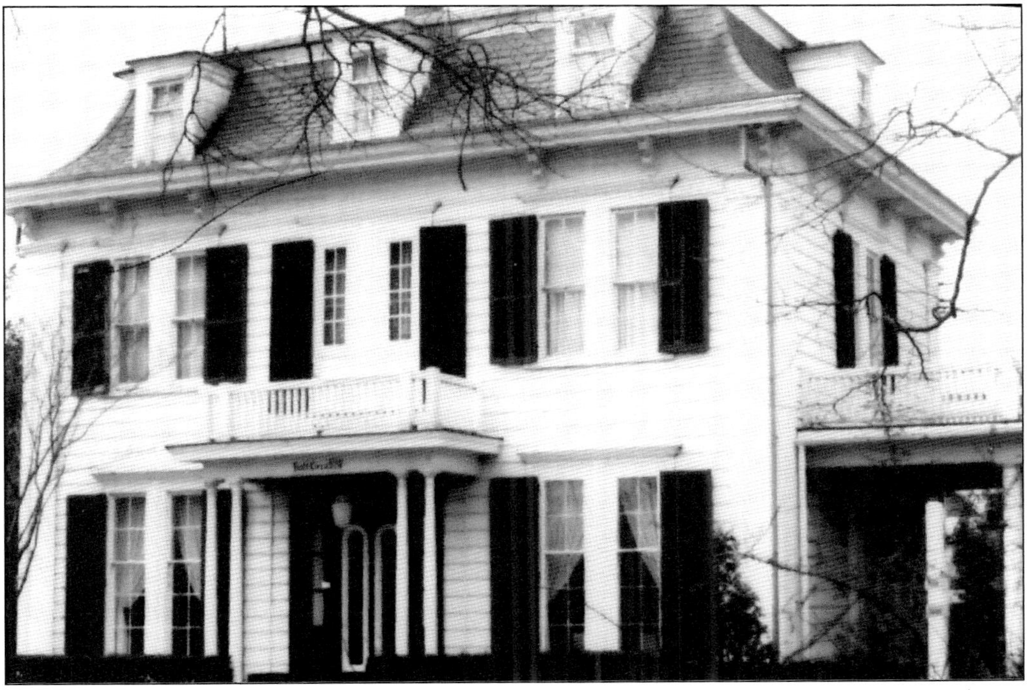

Now in its third location, the house at 16 West Rosedale Avenue was built c. 1870 on what is now Wabash Avenue by Elijah Price, brother to Capt. John Price. The house was then moved to Shore Road, opposite Rosedale Avenue. It was moved to its present location in 1926, under the direction of architect William Koelle. Elizabeth Herrick, who taught several generations of Northfield students, was Elijah Price's granddaughter.

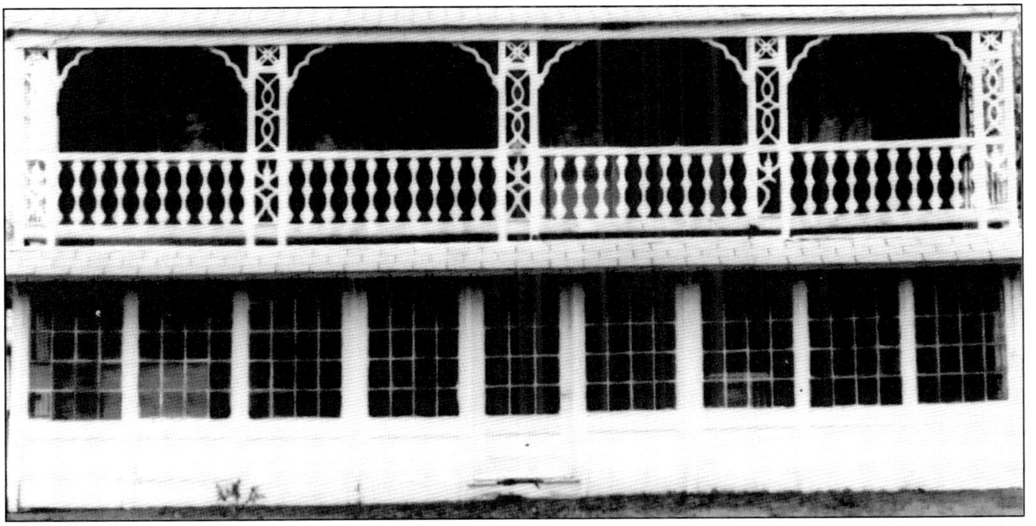

The New Orleans–style façade on this house, at 1905 Cedarbridge Road, differs from the façades seen on typical area homes. Records indicate that Thompson Lake built the house in 1842. As the story goes, he had brought his bride from New Orleans and wanted to make her feel at home. During one of many renovations, it was discovered that trees with bark still on them were used as wall supports.

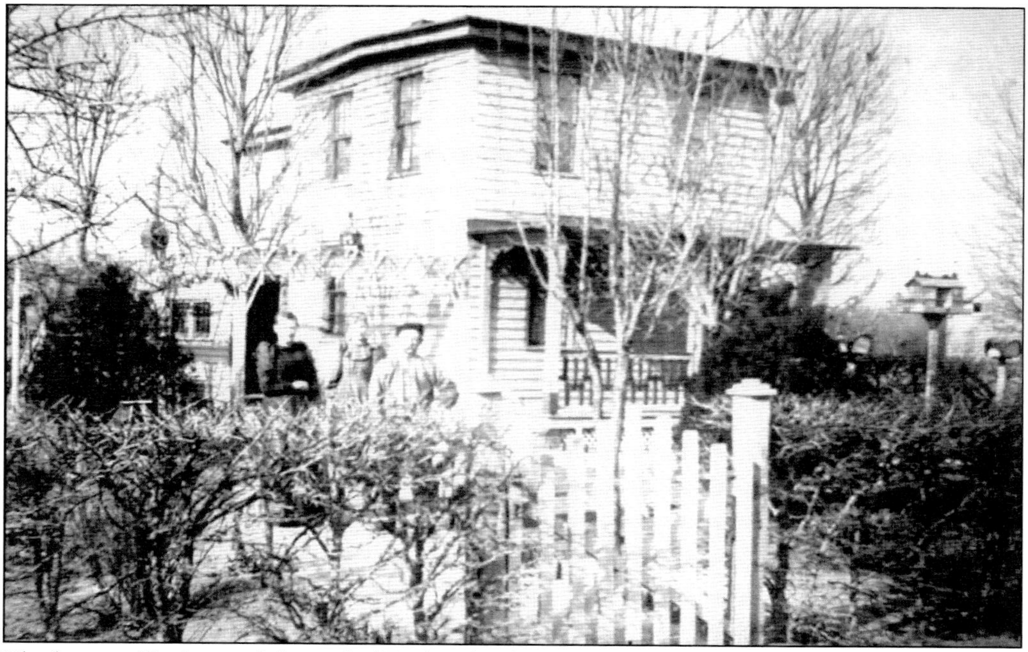

The home of Japhet and Amanda (Toy) Ireland, at 1303 New Road, was the original Sheppard house. It was replaced by the residence located at the address once known as 1311 New Road (see below). The Irelands were the grandparents of the family who owned Scientific Glass Instrument Company, which was located at 1315 New Road, behind the present-day site of the Plaza 9 Shopping Center. Charles Sheppard married Nellie Ireland.

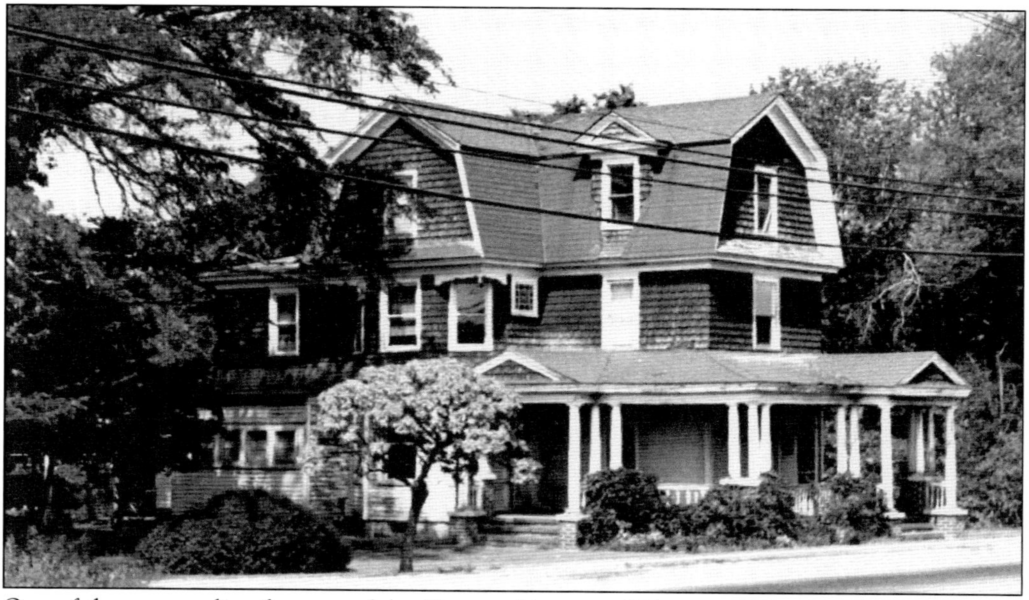

One of the outstanding features of the Sheppard house at Tilton and New Roads was the foyer with its beautiful stained-glass windows. This photograph was taken in 1982, shortly before the house was torn down. For 65 years the Sheppard family owned and operated Scientific Glass, which manufactured laboratory glassware.

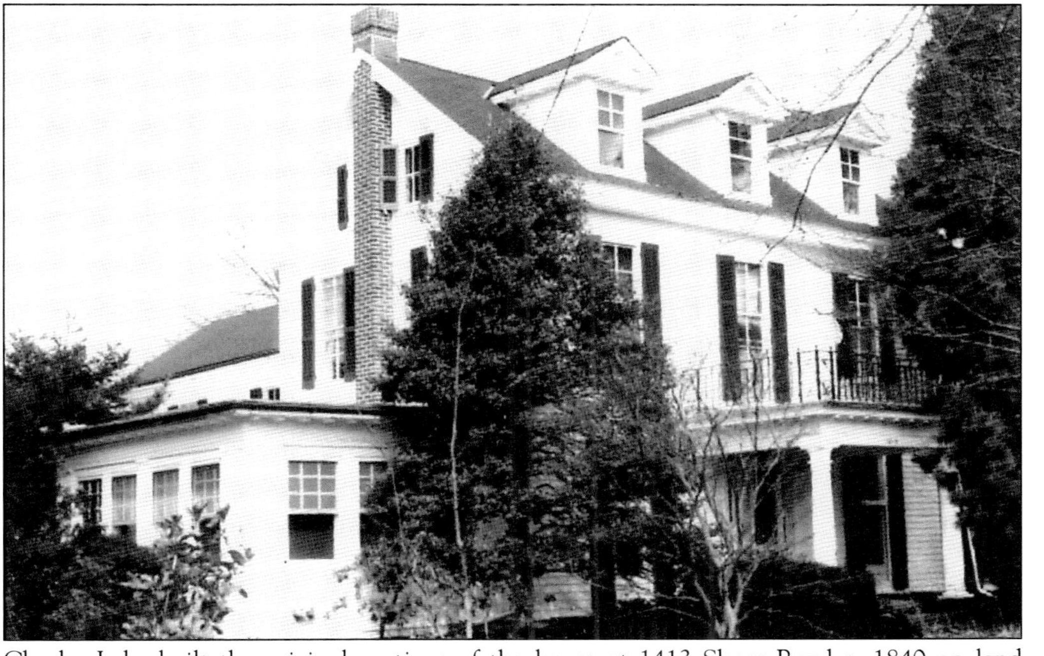

Charles Lake built the original portions of the house at 1413 Shore Road *c.* 1840 on land originally owned by the Fifield family. The main front section was added in 1870, with other rooms dating from 1935. According to old records, the A-shaped window in the roof, now gone, was considered so unusual that visitors from all over the county came to view it.

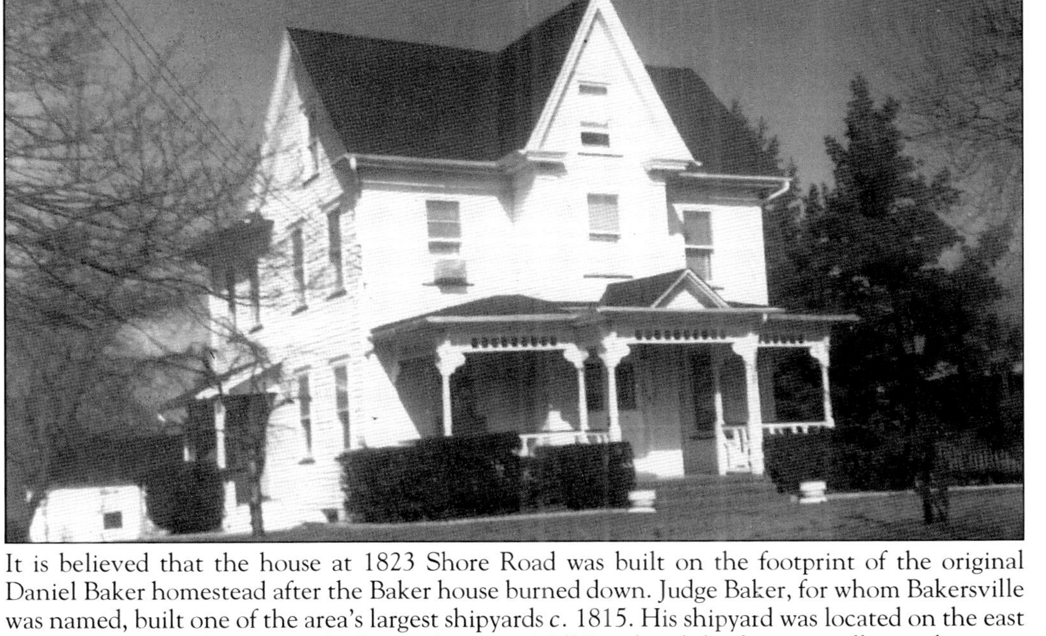

It is believed that the house at 1823 Shore Road was built on the footprint of the original Daniel Baker homestead after the Baker house burned down. Judge Baker, for whom Bakersville was named, built one of the area's largest shipyards *c.* 1815. His shipyard was located on the east side of Shore Road, opposite the house, between Mill Road and the first post office and next to Warren Ryon's home. The rebuilt house was eventually owned by William Boice, mayor of Northfield and owner of the blacksmith shop next door to this house.

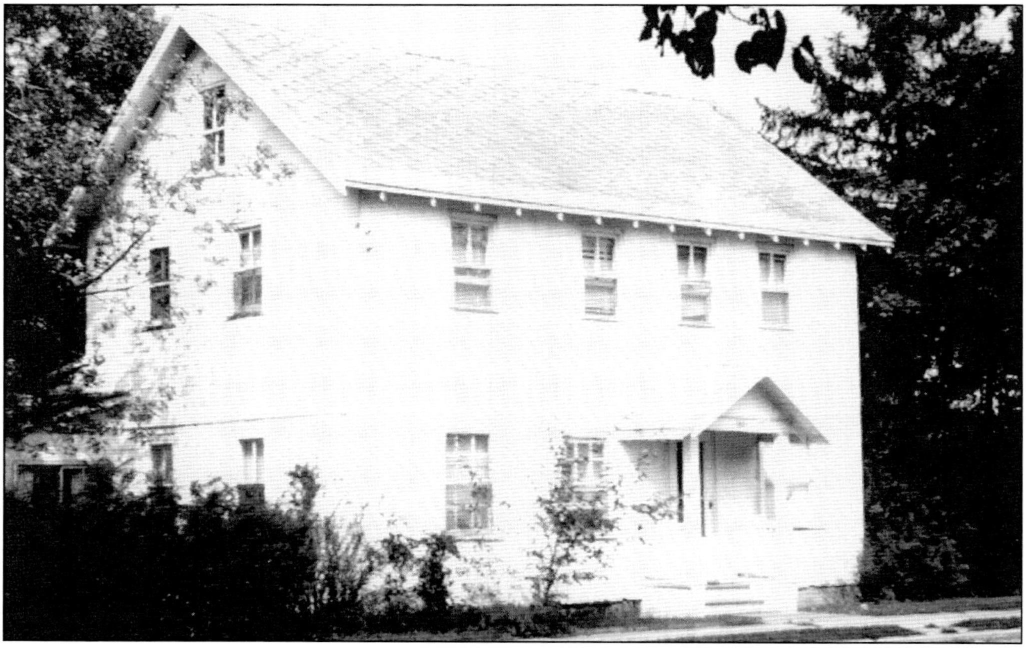

The Deputy house, at 1821 Tilton Road, once stood on Shore Road, adjacent to the store at the corner of Shore and Mill Roads. In the early days, the country store was operated by Jesse Adams, grandfather of Israel G. Adams. Later, Elijah Price ran the store. In 1881, Edward Ryon, grandson of Pardon Ryon, bought the store. In the summer of 1898, he moved the house over to Tilton Road and the store farther north on Shore Road.

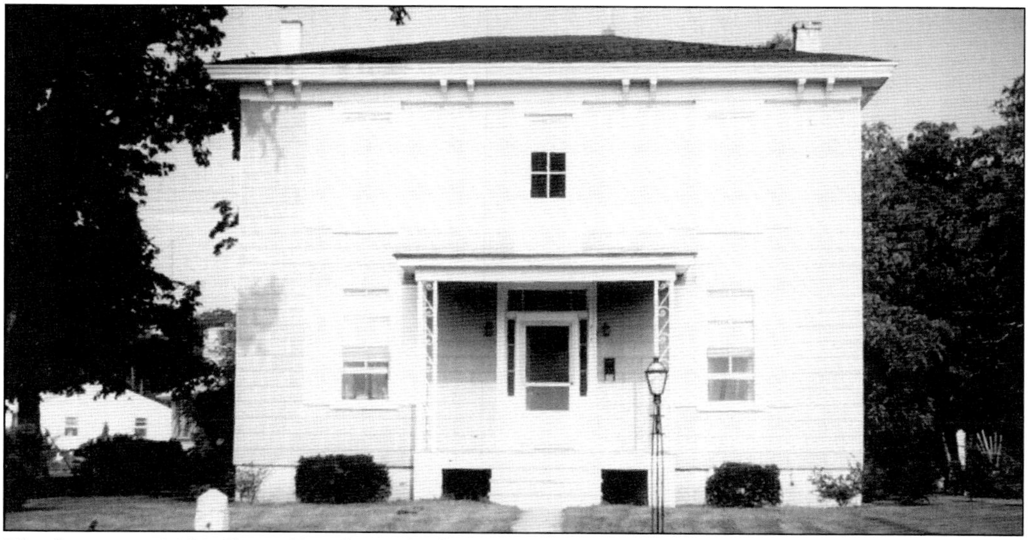

The house at 2151 Shore Road was built in 1866 as the home of Capt. John Price, father of Lizzie, Olive, and Louie Price. A successful sea captain, Price sometimes made routine trips hauling ice or lumber to New York and sometimes voyaged around the world. In an interview, former mayor Otto Bruyns recounted how Lizzie Price used to tell him that her father had a sight (a marine navigational instrument) that he would use to look right over to Margate and see the schooners come in.

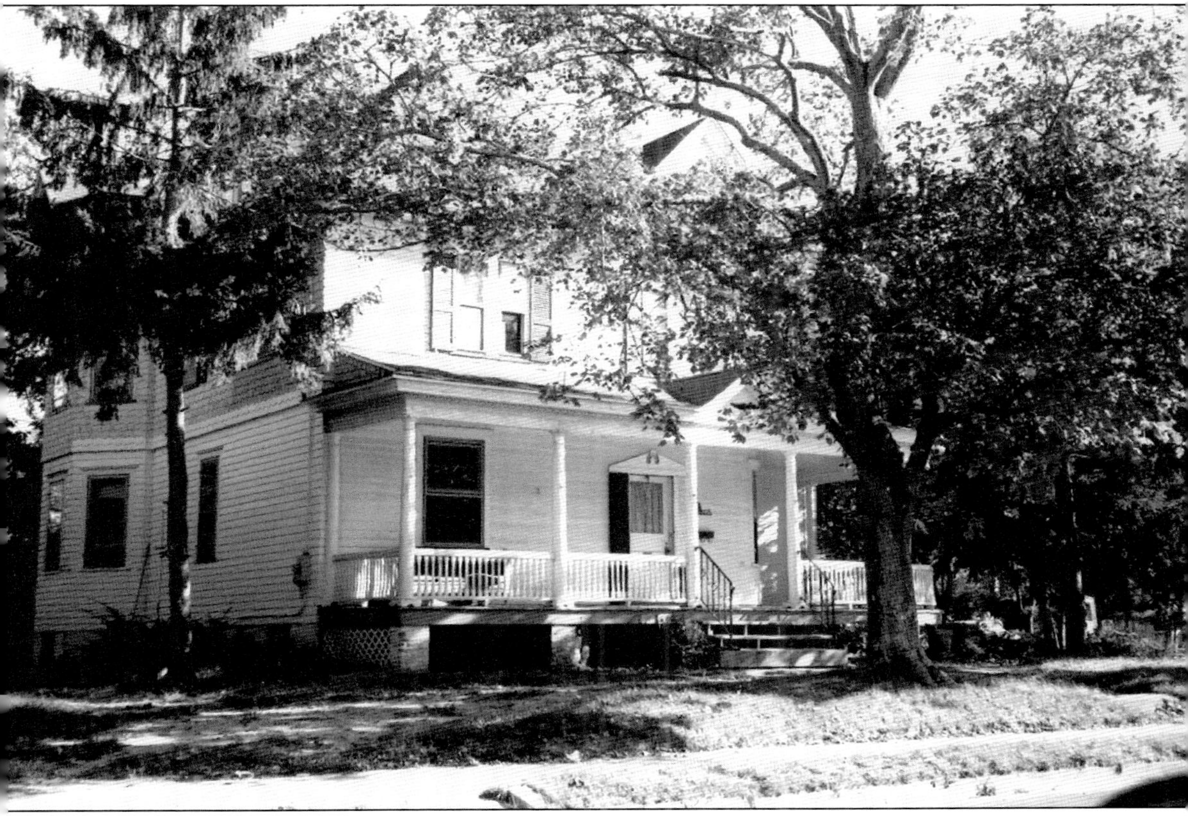

Edward Ryon built the house at 1826 Shore Road in 1889. It was constructed on the foundation of the original house on the site, the Deputy house, now at 1821 Tilton Road. It is a splendid example of Victorian construction, but there is a mystery included with the beautiful chestnut woodwork and sweeping stairway. The third floor is completely open. Was it a game room, a ballroom, or maybe a speakeasy? On the south side of the room, a trapdoor conceals a ladder into a room with no other way out. There are shelves around the walls. Ryon was named Bakersville's first postmaster in 1882 and served in that capacity for 28 years. After he retired, his daughter, Edna, was named postmaster. The post office was located in Ryon's store, which was next door, on the corner of Mill Road. Following Edward Ryon's death, on December 15, 1932, the home at 1826 Shore Road, along with the store, passed to his son, Warren James Ryon.

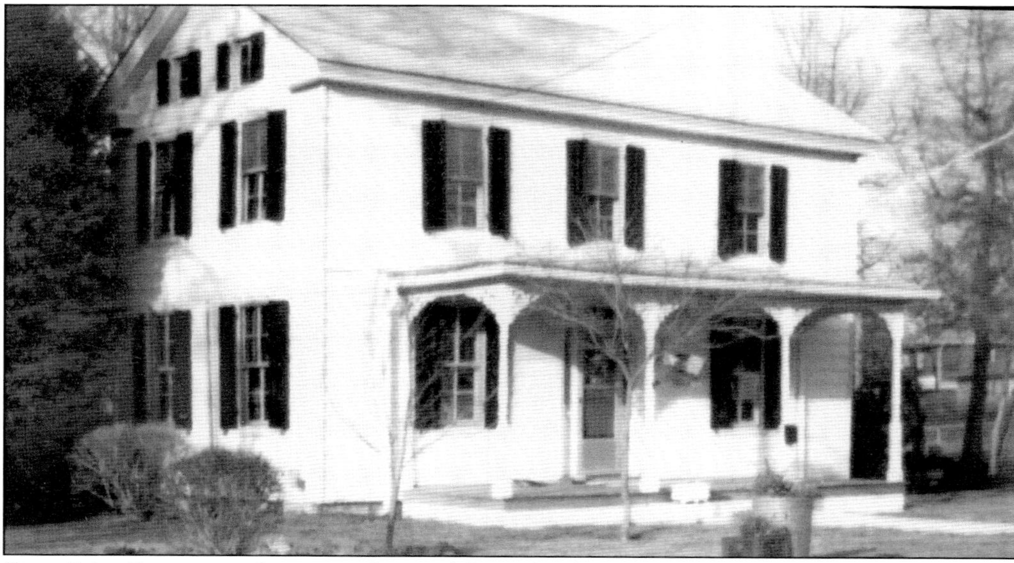

Capt. John Sampson, who married one of the Ireland daughters, built the Sampson homestead on Zion Road c. 1858 on the portion of the extensive Ireland property that had been given to his wife. William Oxley moved to Northfield in 1905. He and his wife, Elizabeth (Sampson), bought the house that had been owned by her parents. A butcher by trade, Oxley provided a rural meat route for the surrounding community.

Fredda Garrett Is Married In Richmond, Va.

A wedding of interest to local residents was solemnized in the chapel of St. Paul's Episcopal Church in Richmond, Va., when Miss Fredda G. Garrett, daughter of Mrs. Fredda Garrett, of Atlantic City and Northfield, became the bride of Leslie Carleton, son of Mrs. Leslie Carleton Sr., of Richmond.

The ceremony was performed by the rector of the church in a candle lighted chancel. Preceding the marriage service a recital of nuptial music was given by Mrs. A. Swann, organist, and Fred McCormic, vocalist.

The bride, who looked attractive in a two-piece dressmaker suit of coral wool with a shoulder corsage of white roses, was attended by her sister, Mrs. Patsy Garrett Hower, of New York, as matron of honor. Mrs. Hower chose a blue gabardine suit and shell pink accessories. An orchid formed her shoulder corsage.

William G. Garrett, brother of the bride, was the best man.

Mrs. Olive Whitlock, Mrs. Audrey Duke and Miss Jean Timberlake, who were attired in soft informal suits of Spring colors, served as ushers.

Mrs. Garrett, mother of the bride, wore an informal green wool ensemble and black accessories, with an orchid of harmonizing shade, while Mrs. Carleton, mother of the groom, selected a street length black faille frock and a white formal hat.

A reception and bridal supper was enjoyed at Byram's for the immediate family, following which the party enjoyed dancing at the Westwood Club.

After a brief honeymoon the young couple will be at home at 2412 Hanover st., Richmond.

* * *

Fredda Oxley Garrett was the daughter of William and Elizabeth Sampson Oxley. Her daughter Patsy Garrett was a successful entertainer from the 1940s to the 1990s, singing with Fred Waring's Pennsylvanians, considered one of the country's top bands, and performing on radio and television and in film. Among her many acting credits were roles in the movies *Benji*, *Mississippi Masala*, and *The Parallax View*, as well as guest-starring roles on many TV series.

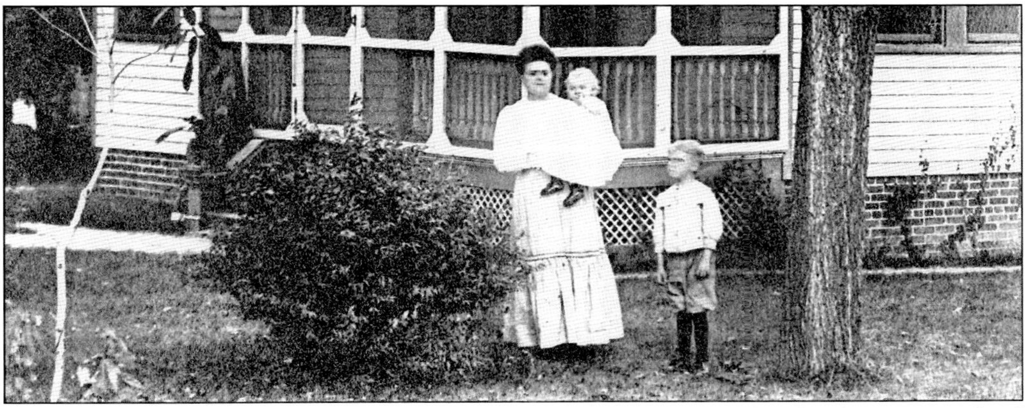

H. Russell Swift is the young boy shown on the right in this photograph. The elementary school in Egg Harbor Township is named after him. The house, located at 309 Shore Road, can also be seen in the photograph below.

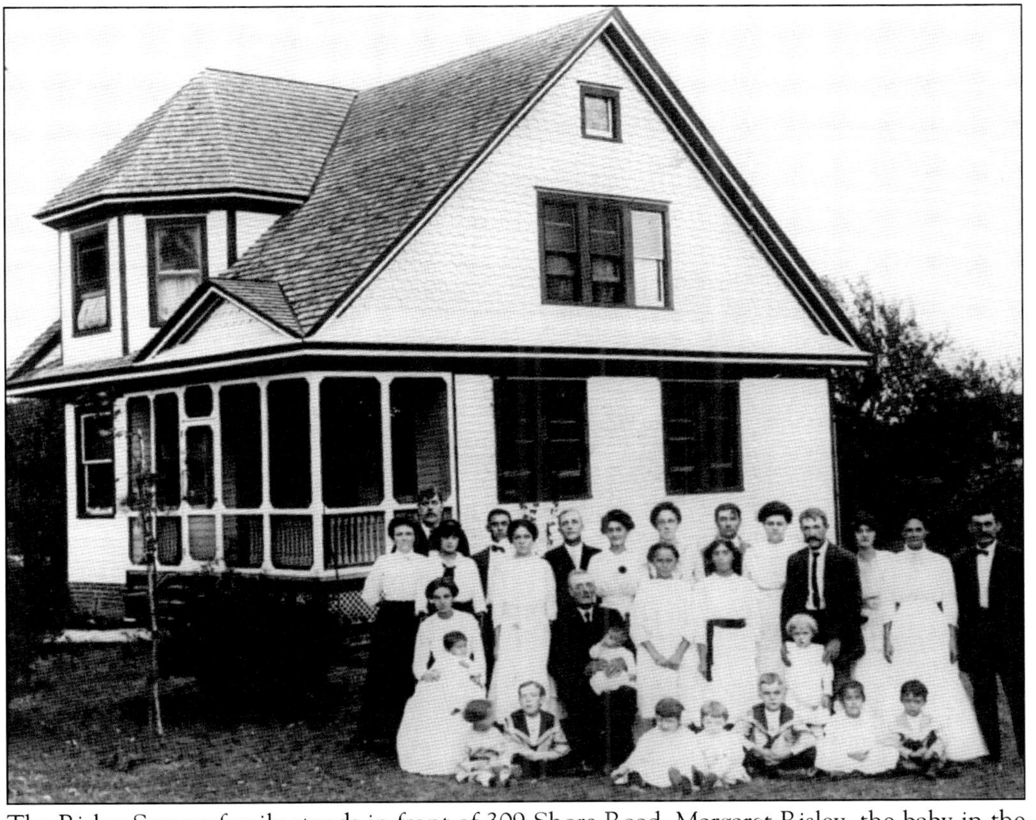

The Risley-Somers family stands in front of 309 Shore Road. Margaret Risley, the baby in the lower left of the photograph, identified these family members, from left to right: her parents, Ernest and Mabel (Mulford) Risley; their children, Margaret and Anna Mae; her grandparents Margaret (Somers) and Edward Risley; and her great-grandfather Risley. Laura and Eugene Conover, who owned this house, were the children's aunt and uncle. Ernest Risley's sister Addie Risley, Aunt Ella and Uncle Ernest Swift, Ernest's sister Joy Finegan, and Uncle Ed Risley are also present.

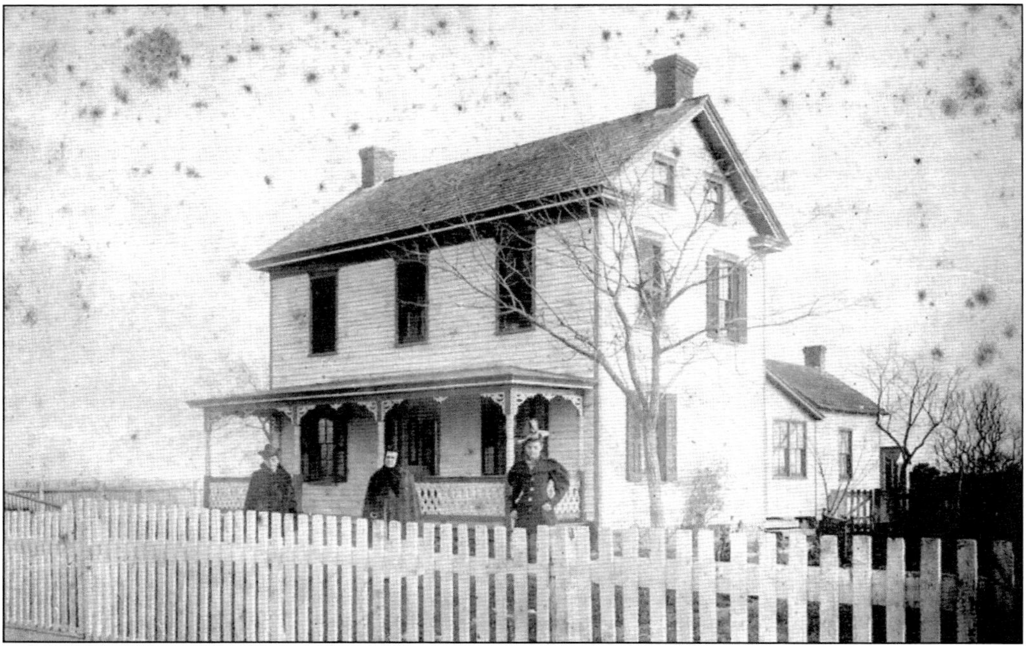

The house at 1712 Shore Road was built for the daughter of Jeremiah Baker. The home of the James Turner family, it appears on the 1872 map of Bakersville. Standing in front of the house (above) are James Turner's daughter, Mamie Turner Cavilier, his wife, Mary Baker Turner, and Mina Turner Young. The first phone call to Atlantic City was made from this house. The photograph below shows the house at it looks today.

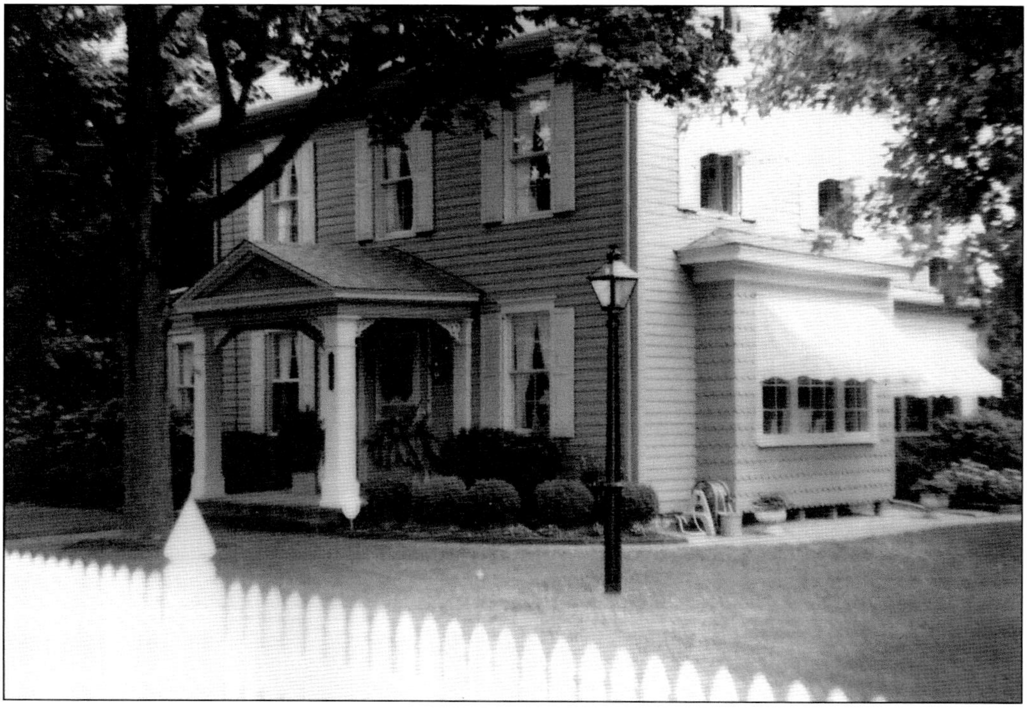

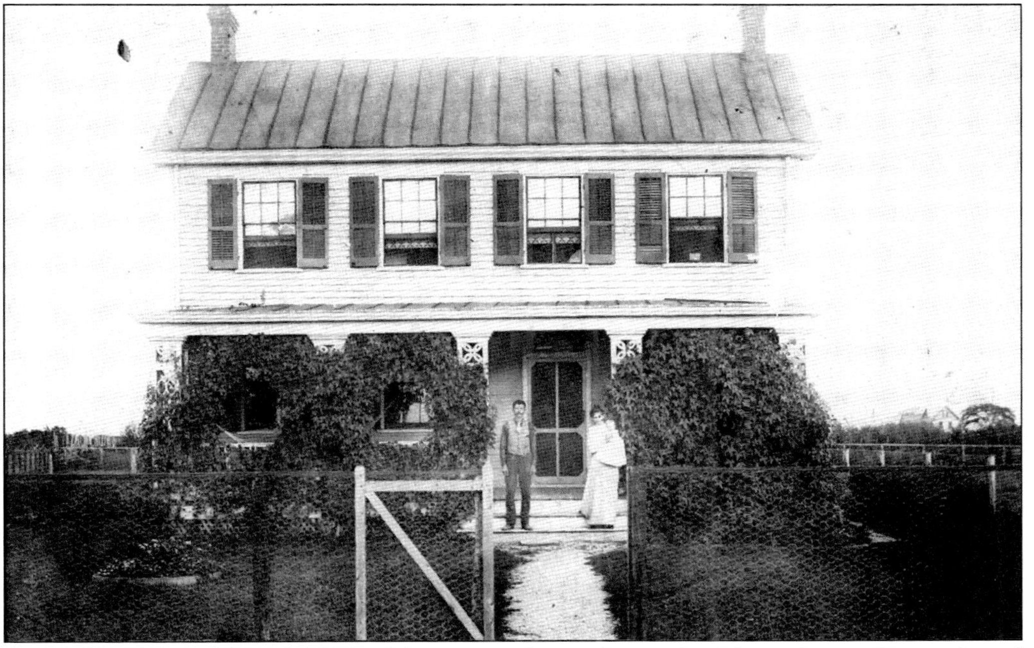

Pictured in front of their Mill Road home are, from left to right, Henry, Lizzie (Brower), and John Price. Henry Price was superintendent of construction when the brick Mill Road School was built in 1914. He became the first president of the Northfield Board of Education, and he helped build the Atlantic City Country Club. Born on a Mill Road farm located at the site of the Ezra Hackett farm, he lived on Mill Road until he was 83, and then he went to live with his granddaughter.

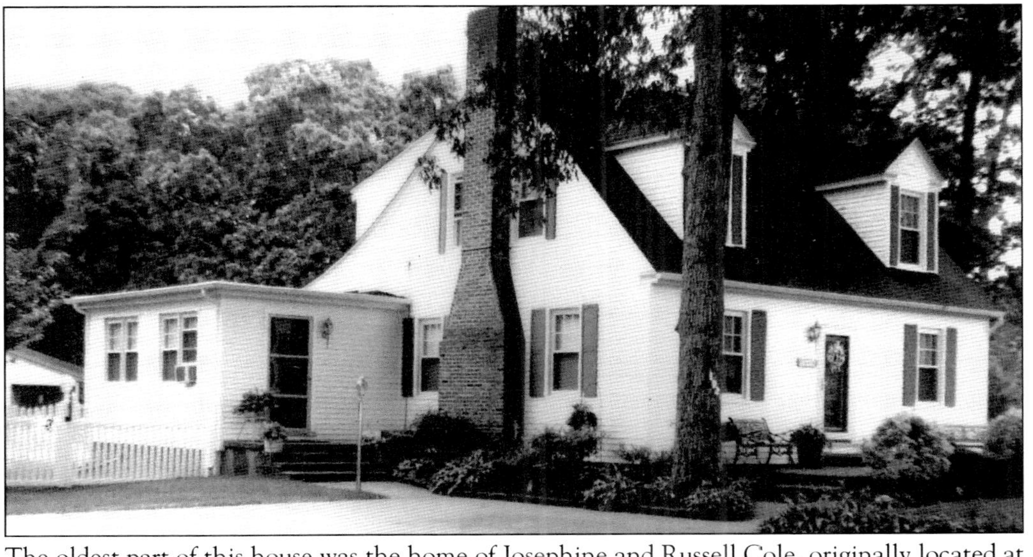

The oldest part of this house was the home of Josephine and Russell Cole, originally located at the Somers Brick Company. Russell Cole was the assistant superintendent of the Somers Brick Company until it went out of business c. 1930. Jesse Hannum, Northfield's road foreman, bought the Coles' bungalow from Birch Grove Park and rebuilt it on Cedarbridge Road as his family home. (Courtesy of the Cole family.)

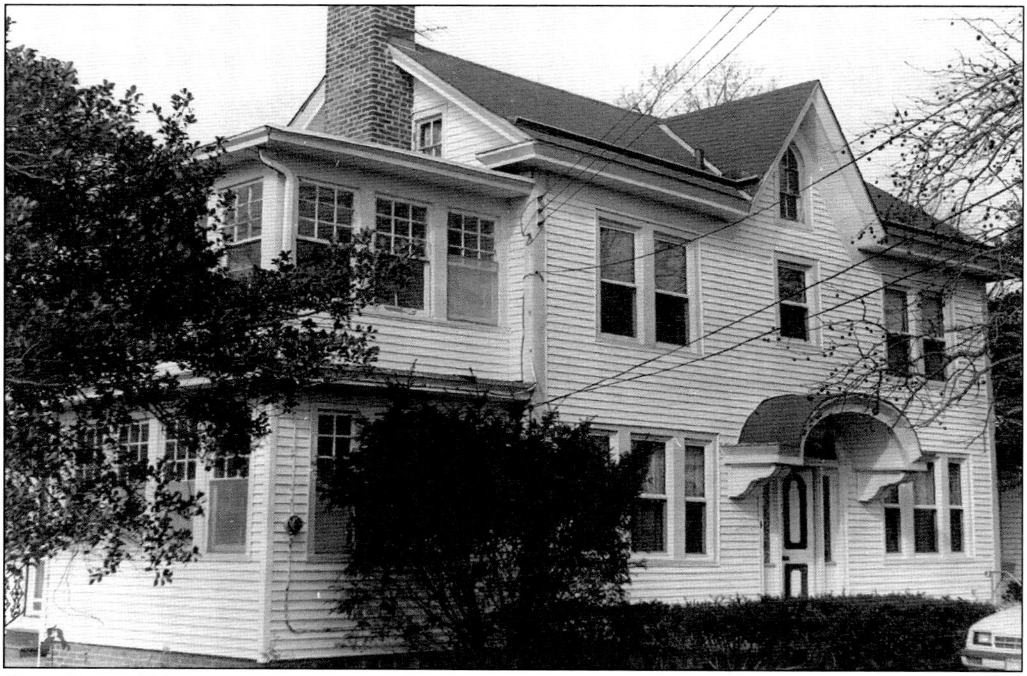

Capt. Lewis Tilton, a sea captain and early Bakersville resident, built this house at 1513 Shore Road in the 1860s. Records indicate that his wife rented rooms and operated a store in one room of the house. The house has been extensively remodeled over the years, but the original floor plan remains. This house has also been home to the Burkard family and the Johnson family.

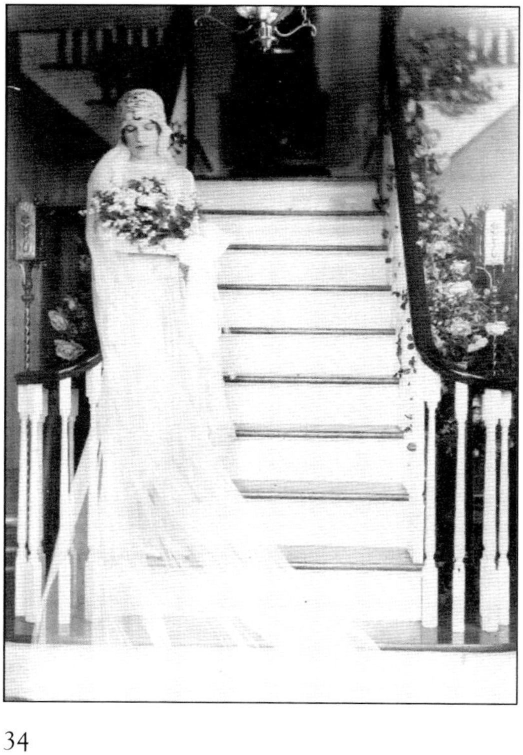

This June 1928 wedding photograph of Celeste Burkard was taken at the family home, at 1513 Shore Road (see photograph above). Celeste Burkard married Edward Bader, son of Mayor Bader of Atlantic City. Her father, William H. Burkard, was founder and president of the Burkard Coal Company. Early city tax records show that the Burkard family purchased the house in 1902. (Courtesy of Edward Bader.)

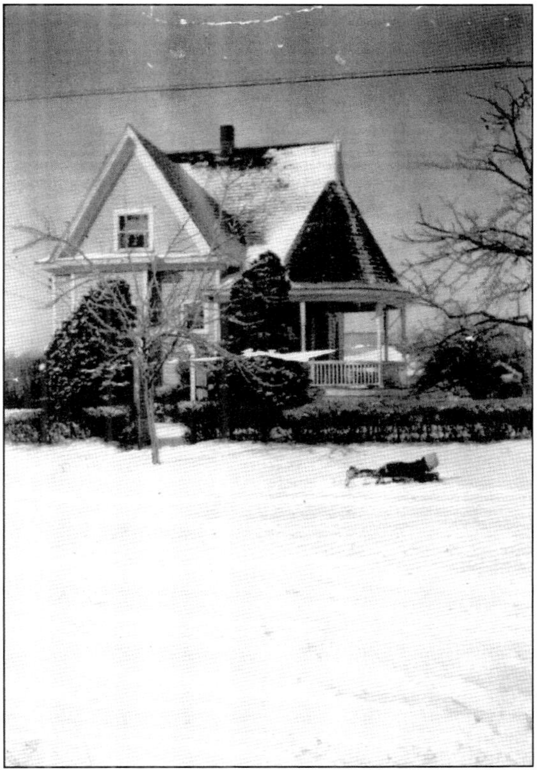

A child enjoys sledding past 1101 Broad Street after a snowstorm during the winter of 1930. One of the earliest built on Broad Street, this house was noted for its interesting porch turret. One longtime Northfield resident remembers that many considered Broad Street "the sticks" until well into the 20th century.

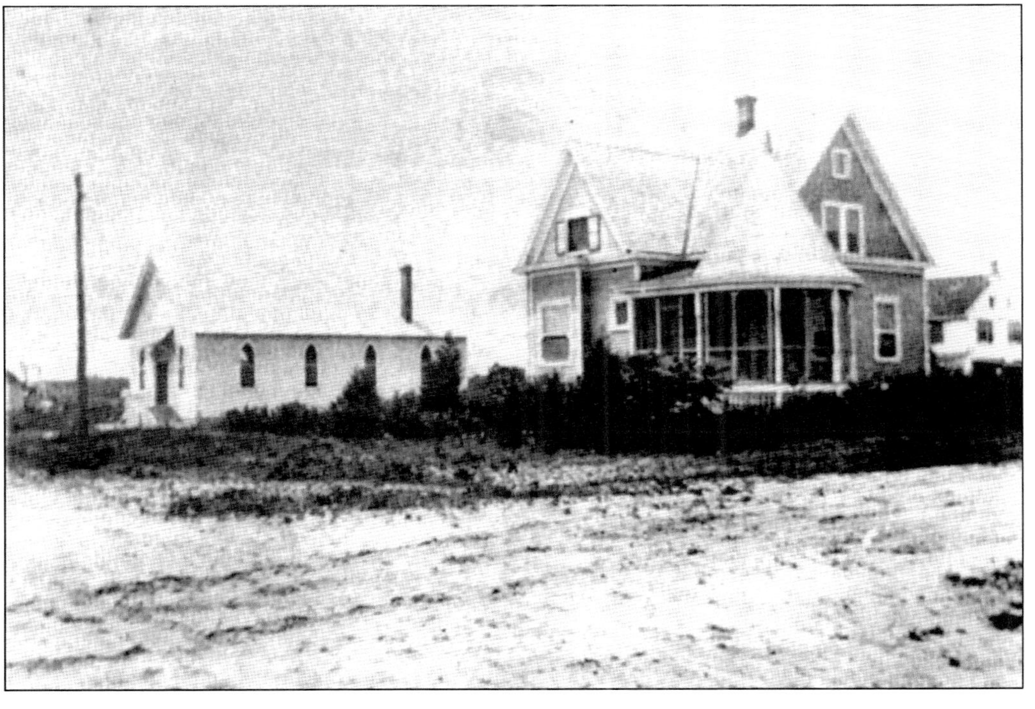

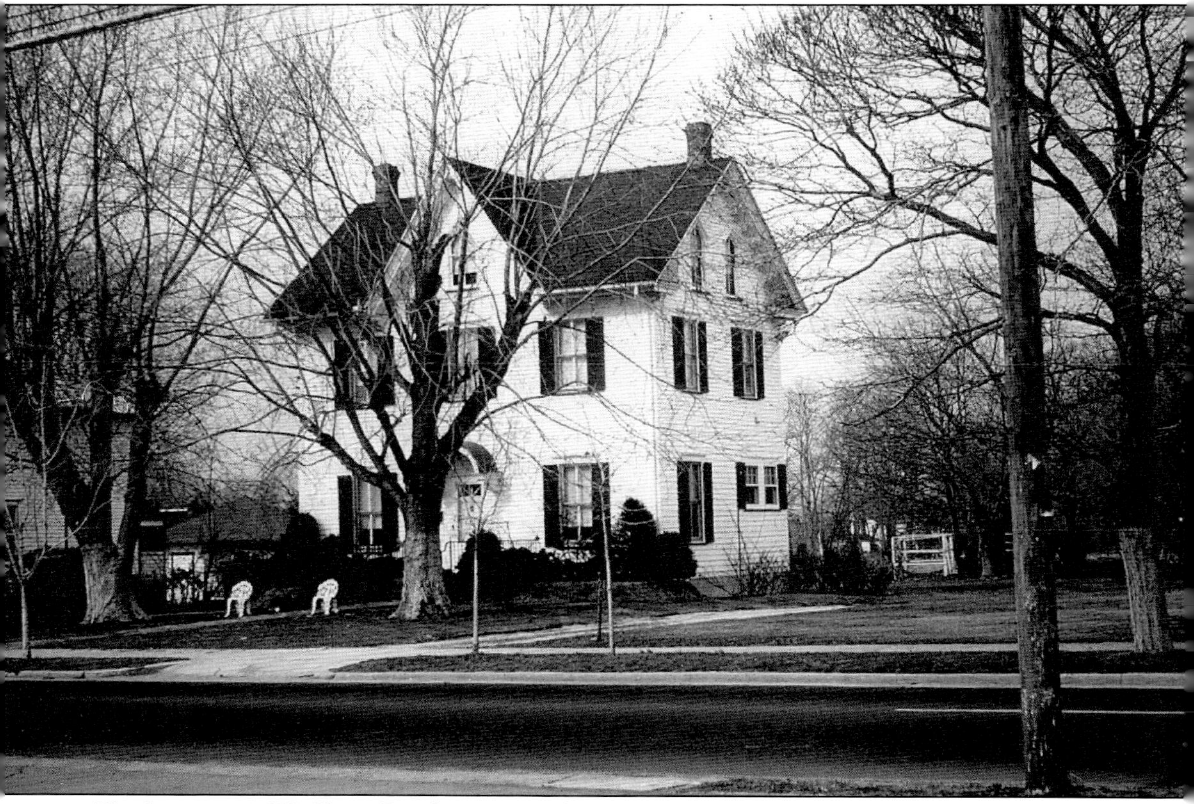

The house at 1607 Shore Road was once the site of the famous garden known as Rose Tree. This garden, started in 1950 by Mrs. Peter Paul and Mrs. George Tomlinson, was planted with more than 900 rose trees, rosebushes, and climbing roses. The garden was open to the public, and it is reported that sightseeing buses stopped there three times a day and that, at the time of peak bloom, there were 1,000 visitors a day. According to Carol A. Patrick in *Historic Houses of Northfield*, "Mrs. Paul and Mrs. Tomlinson discovered the words 'Captain William Price—1870' scratched into the plaster. This was one of three houses built by Captain Lewis Tilton. It was bought by Captain William Price, father of Mrs. Hannah Duberson. . . . In 1928 the Northfield Public Library moved from the mayor's office in the old City Hall across the street to a second floor room in Mrs. Duberson's home."

Three

Where We Worked and Shopped

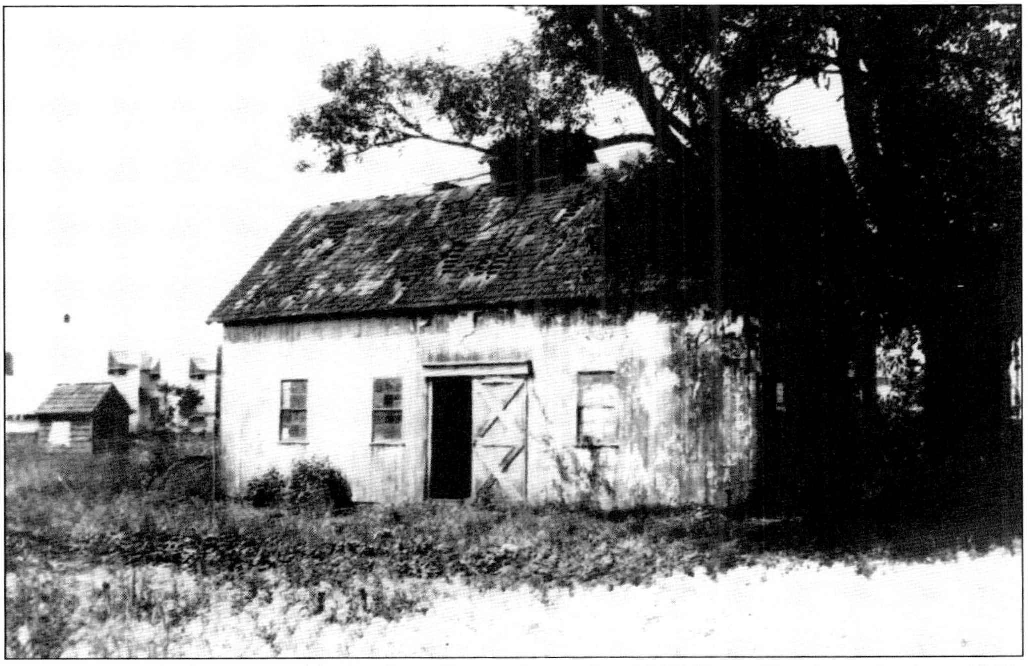

The blacksmith shop owned by William Boice, located at 1807 Shore Road, was built in 1861. This picture was taken in 1926 by Mrs. Walter Block. The shop was torn down in 1938, and its timbers were used to build Block's garage on Tilton Road. William Boice was Northfield's second mayor (1908–1909) and its fourth (1912–1920). Longtime Northfield resident Lawrence Hampton, who lived nearby, recalled going over to the blacksmith shop to "help" Boice: "I would brush the flies off the horse and pump the bellows. He was a very small man, about five feet tall, and I remember thinking that one of these days a horse would knock him over." The horse's hooves were cut with a rasp, and the nails were hammered into the side so that it did not hurt the horse. Boice also made clam tongs (called the best in the South Jersey area) and put iron rings onto wooden wagon wheels.

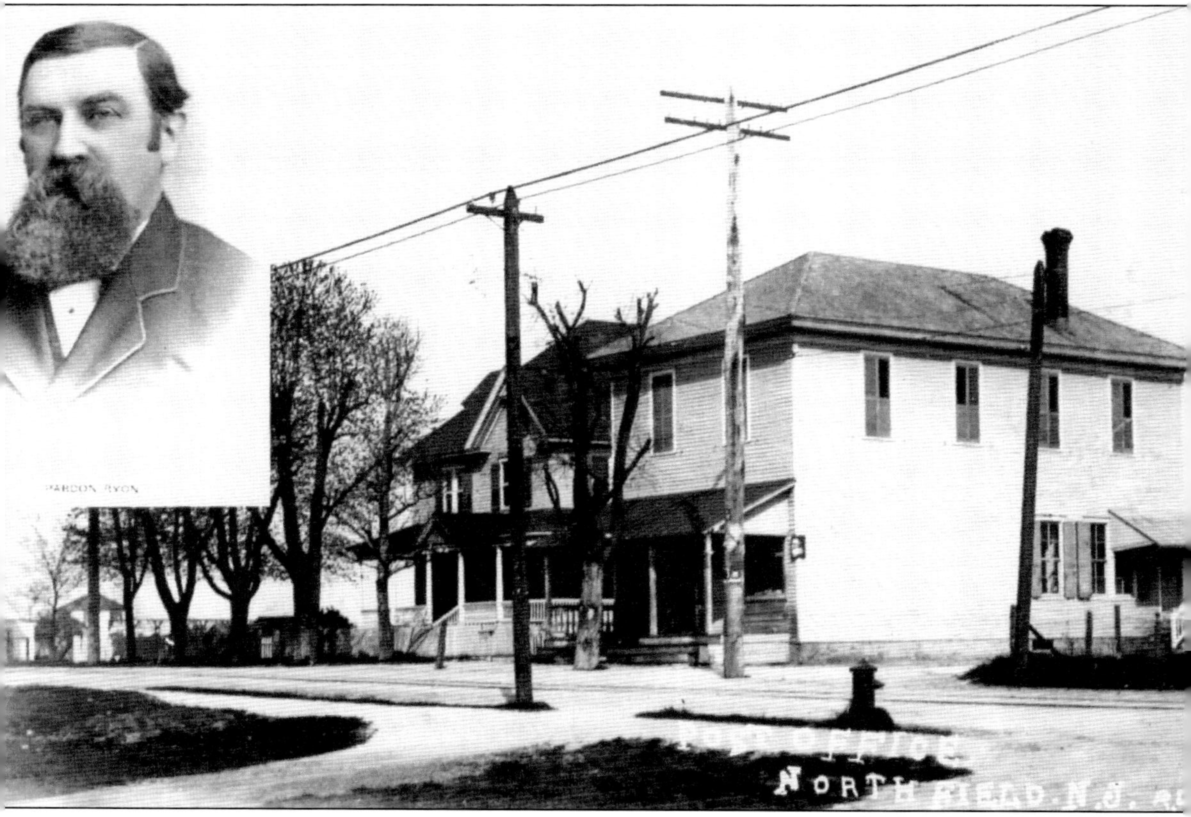

Pardon Ryon, the patriarch of the Ryon family in this area, was born in East Lyme, Connecticut, in 1793. Legend has it he was persuaded by Daniel Baker to settle here, but the attraction may have been Elizabeth Adams, the daughter of Jesse and Deborah Adams of Bakersville, whom he married in April 1825. For a time he had a store and was postmaster in Bargaintown. He later had a store in Bakersville, but in 1833, he moved a little to the north, to Smith's Landing (now part of Pleasantville), where he also had a store and was named postmaster. Pardon Ryon fathered eight children. The third, James Ryon, was born in Bakersville on June 8, 1830. He married Caroline Cordery on November 19, 1853. His son, Edward C. Ryon, is believed to have been the builder of the house at 1826 Shore Road, which is known as the Ryon House, although this has not been confirmed. (Information courtesy of Carolyn Collins Martin, from the *Ryon Genealogy*.)

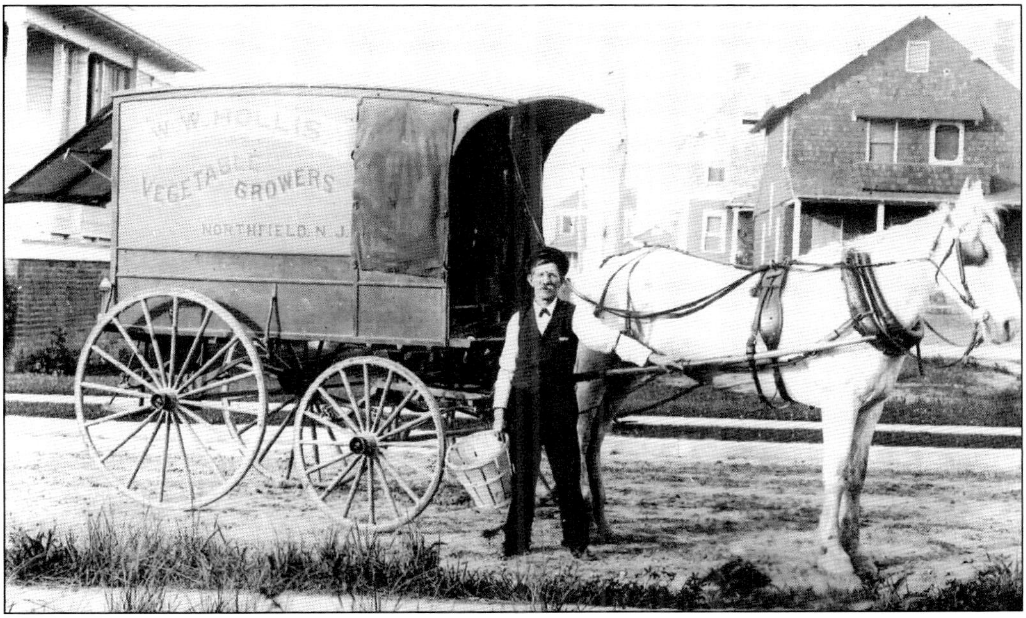

Jesse Lever, shown here with a horse and wagon belonging to W. W. Hallis, was a huckster in Northfield; he peddled fruits and vegetables door-to-door for a few years in the early 1900s. According to one of his account books, his expenses for June 12, 1912, included "set of shoes on mare, $1.25, postage stamps, $.04," and, for June 13, "lunch for myself, $.10." Lever was the father of W. Everett "Bud" Lever, Northfield's chief of police from 1929 to 1961. (Courtesy of the Lever family.)

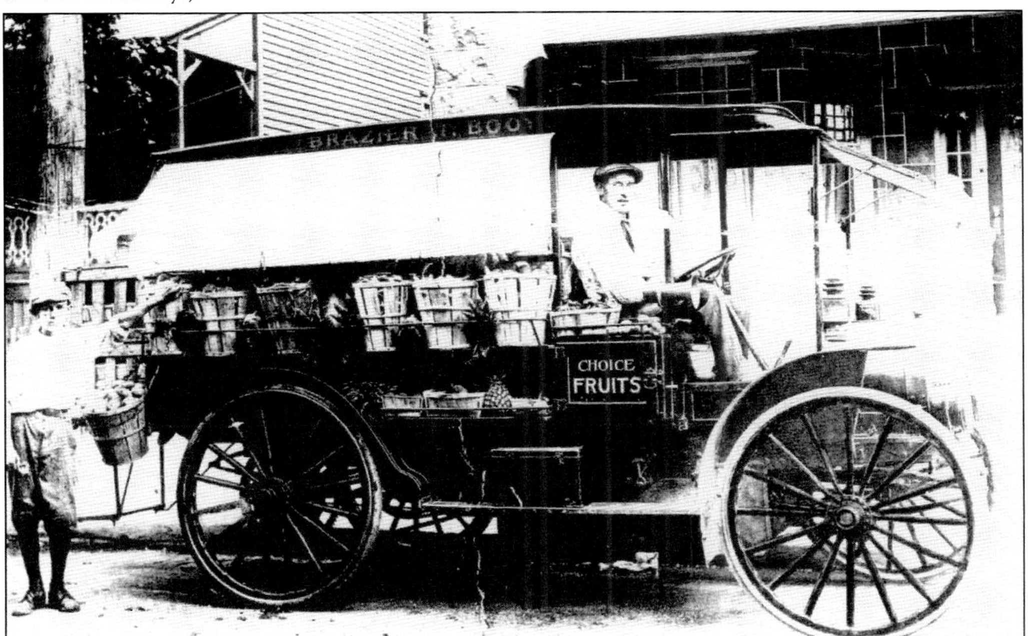

Brazier Booye was a huckster who sold fruits and vegetables in Atlantic City, Ventnor, Margate, and Longport. He then went into the business of building and house moving.

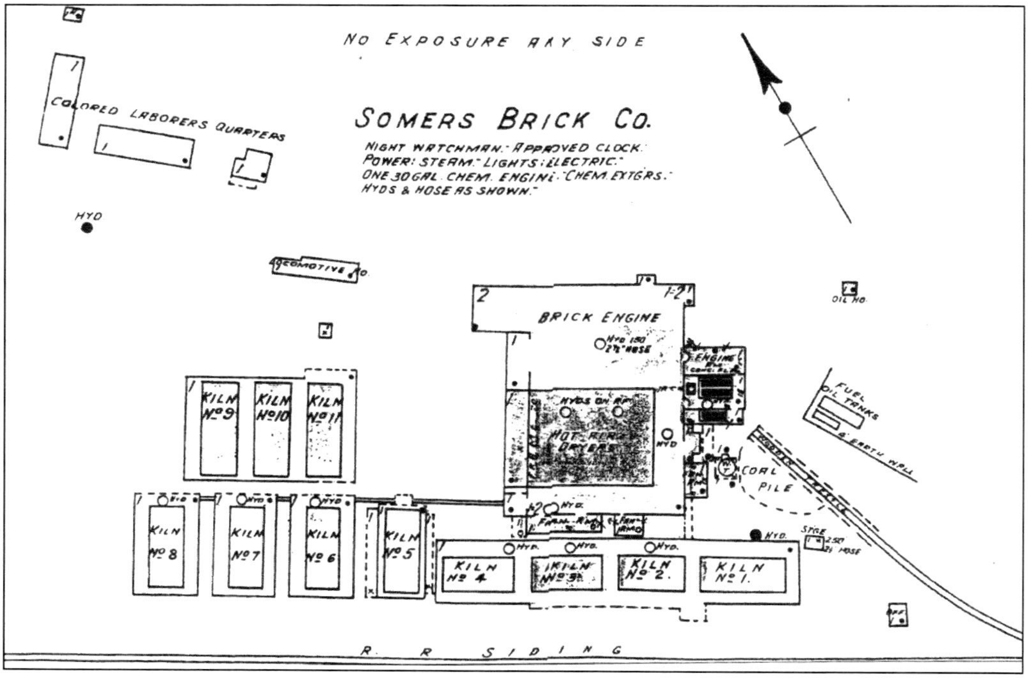

This map of Somers Brick Company shows 11 kilns, a railroad siding, and quarters for "colored laborers." The Northfield Museum currently occupies the site of one of the kilns. In preparing to construct the foundation for the new museum building, a massive amount of brick was excavated. Records indicate that the Somers Brick Company began operations in 1847 and started making bricks c. 1900. The company went out of business during the Great Depression. (Courtesy of the Atlantic County Historical Society.)

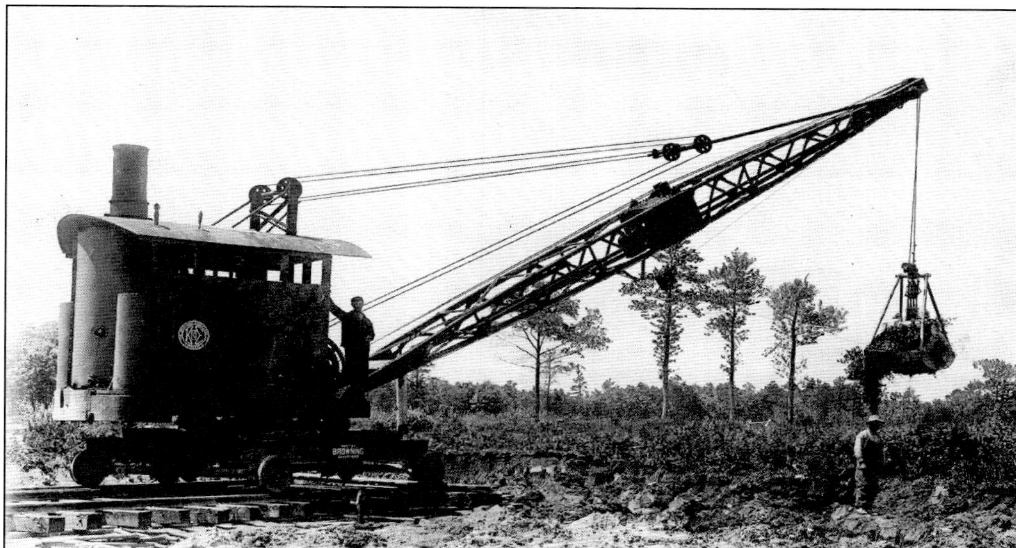

A crane at the Somers Brick Company scoops sand in this 1914 photograph. Joseph L. Price is one of the men in the photograph. The brickyard, located where Birch Grove Park is now, was for many years the largest business in Northfield.

These two men are working one of the Somers Brick Company kilns. The man on the right, Joseph Mazza of Northfield, had worked in the sulfur mines in Sicily and, by *c.* 1910, was employed at the brickyard, as recounted by Carol A. Patrick in *More Historic Houses of Northfield*. Mazza began to acquire farmland and worked night shifts at the brickyard and farmed his land during the day. He also operated a little store behind the brickyard, where he sold small necessities, such as tobacco, to the workers. The company used a machine called AutoBrik to make bricks. Bricks made in Northfield were known as New Jersey Red Colonials. Lettering on bricks made here includes "S B Co," "Somers," "S. & F. CO.," and "S&FBCo."

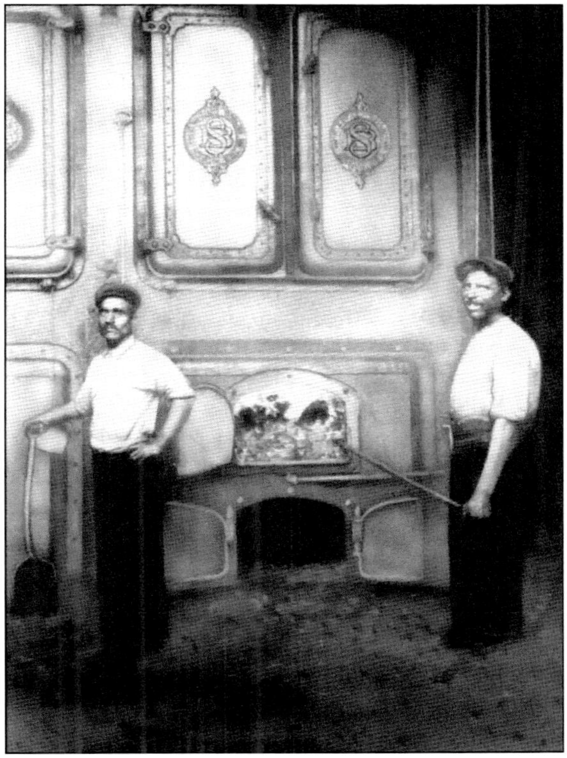

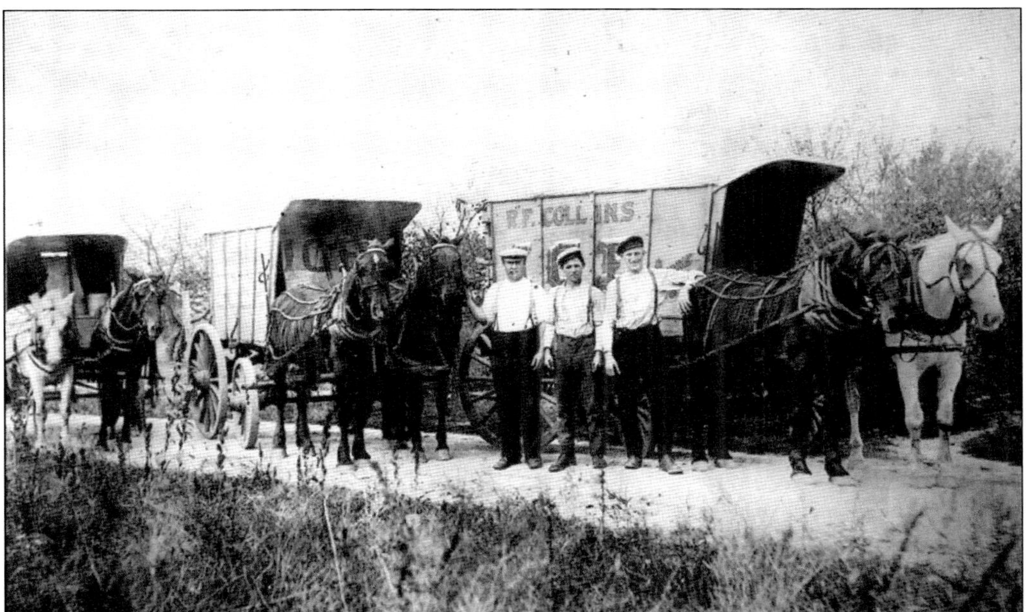

These R. F. Collins ice wagons served the local area, including Northfield, with ice taken from Bargaintown Pond. From left to right are Henry Rankin, Bakersville resident Roy Collins (son of Richard F. Collins), and William Barrett of Linwood. (Courtesy of the Egg Harbor Township Historical Society.)

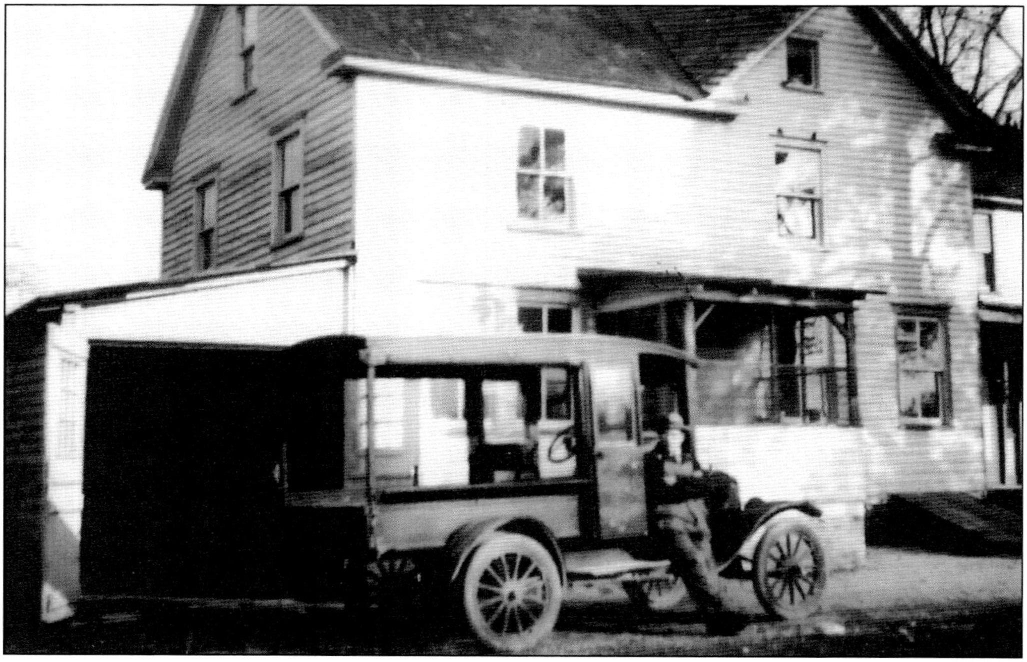

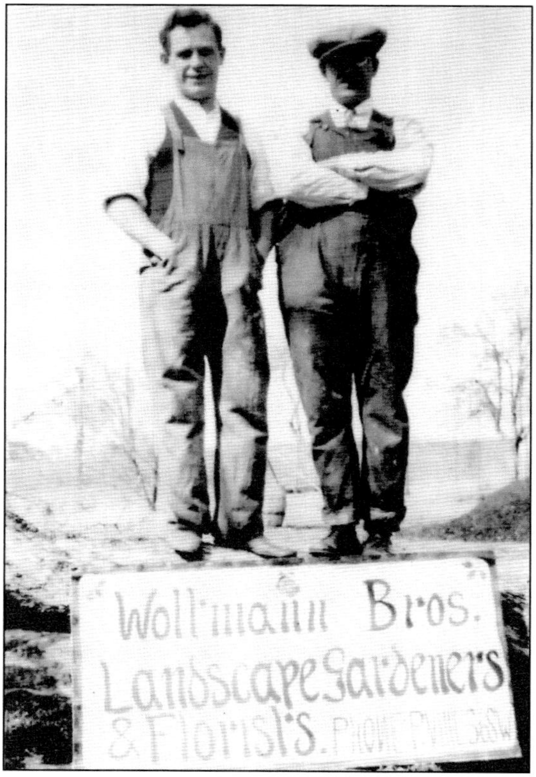

Woltmann Brothers Landscape Gardeners & Florists was on Dolphin Avenue, and the florist shop was in Pleasantville. The telephone number was 368W. Greenhouses and farmland were to the right and rear of the property. The delivery truck is parked in front of the house (which is still standing) at the homestead. In the lower photograph, Edward Woltmann (left) and Fred Woltmann stand with a sign advertising their business in 1927. (Courtesy of Laura Woltmann Forshaw.)

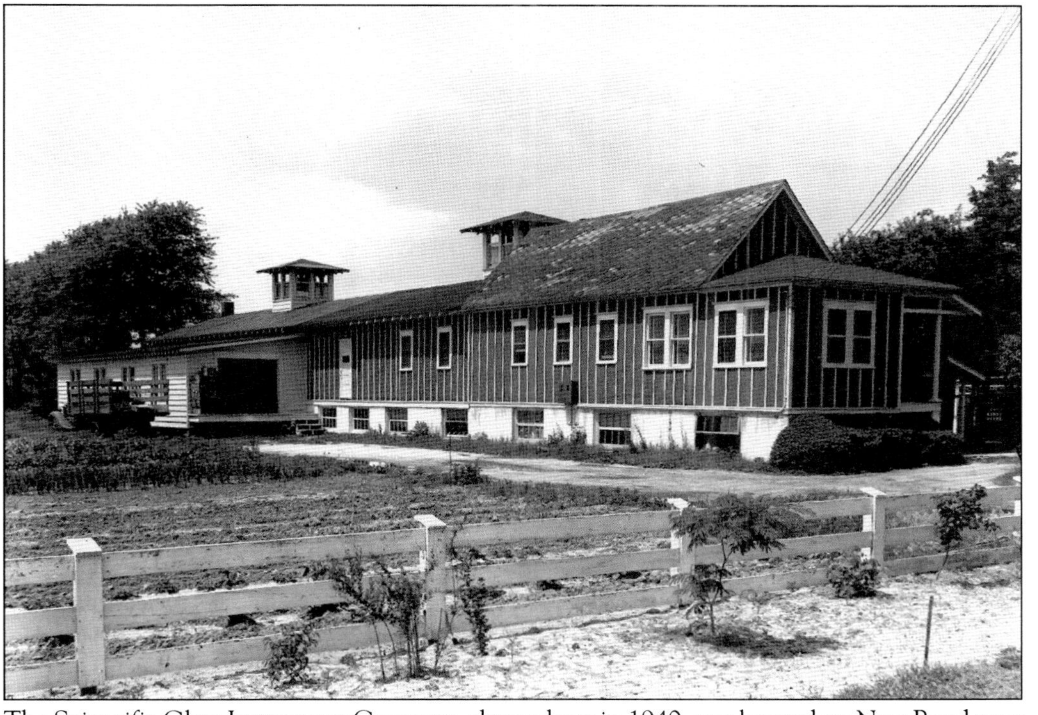

The Scientific Glass Instrument Company, shown here in 1940, was located on New Road near Tilton Road, behind the property now occupied by Eckerd Drugs and Plaza 9. Owned and operated by the Sheppard family, the company was in business in Northfield from 1914 to the 1960s. It made tubes for blood testing and for milk sampling. Records show that customers included E. I. Lilly & Company and Jonas Salk. Salk, who developed the polio vaccine, ordered test tubes from the company in the early 1950s.

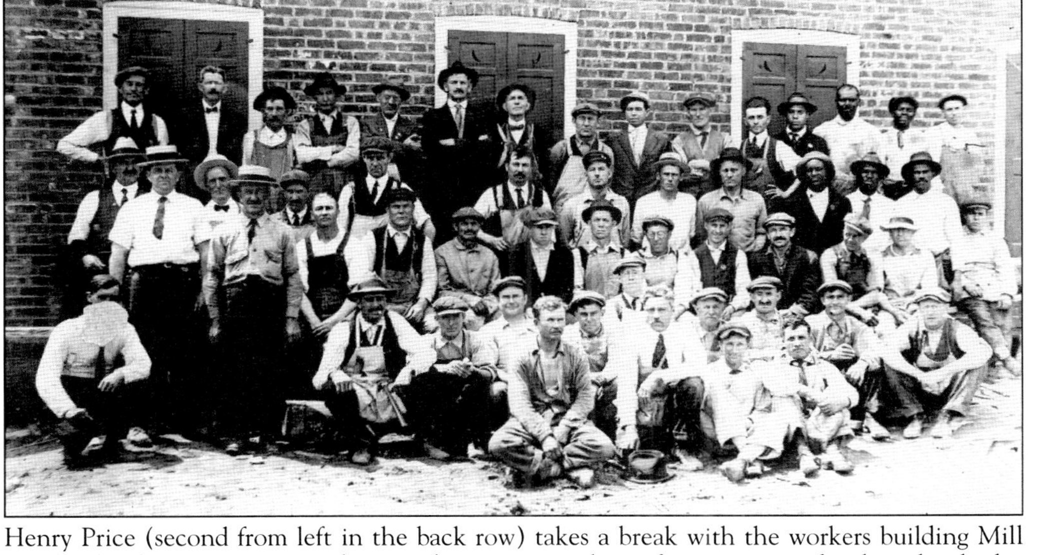

Henry Price (second from left in the back row) takes a break with the workers building Mill Road School in 1914. Price, who was the superintendent of construction for the school, also helped build the Atlantic City Country Club.

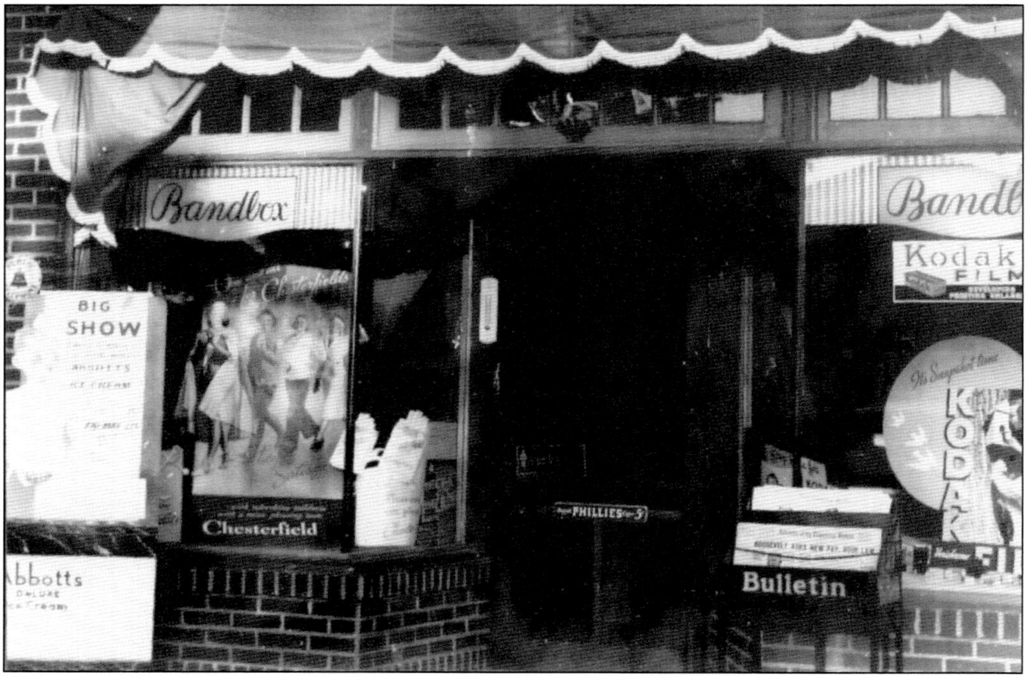

The Bandbox sold cigars, newspapers, ice cream, and sandwiches and also had a soda fountain. From 1930 to 1940, it was operated by Eugene Guion. It was subsequently operated by Mr. Grist and then by Walter Schmid. It was in a row of stores on the east side of Shore Road, across from Fifield Avenue. The lower photograph dates from *c.* 1939 or 1940. The American Store was a grocery store. The post office was the building to the right of this strip of stores. (Courtesy of Tom Guion.)

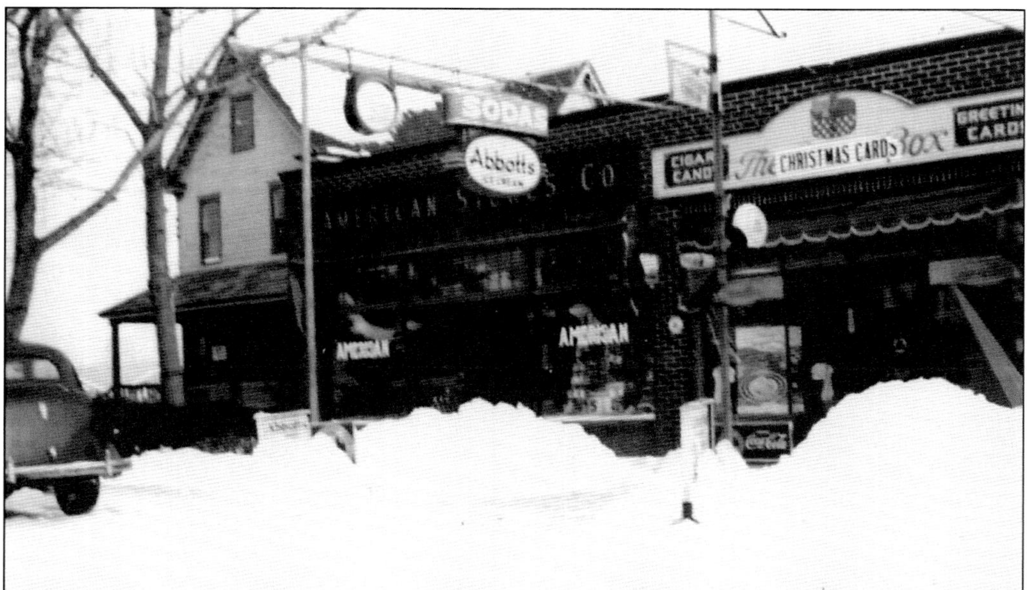

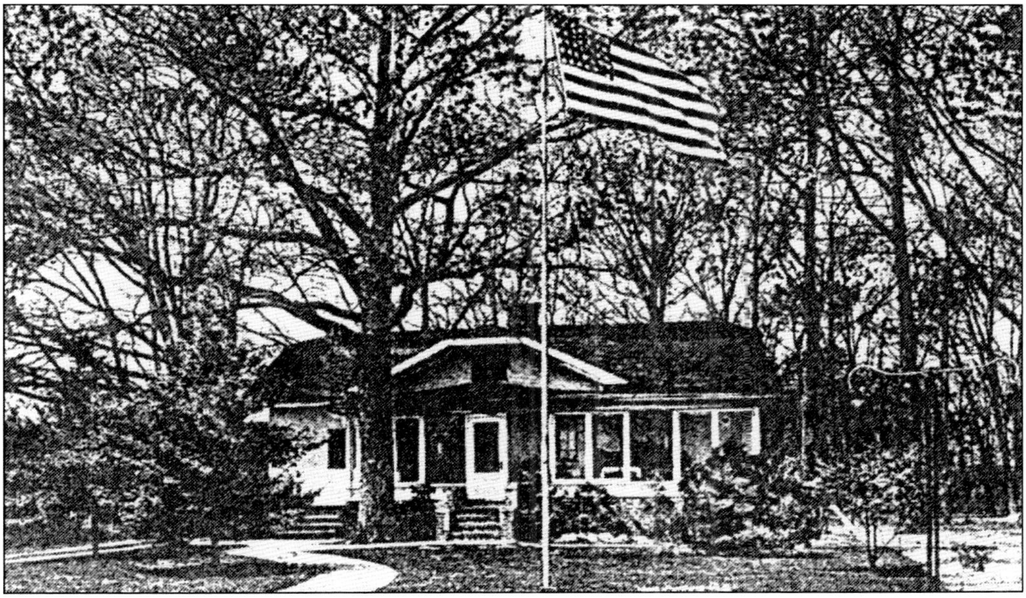

Acorn Lodge was located on Shore Road, just south of the intersection with Mill and Tilton Roads, near the current location of Ventura's Offshore Cafe. Miriam Metz opened this restaurant in her family home following the death of her husband, Thomas Metz Sr. The Metzes' two sons, both second lieutenants, were killed during World War II. Thomas O. Metz Jr. (right) was killed in January 1944 in an airplane collision north of his base in Monroe, Louisiana. He was buried in Arlington National Cemetery. Walter E. Metz was killed in May 1945. Originally buried in England, his remains were exhumed in 1948 and brought to the United States for burial at Arlington.

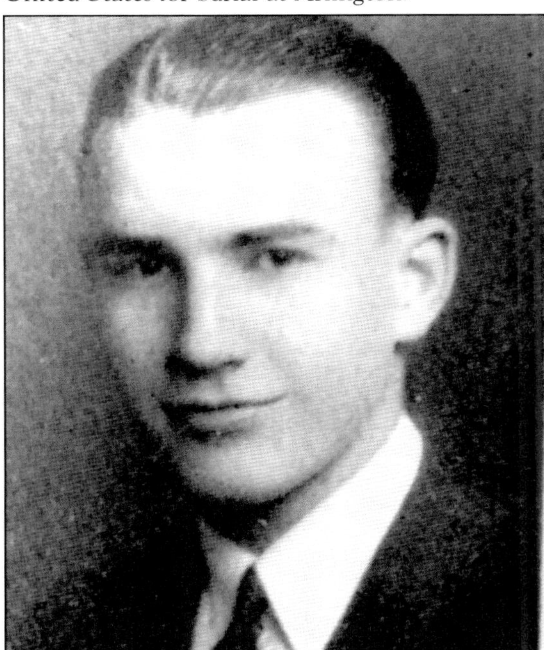

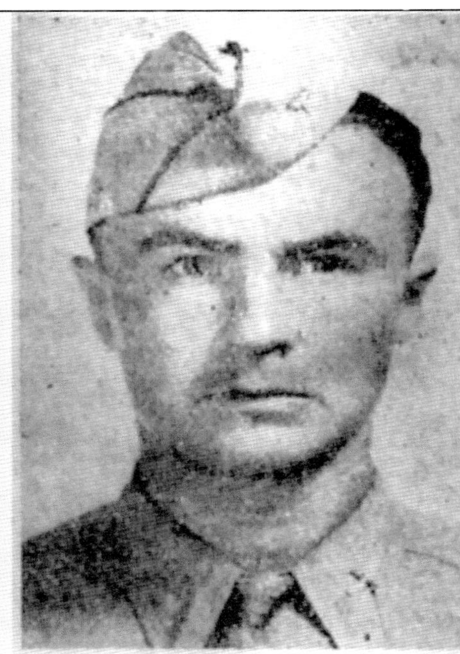

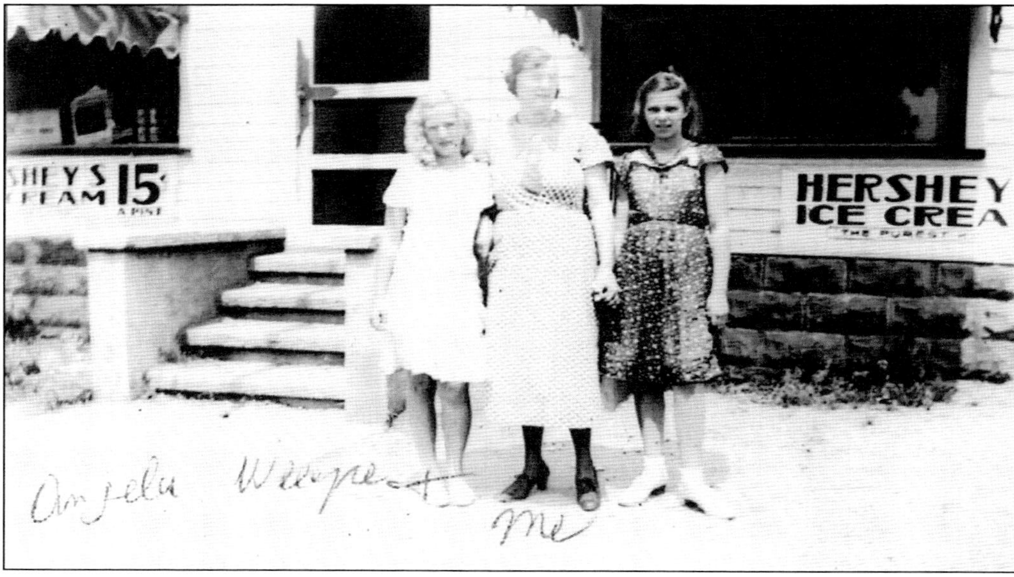

DeKluyver's Quality Bakery, owned by Dirk and Louise DeKluyver, was located at Dolphin and New Roads. The actual baking was done in a concrete block building situated behind the store, on New Road. Both of the buildings at Dolphin and New Roads are still standing today. The bakery moved *c.* 1927 to the Black Horse Pike in Pleasantville, where it operated as DeKluyver's Bakery. Pictured above are, from left to right, Angela, Louise, and daughter Louise "Weeze" DeKluyver. Below are, from left to right, Louise, Dirk, Angela, and Weeze (Louise DeKluyver Kuppel). After Dirk DeKluyver's death in the late 1930s, the bakery was moved from its Northfield location to the Black Horse Pike in Pleasantville, to the site where Hornberger's and Minos were later located. (Courtesy of the DeKluyver family.)

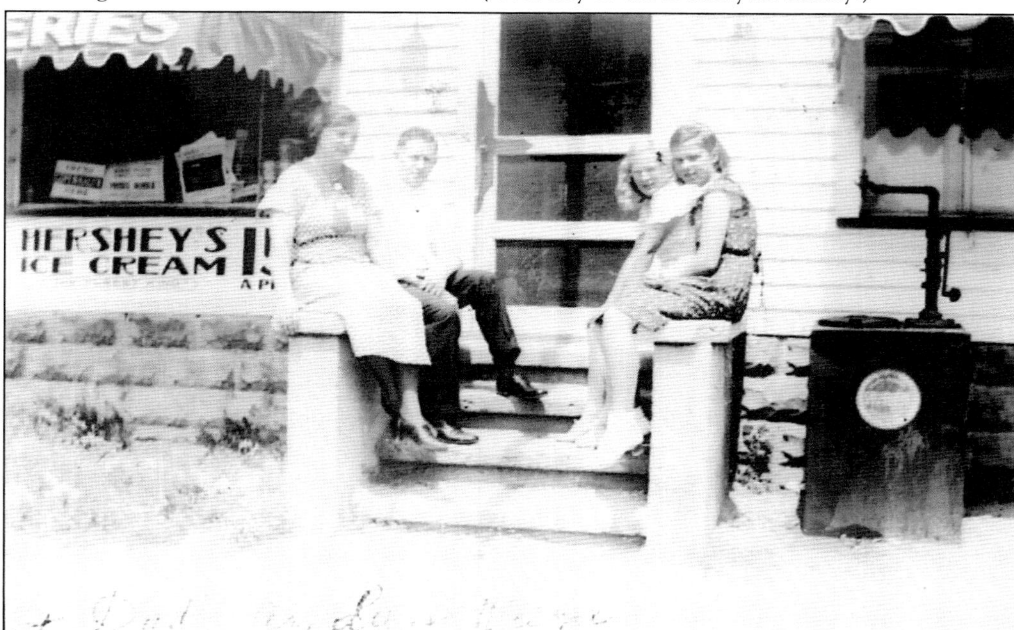

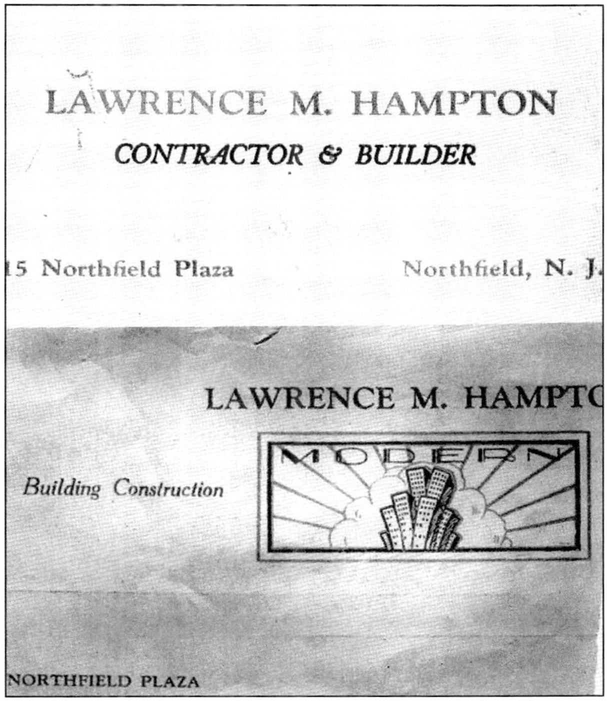

Lawrence M. Hampton (1903–2001) was a building contractor who learned the trade from his father, Nicholas G. Hampton, and his uncle, Wade Hampton. The Hampton Brothers built Northfield Plaza. When the Depression hit in 1929, Lawrence Hampton borrowed money from the bank and built a restaurant, the Log. In 1941, he added a large dining room, which opened just at the start of World War II. Lawrence and Jewel Hampton were the parents of Joyce Hampton Pullan, one of the founding members of the Northfield Cultural Committee and the Northfield Historical Society. (Advertisement courtesy of the *Pleasantville Press*; information courtesy of J. H. Pullan.)

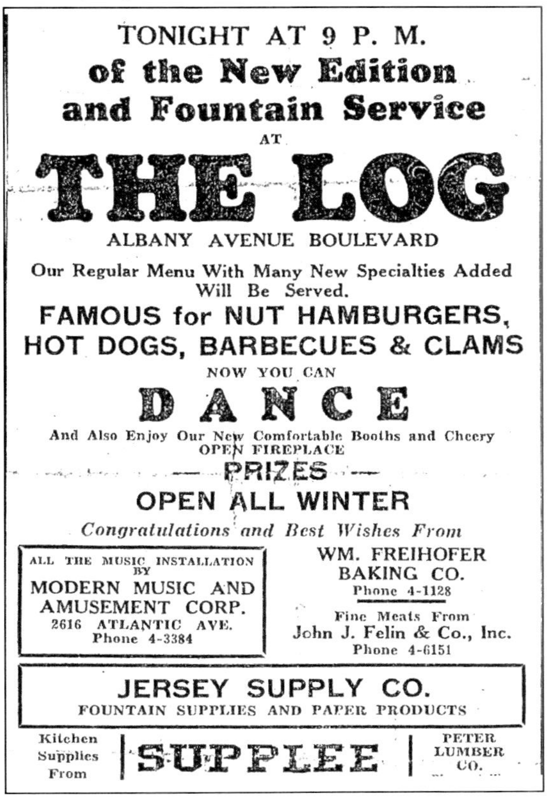

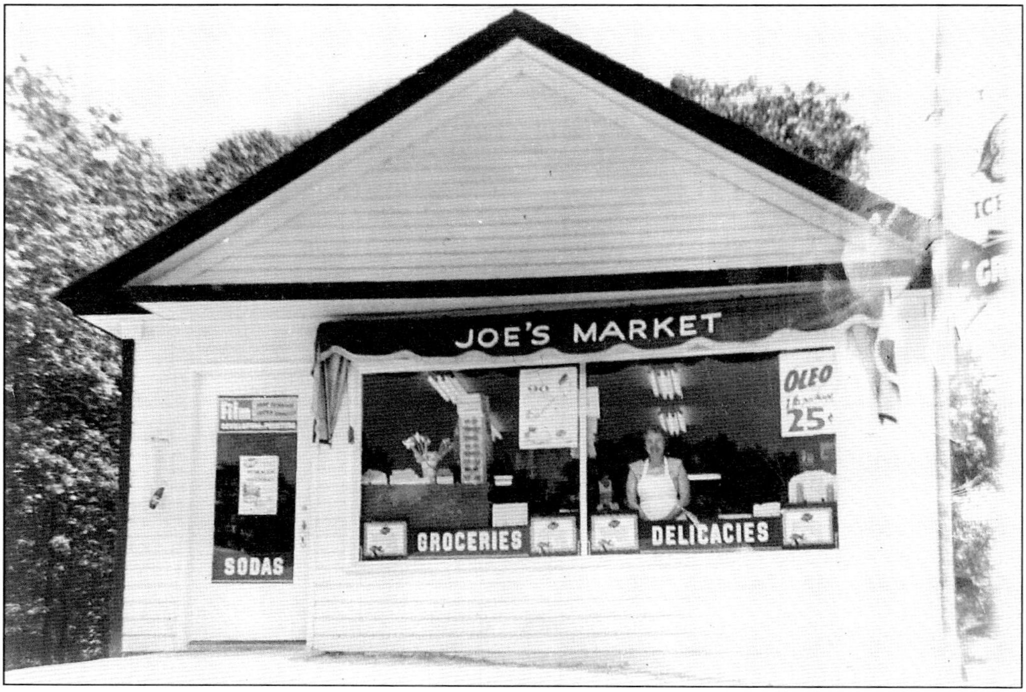

Joe's Market was originally the James Candy store. It sold candy and cigarettes on one side and dry goods on the other. "Aunt Jennie" Rotan ran the store and lived in the back. In 1955, it was purchased and enlarged by Joe Guerrier and renamed Joe's Market. Muriel Morton can be seen looking through the display window in the photograph above. Tilton Market now occupies this location, at Tilton and Zion Roads. (Courtesy of Joe Guerrier.)

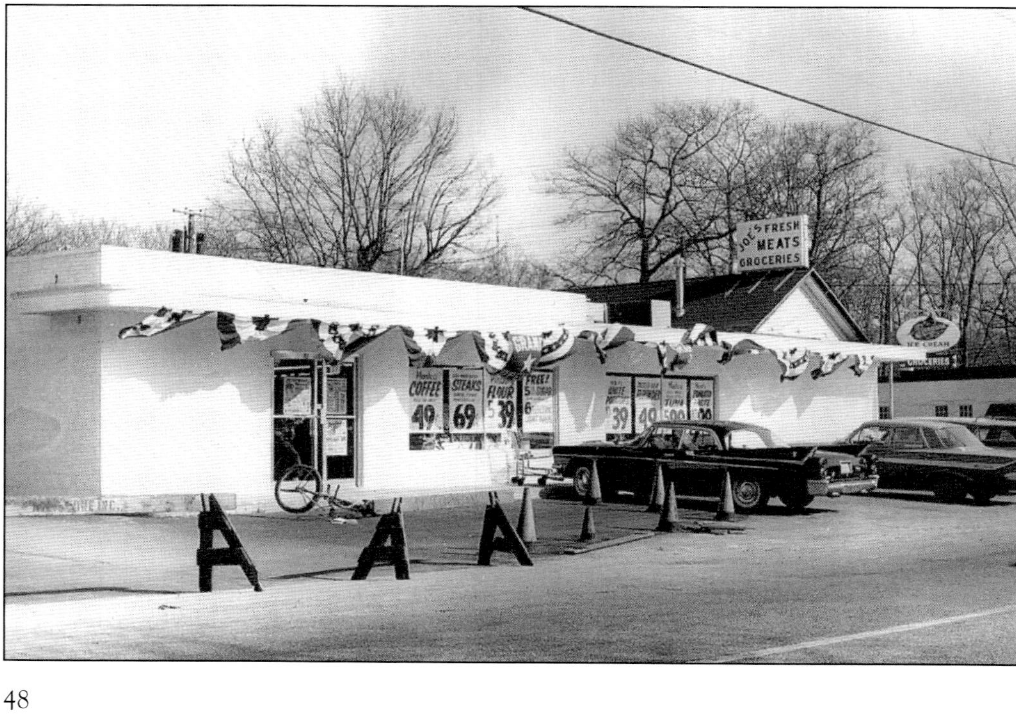

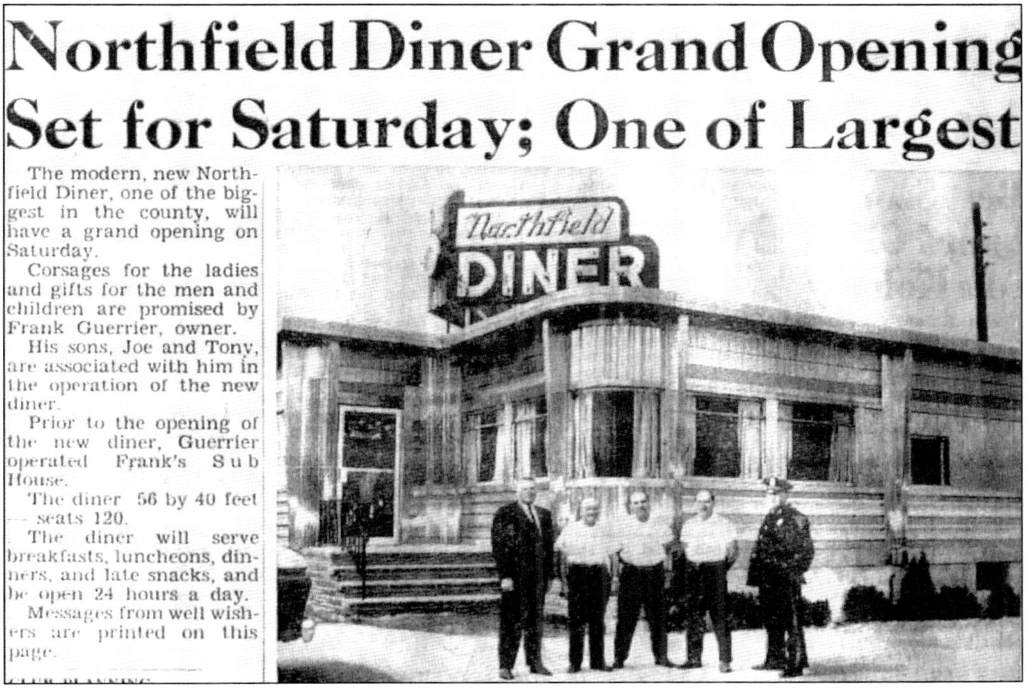

Northfield Diner Grand Opening Set for Saturday; One of Largest

The modern, new Northfield Diner, one of the biggest in the county, will have a grand opening on Saturday.

Corsages for the ladies and gifts for the men and children are promised by Frank Guerrier, owner.

His sons, Joe and Tony, are associated with him in the operation of the new diner.

Prior to the opening of the new diner, Guerrier operated Frank's Sub House.

The diner 56 by 40 feet — seats 120.

The diner will serve breakfasts, luncheons, dinners, and late snacks, and be open 24 hours a day.

Messages from well wishers are printed on this page.

The Northfield Diner opened on May 5, 1966. Owner Frank Guerrier (second from left) stands outside with his sons, Joseph (center) and Anthony, flanked by Mayor Otto Bruyns (left) and Police Chief Howard Chambers. Frank had originally operated Frank's Sub House at this same New Road location, today occupied by Athena's Family Restaurant and, before that, by the Sunset Diner. (Courtesy of Helen Rando, the *Pleasantville Press*, and the Hinman family.)

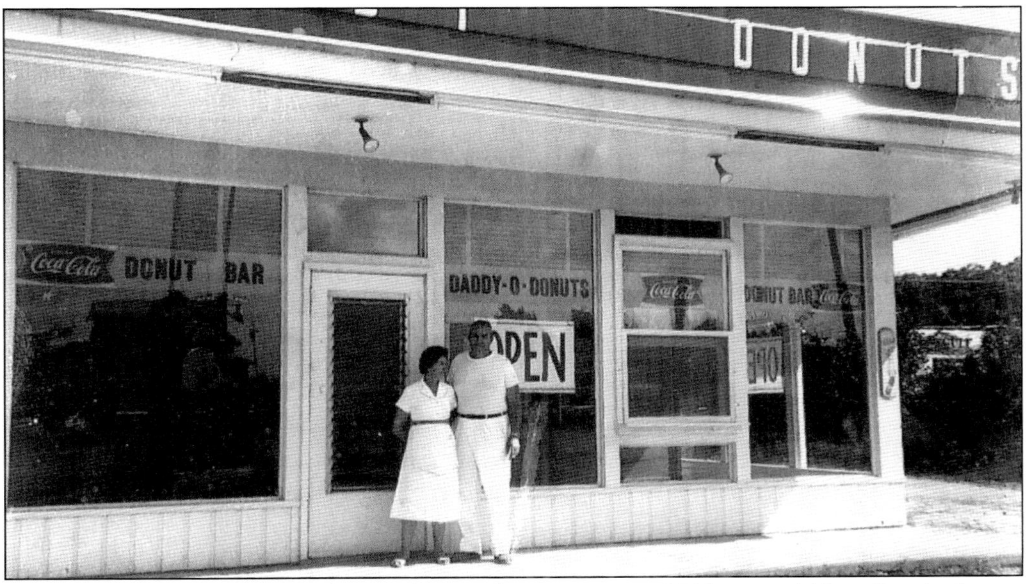

Daddy-O Donuts was located near the northwest corner of Tilton and New Roads. It was owned and operated by Mary and Frank Gurney, shown in this photograph. (Courtesy of Mary Ellen Galina.)

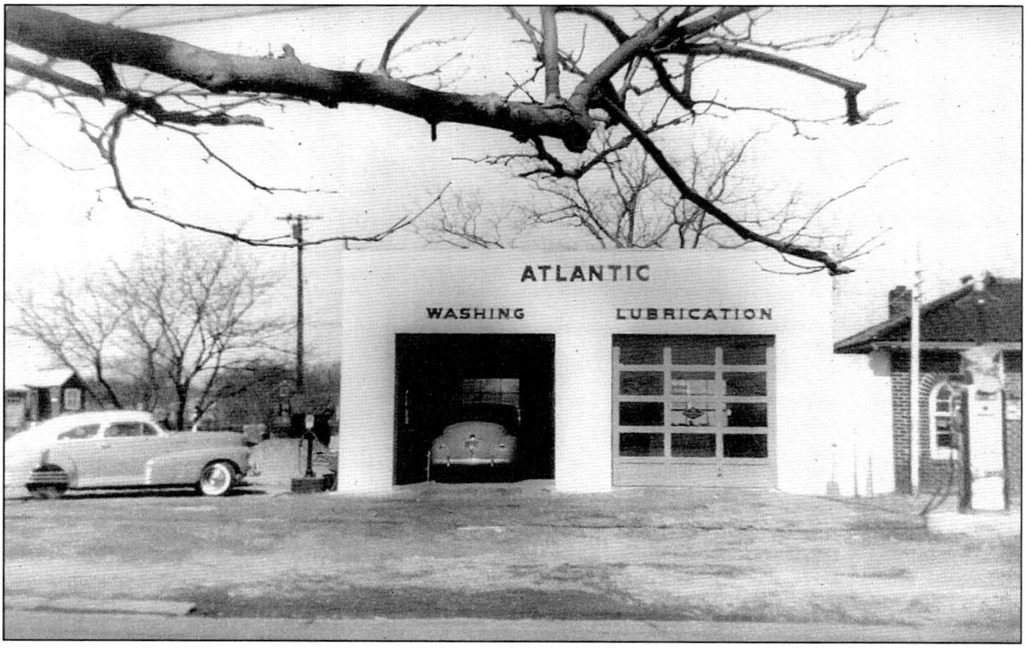

The original building at 517 Shore Road was constructed in 1926 as a gas station for Atlantic Refinery. In 1949, Frank Perri Sr. purchased the building from Sadie G. Kline, and it was renovated as a garage in 1955. Today, it is an auto service center and is located at Shore Road and Haddon Avenue. Jim Steelman of Somers Point is pictured below. (Courtesy of the Perri family.)

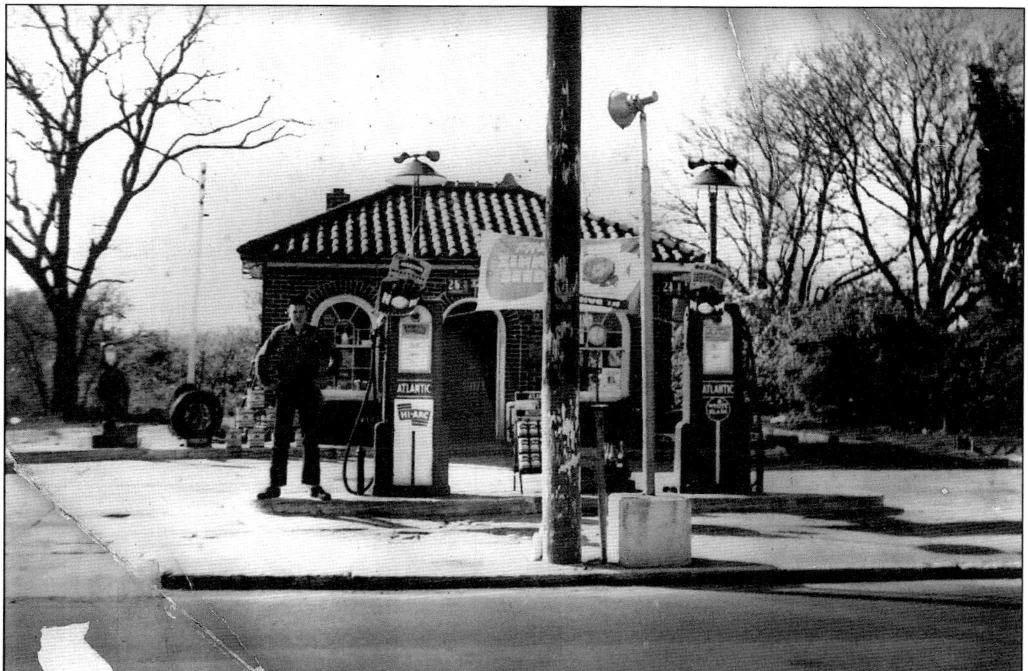

Many people who grew up in Northfield in the 1930s and 1940s have fond memories of the horses in the stable behind Rugby Hall. One longtime resident recalled, "As children, we were allowed to 'visit' them after school. The path to Mill Road School led from Shore Road through the woods." The Rugby is now Ventura's Offshore Cafe. Wayne's Inn was on New Road, where the Owl Tree is now located.

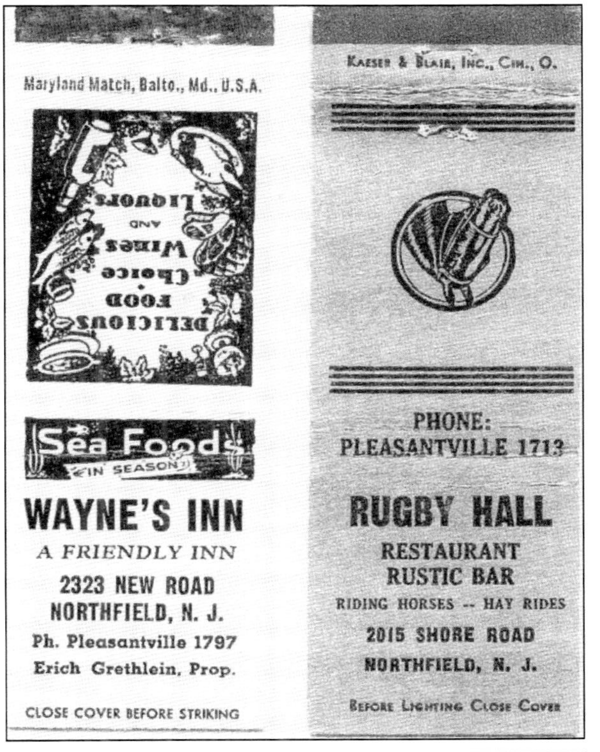

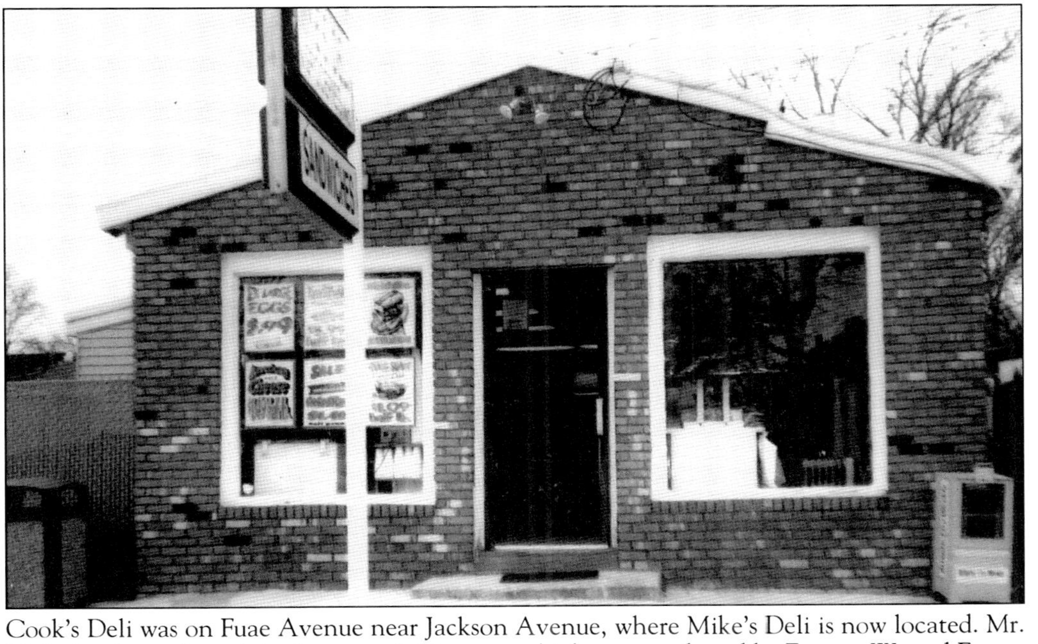

Cook's Deli was on Fuae Avenue near Jackson Avenue, where Mike's Deli is now located. Mr. McFarland was the original owner of this store, which was purchased by Eugene W. and Emma J. Cook in 1948. Operated first by the Cooks and then by their son and daughter-in-law, Donald R. and Madeline L. Cook, the delicatessen became known as the place to go for penny candy on a Sunday afternoon. After the store was sold in 1983, it was renamed Mike's.

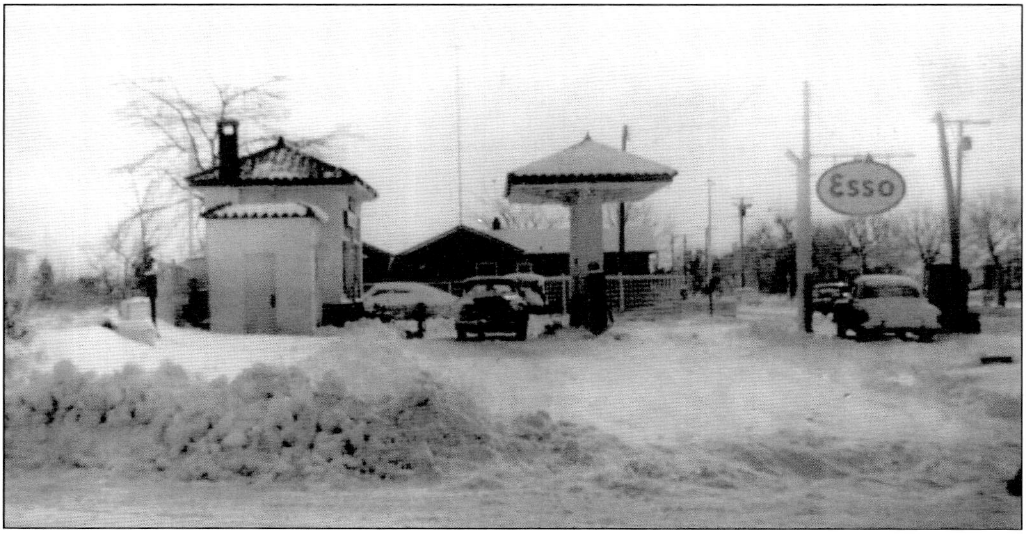

Ike Heckman built this gas station at Shore and Mill Roads in 1929. James Clark began operating the station in 1954 after Heckman died while at work at the station. In 1969, Tom Clark took over from his father and operated the station until it closed in 1991. This photograph was taken in the 1950s. The lift at the original station was outdoors; the lift at the new station, built in 1963, was inside. (Courtesy of Tom Clark.)

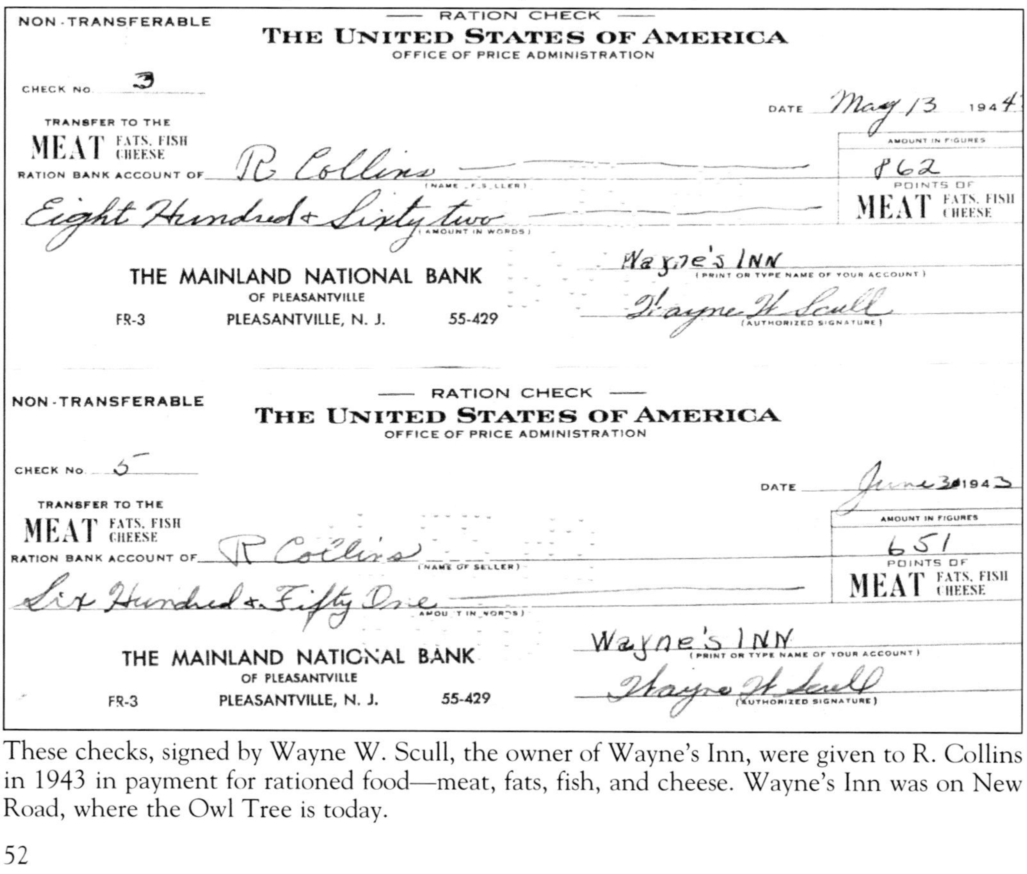

NON-TRANSFERABLE — RATION CHECK —
THE UNITED STATES OF AMERICA
OFFICE OF PRICE ADMINISTRATION

CHECK NO. 3
DATE May 13 1943
TRANSFER TO THE MEAT FATS, FISH CHEESE RATION BANK ACCOUNT OF R Collins (NAME OF SELLER)
AMOUNT IN FIGURES 862 POINTS OF MEAT FATS, FISH CHEESE
Eight Hundred & Sixty two (AMOUNT IN WORDS)
THE MAINLAND NATIONAL BANK OF PLEASANTVILLE PLEASANTVILLE, N. J. FR-3 55-429
Wayne's INN (PRINT OR TYPE NAME OF YOUR ACCOUNT)
Wayne W. Scull (AUTHORIZED SIGNATURE)

NON-TRANSFERABLE — RATION CHECK —
THE UNITED STATES OF AMERICA
OFFICE OF PRICE ADMINISTRATION

CHECK NO. 5
DATE June 30 1943
TRANSFER TO THE MEAT FATS, FISH CHEESE RATION BANK ACCOUNT OF R Collins (NAME OF SELLER)
AMOUNT IN FIGURES 651 POINTS OF MEAT FATS, FISH CHEESE
Six Hundred & Fifty One (AMOUNT IN WORDS)
THE MAINLAND NATIONAL BANK OF PLEASANTVILLE PLEASANTVILLE, N. J. FR-3 55-429
Wayne's INN (PRINT OR TYPE NAME OF YOUR ACCOUNT)
Wayne W. Scull (AUTHORIZED SIGNATURE)

These checks, signed by Wayne W. Scull, the owner of Wayne's Inn, were given to R. Collins in 1943 in payment for rationed food—meat, fats, fish, and cheese. Wayne's Inn was on New Road, where the Owl Tree is today.

Four

Reading, 'Riting, and 'Rithmetic

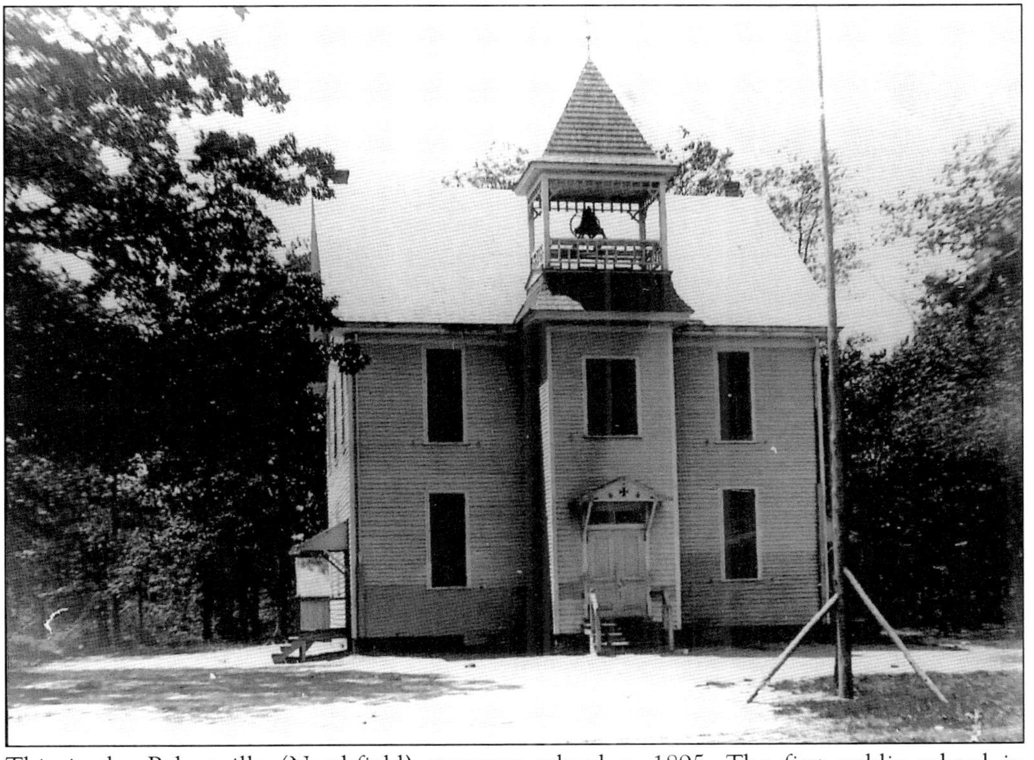

This is the Bakersville (Northfield) grammar school *c.* 1895. The first public school in Bakersville was the Brick School and Meeting House, a one-room brick building constructed in 1817 on land donated by James Tilton on the northwest corner of Tilton and Zion Roads. In 1872, a two-story wood-frame school was constructed on Mill Road, on a one-acre property that had been donated for that purpose. This building was then moved west to make room for the brick Mill Road School, the original portion of which was built in 1914. The frame building was used as a school through 1915; classes commenced at the brick school in 1916.

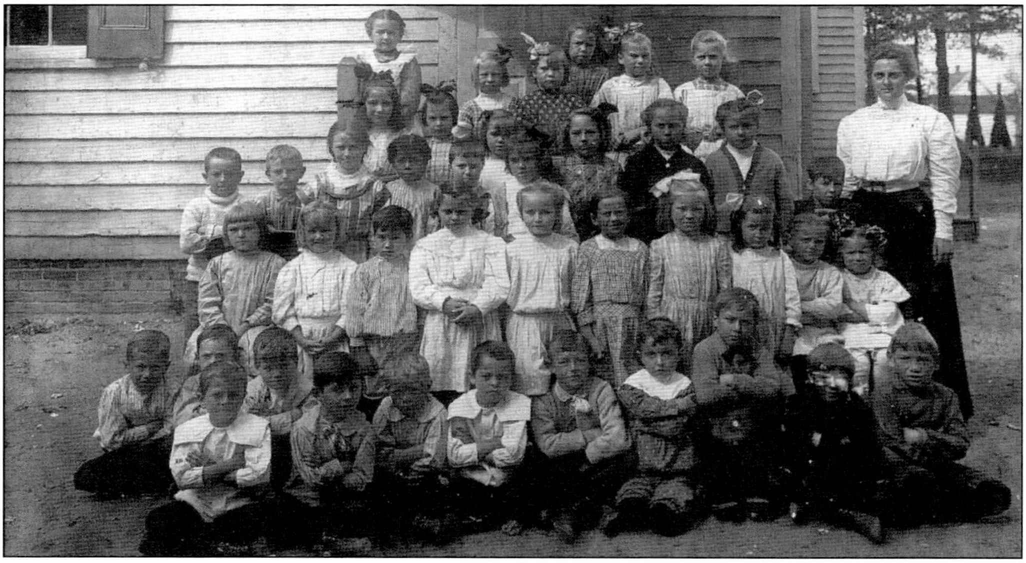

This photograph shows Northfield School's first and second grades in 1909. Their teacher, Ethel Bartlett, came from Absecon.

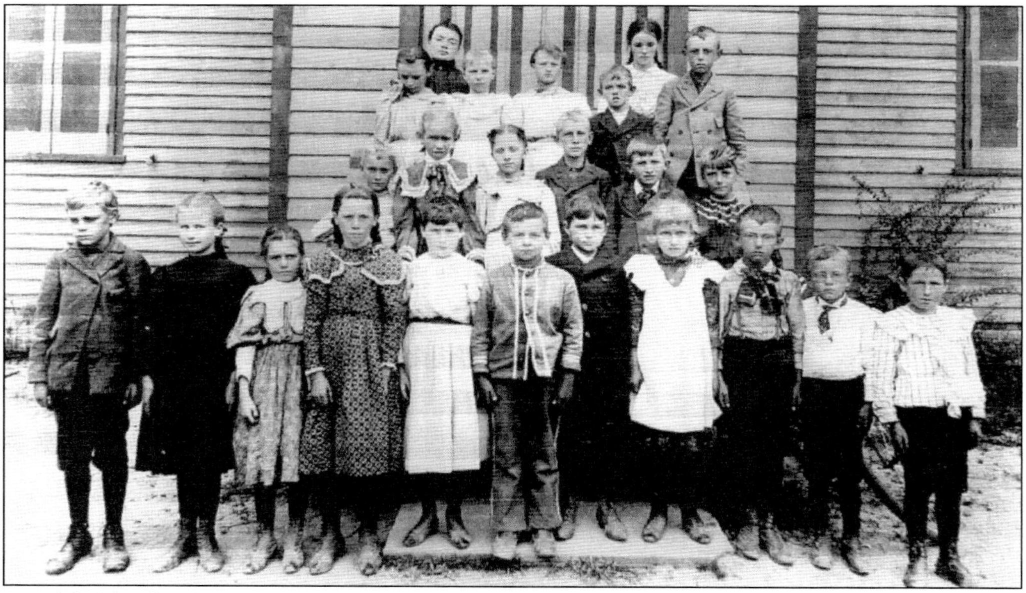

Northfield School students are pictured here *c.* 1895, as recollected by Lewis Lake. They are as follows: (first row) Walter Sutton, Mary Roberts (Mrs. W. Stewart), Gertrude Hingston (Mrs. John Turner), Ida Murray (Mrs. Howard Conklin), Jessie Vickers (Mrs. Raymond Somers), Winfield Moffit, Wilbur Steelman, Bertha Kears (Mrs. Clarence Dixon), Warren Ryon, Seaward Leeds, and Harry Dougherty; (second row) Gertrude Leeds (Mrs. Fred Elmer), Emma Fifield (Mrs. Morris Snyder), Abbie Fifield (Mrs. Charley Cochlin), Lewis Lake, Harry Adams (brother of Constant Adams), Dora Fabian, and Joseph Price; (third row) Rena Contale, Lilly Small, Mabel Roberts, Mark Kears (a boatbuilder), and Phoebe E. Price (Mrs. Ralph Hackett). In the back left is the teacher, Olive Mier, who came from Hazelton, Pennsylvania. She taught in Northfield for only one year.

Louisa Somers attended Mill Road School. During the 1908–1909 school year, the school register indicated that she was one of 27 students in the classroom taught by C. W. Kean, whose annual salary was $720. This classroom contained one 11-year-old, four 12-year-olds, six 13-year-olds, ten 14-year-olds, four 15-year-olds, and two 16-year-olds. School was in session from September 8, 1908, to May 17, 1909. The register classifies this as a "grammar" grade and notes that there were three classes in the room.

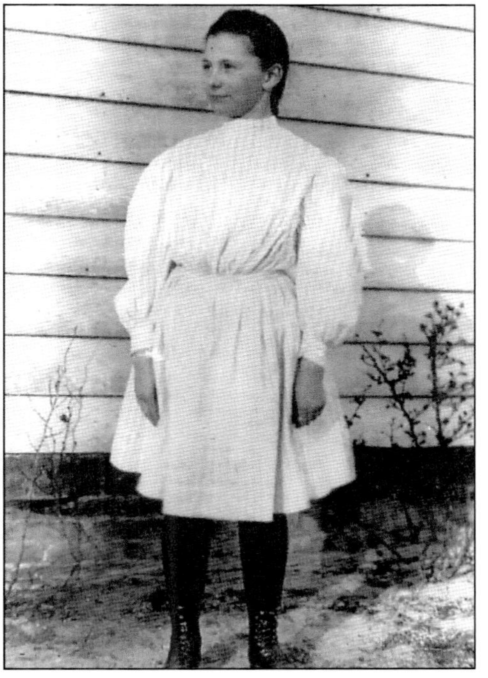

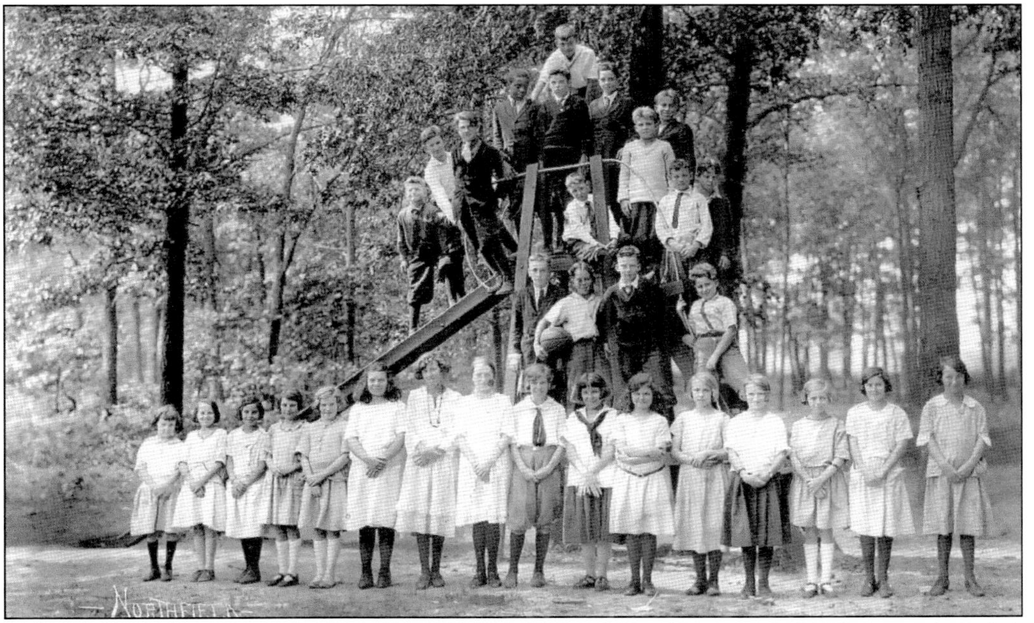

Seen here are Mill Road School sixth- and seventh-grade students in 1923. They are, from left to right, as follows: (first row) Milta Price, Betty Snyder, Elsie Lucas, Ethel Thomas, Elizabeth Godfrey, Vira Burroughs, Elsie ?, Emma Somers, Ida Mae Hampton, Frances Risley, Nellie Hambleton, Elsie Higbee, Anna Morton, Evelyn Rentschler, Hilda Lucas, and unidentified; (second row) unidentified, Bruno Garr, George Walters, and Herbie Trautenberg; (third row) Eugene Hewitt, Emerson Dougherty, Joe Lindner, and unidentified; (fourth row) Bill Bishop (in knickers), unidentified, Chris Whitehead, Floyd Walker, Andy Bozarth, and unidentified.

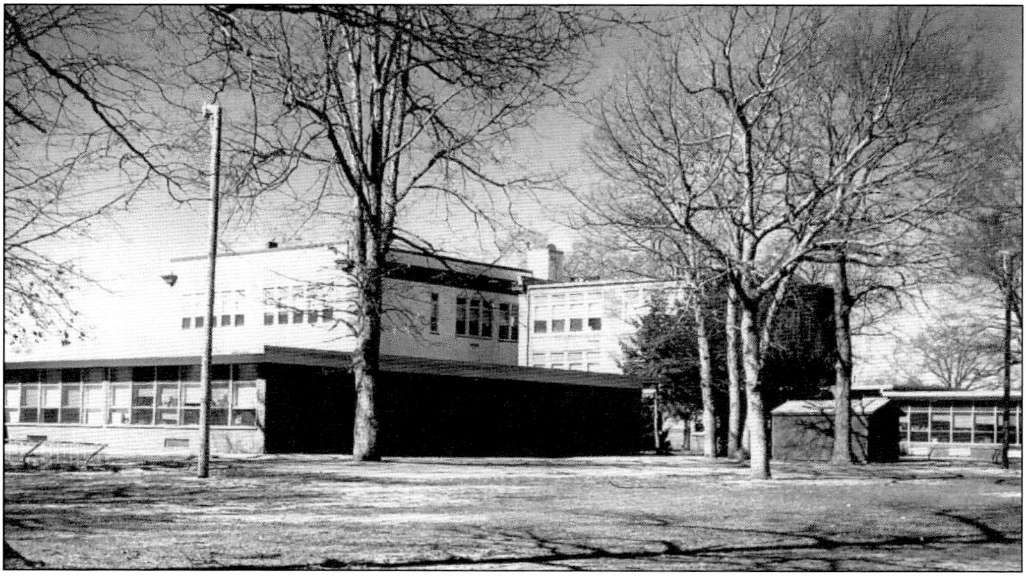

Construction of the original portion of the brick Mill Road School began in 1914, and the school became operational in 1916. The white-painted addition, built in 1927, included the auditorium. It held grades six through eight when it closed in 1997. Replaced by the Northfield Community School, the building was torn down in 1998.

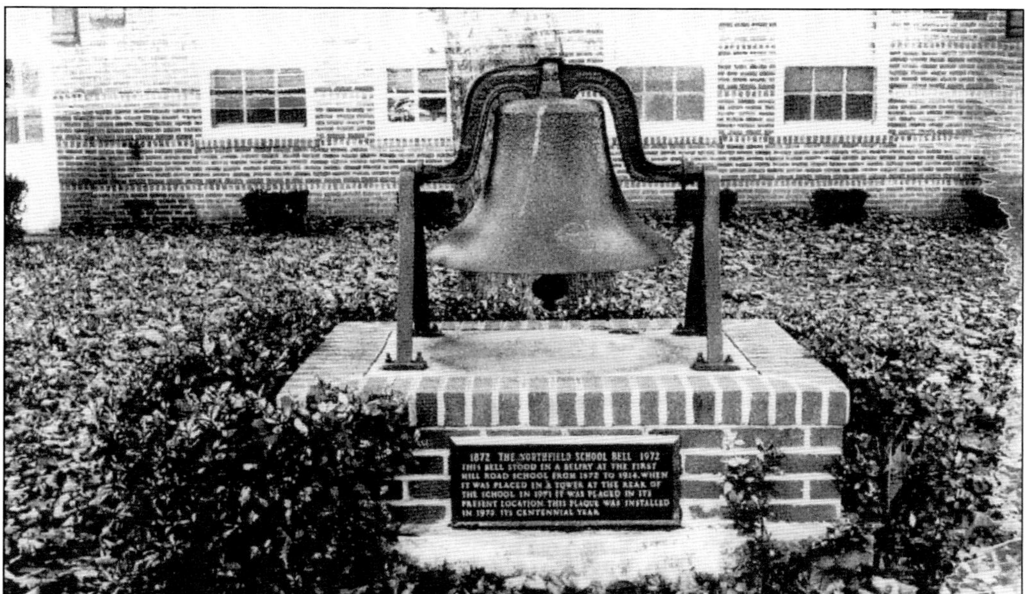

The Mill Road School bell originally hung in the front tower of the old wooden schoolhouse. In 1914, when the brick school was built, the bell was placed in a tower behind the building. Occasionally, it was rung in the middle of the night by pranksters. The bell rope was tied into a classroom to which only special students were permitted access—in order to reach it, the pranksters had to climb the tower. In 1972, the tower was removed, and eighth-grade National Honor Society students arranged to have the bell placed on a monument in front of the school. When the community school was built, the bell was moved to the school atrium.

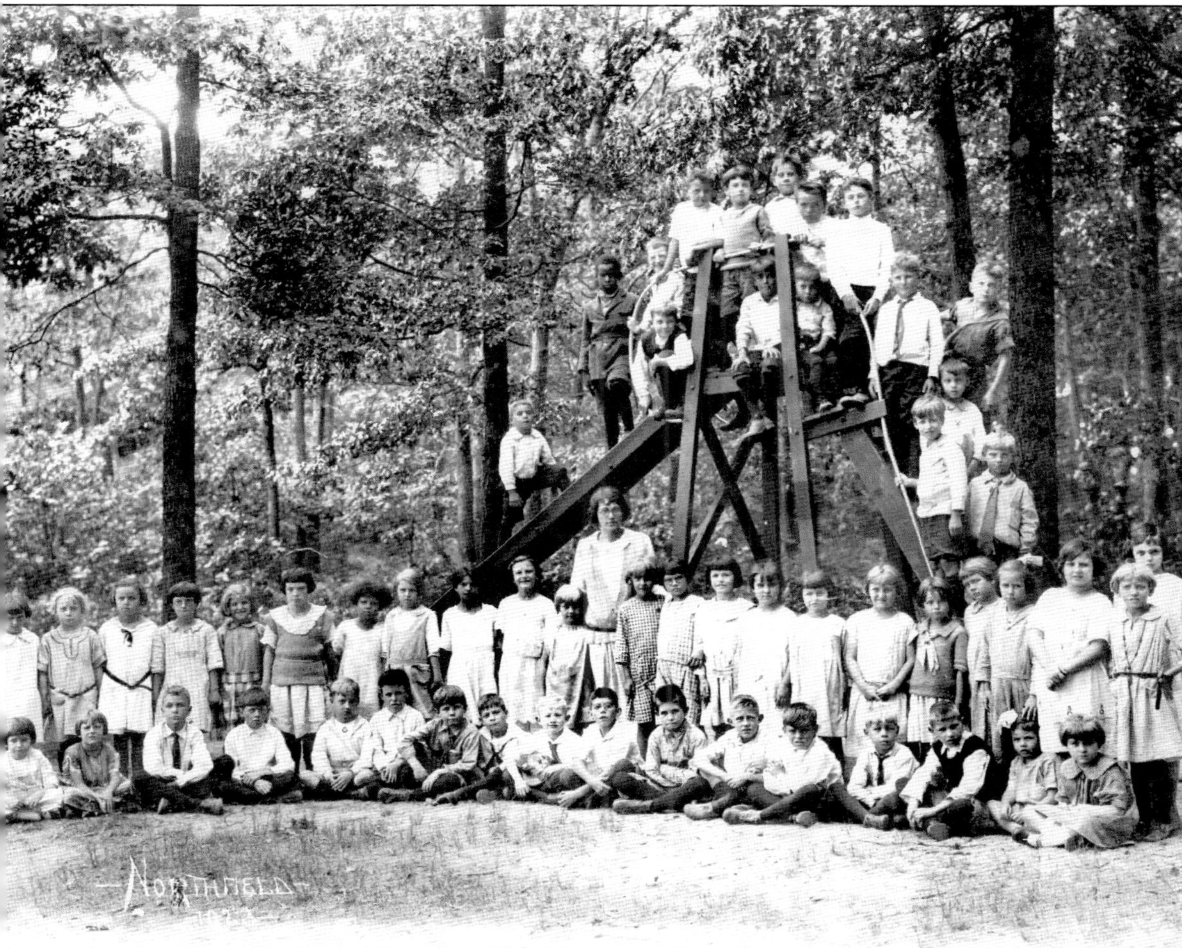

This photograph shows third-grade students at Mill Road School in 1923. They are as follows: (first row) Helen Duble, Henrietta Van Dyke, Lambert McGee, Evelyn Chambers, Edith Higbee, Louise Harman, Antoinette Majane, Eleanor Lucas, Dorothy Chambers, Virginia Bayen, Almeda Dougherty, Mary Maden, Jeanette Hinman, Melvin Dougherty, Bobby Marsh, Carl Walker, and Carlton Hackett; (second row) Ruth Mihian, Jacinia Mazza, Alvenia Lee, Hannah Shappel, Maurice Lake, Thomas Creasy, ? Risley, Mrs. Rockleman (teacher), Edward Duble, Henry Swain, Ruth Ryon, Cara Banning, Edward O'Donald, Thomas Marsh, Anna Lucas, Morris ?, Eugene Swilkey, Bobby ?, John Burroughs, Christina Pettinelli, Everett Steward, ? Risley, Ethel Lucas, Maurice Dougherty, Florence Morton, Paul Taylor, Lorene Lee, William Schoenleber, and 13 unidentified students.

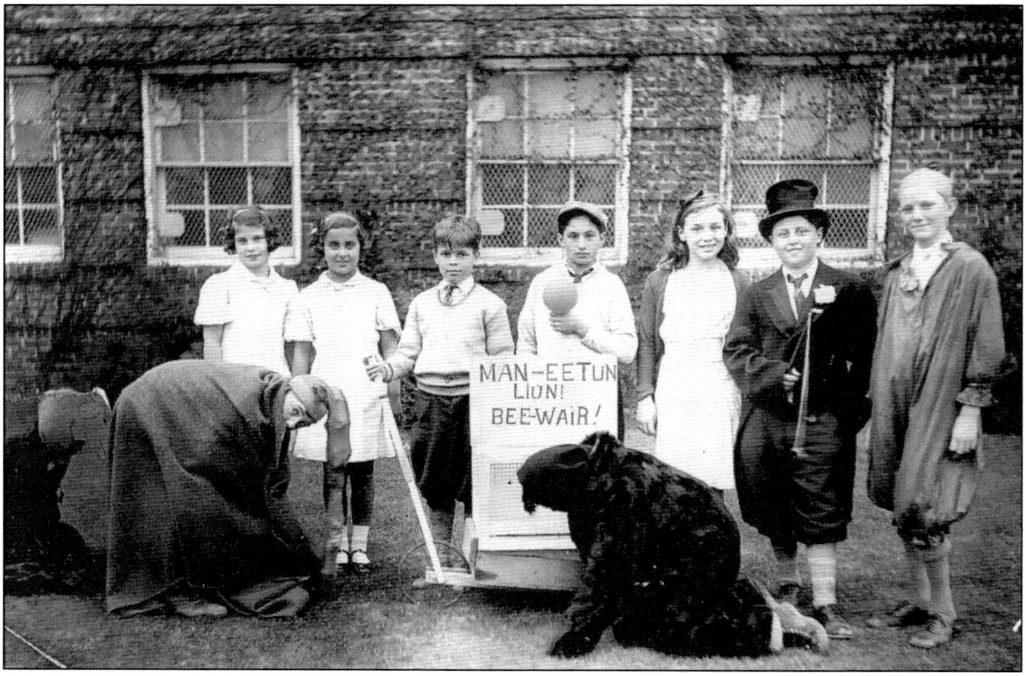

Costumed Mill Road School students in the late 1930s are seen with a sign reading "MAN-EETUN LION! BEE-WAIR!" From left to right are Glenn Lee, George Banning, ? Hewitt, Sam Mazza, Fred Carney, Marion Curlette, Florence Probst, and two unidentified students.

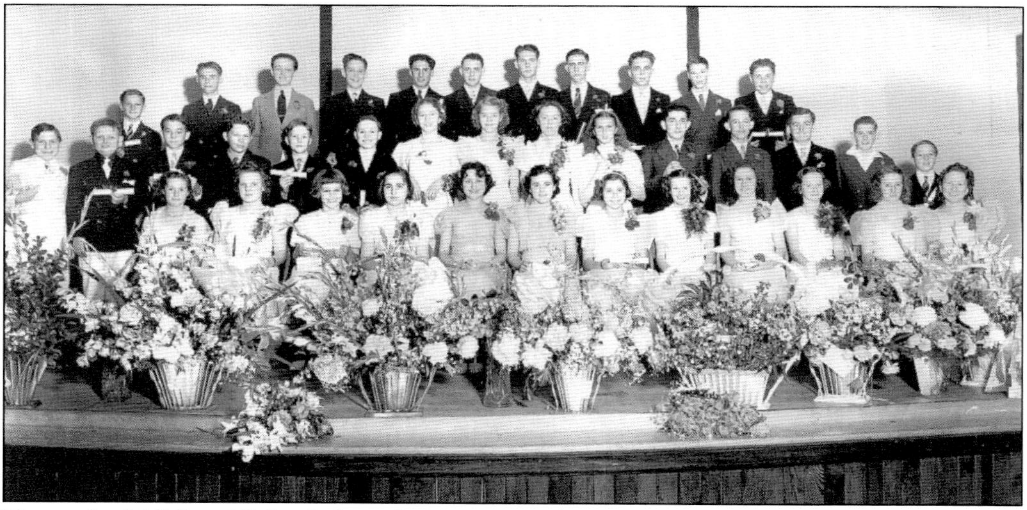

This is the Mill Road School class of 1938. Pictured are, from left to right, the following: (first row) unidentified, Elaine Southard, Marian Delmar, Phyllis Plumbo, unidentified, Emma Schoenleber, Roberta Seifred, Virginia Wray, Maybelle Stewart, Gertrude Shearer, Anna Hand, and unidentified; (second row) Victor Trevitt, Bob Price, Bill Chambers, Tom Haughey, Charles Nugent, Tom Sykes, Doris Bates, Hilda Block, Elva Albertson, Angela DeKluyver, William Paulus, Bill Block, Frank Mason, unidentified, and Elmer Walton; (third row) Harry Walton, Clyde Weiss, David Drysdale, Jack Conover, Sam Mazza, Grover Hinmon, Arthur Raye, George Ryon, Bob Eble, Jim Wray, and David Trevitt.

Dorothy Rohr (left) and Leah Rumbel, photographed here on June 8, 1933, taught sixth-, seventh-, and eighth-grade classes at Mill Road School. Leah Rumbel came to Northfield from Pennsylvania in 1924. According to old records, she was known for keeping order in her room and for her contributions toward developing the school library.

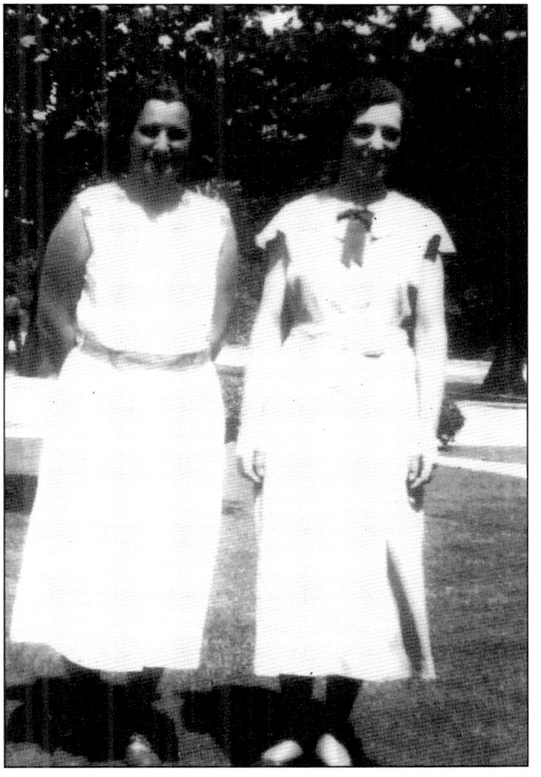

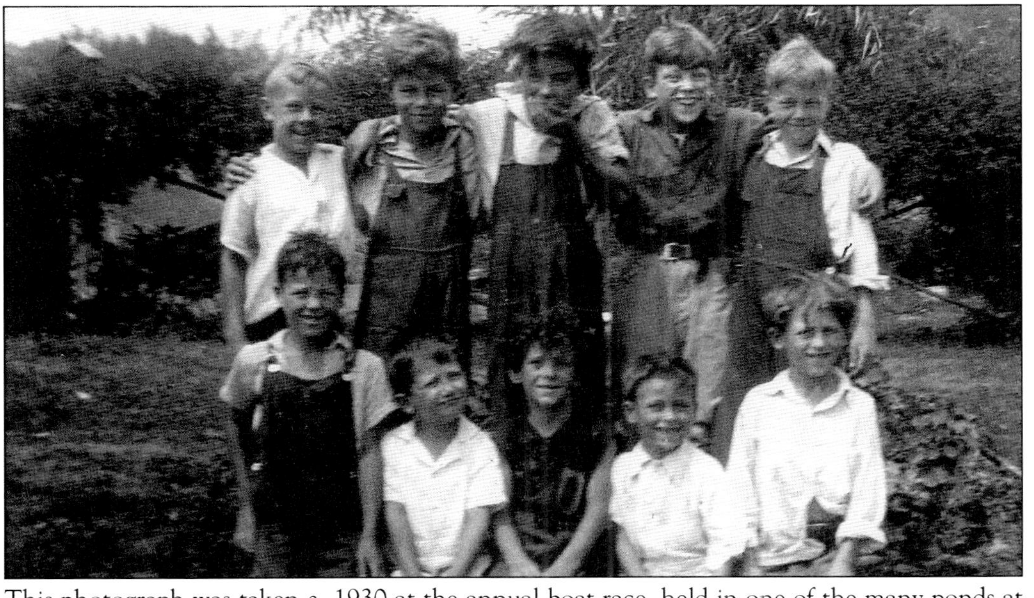

This photograph was taken c. 1930 at the annual boat race, held in one of the many ponds at the brickyard, which is now Birch Grove Park. Sailboats were made by the participants. From left to right are the following: (first row) Jack Nugent, John Himmelriech, unidentified, Arthur Murray, and George Murray; (second row) Ed Forshaw, Dan Delmar, Bob Delmar, Charles Purcel, and Frank Nugent.

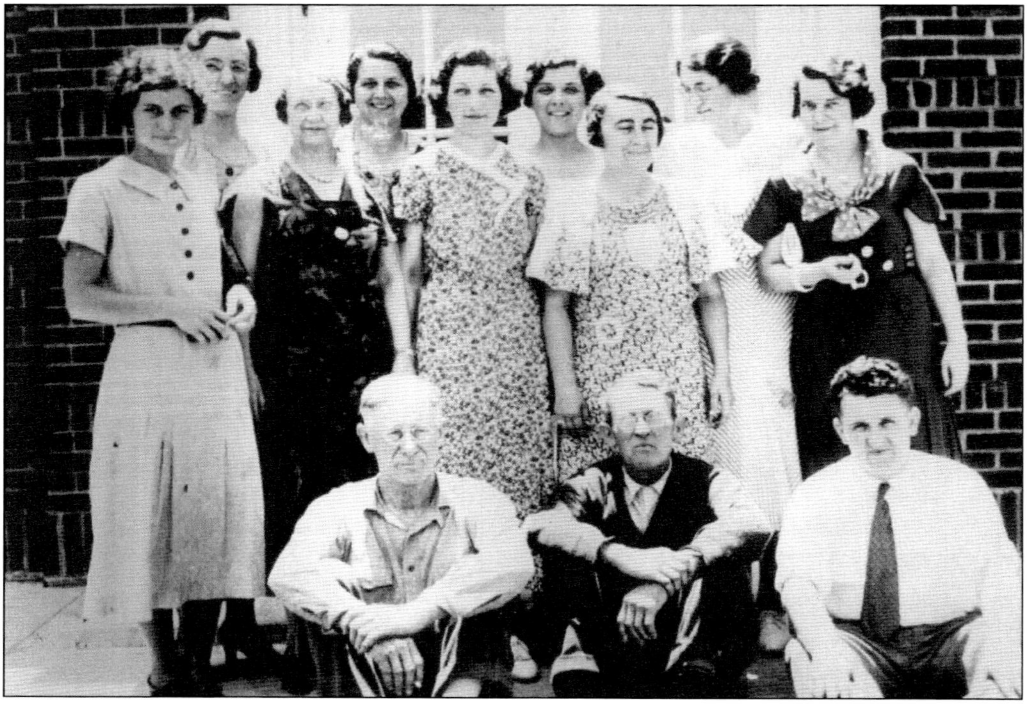

This photograph shows some Mill Road School teachers. From left to right are the following: (first row) Mr. Latta, Mr. Boyd, and Raymond Moyer (who taught arithmetic and history, and died at the school in 1958); (second row) unidentified, Mrs. Beidelman, unidentified, Mrs. Daily, and two unidentified teachers; (third row) Leah Rumbel and two unidentified teachers.

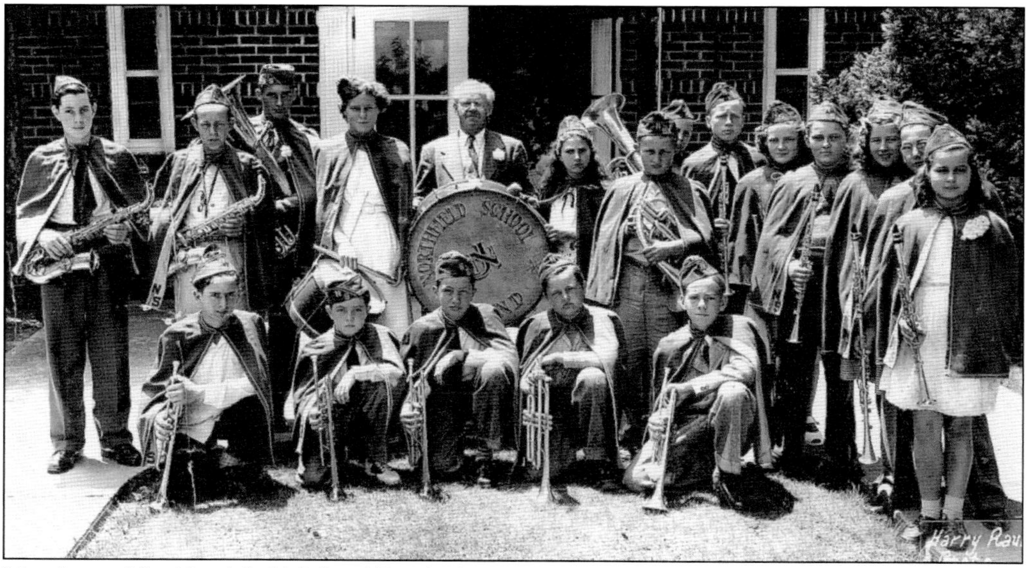

Members of the Northfield School Band of 1946–1947 are seen in uniform in front of Mill Road School with their director, Walter Hauck. They are James English, Charles Sheppard, Ed Woltmann, Jay Scull, Richard Cote, Jerry Hampton, Klaricka Cote, Dorothy Zimmerman, Mona Frisbie, and eight unidentified students.

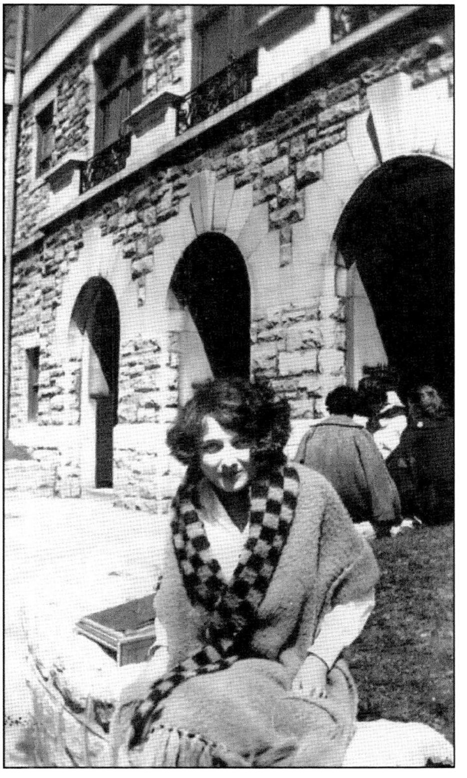

Several generations of students at Mill Road School remember Mary Hannum, a teacher of almost legendary status. She taught art, reading, and penmanship. In addition, she produced and directed school plays, such as *Alice's Tea Party*. She graduated from Montclair State Normal School in 1926. The photograph on the right was taken in 1922, when she was about 18. The photograph below shows her and her friend Julia in 1923.

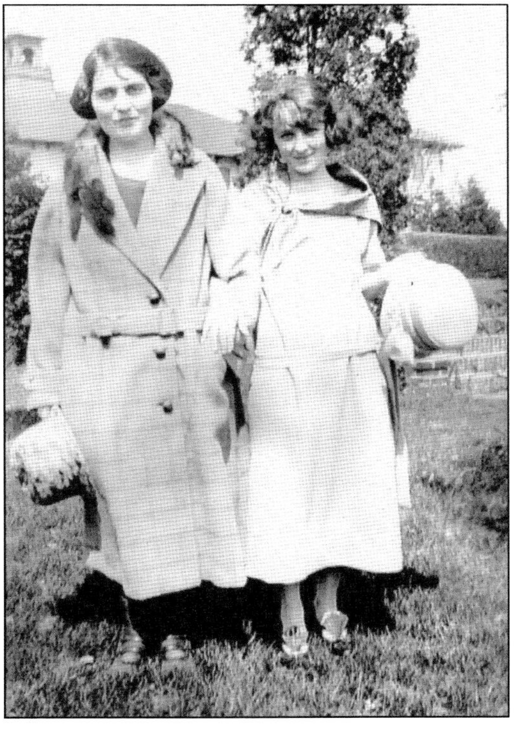

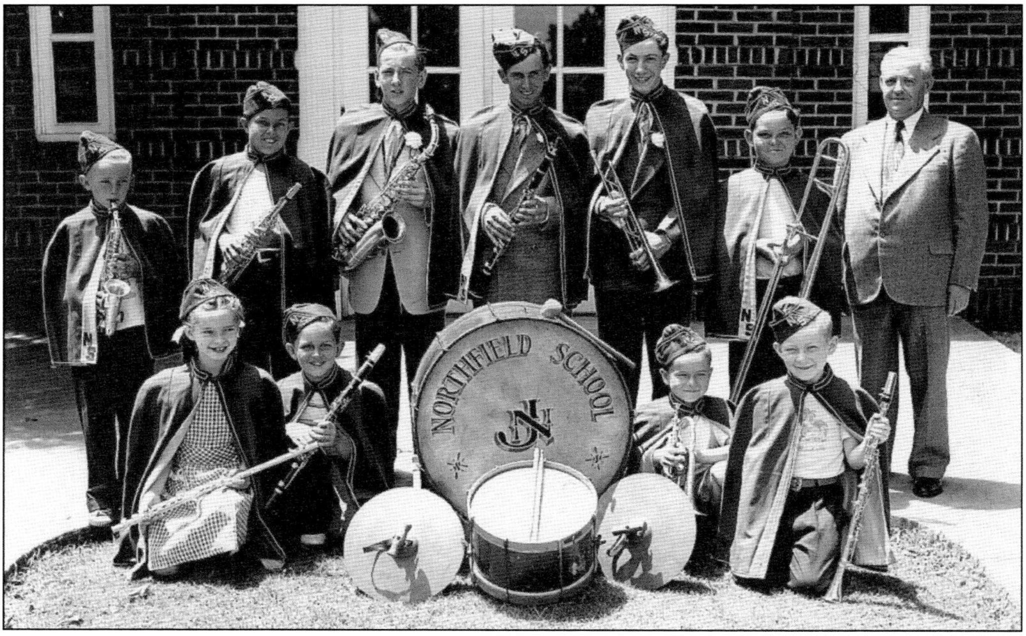

This is the Mill Road school band in 1950. Those who have been identified are Klaricka Cote, Ulf Ernst, John Fuss, James English, Charles Sheppard, Ed Woltmann, and Walter Hauck (director).

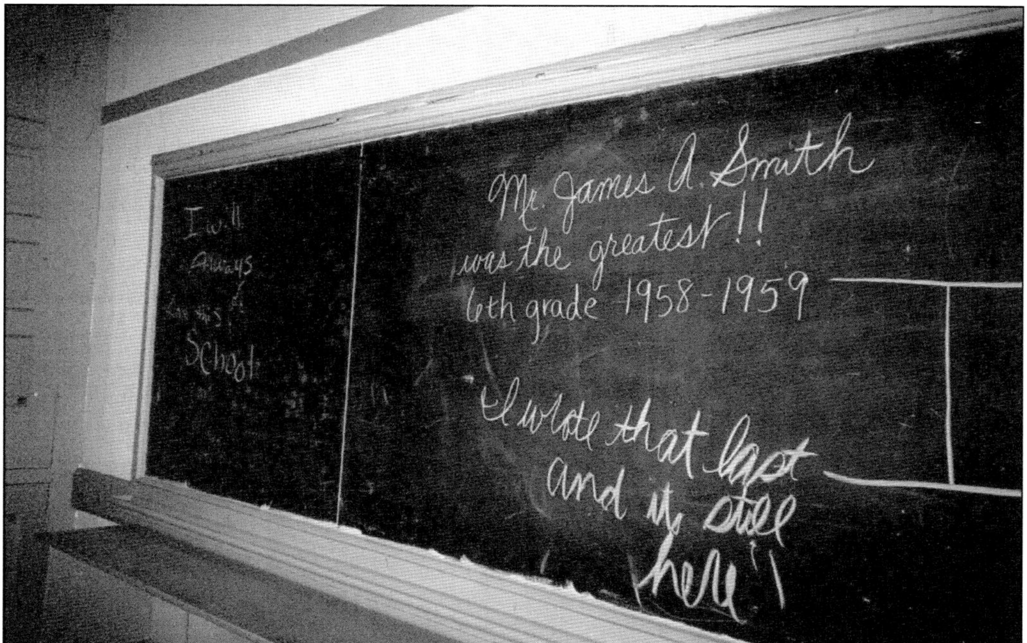

At the October 1997 reunion for all Mill Road School alumni, one former student left this fond message on a blackboard: "Mr. James A. Smith was the greatest!! 6th grade 1958–1959." The following year, Mill Road School was torn down to make way for the new Northfield Community School.

George Carey was the custodian and worked in the boiler room at Mill Road School for many years. Former students recall that he could be counted on to help whenever students were assigned to carry books from the summer storage area behind the auditorium stage to their classrooms at the beginning of the new school year.

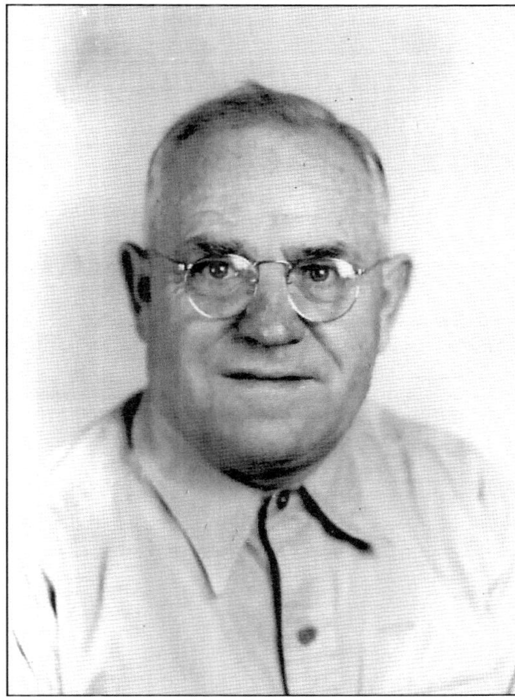

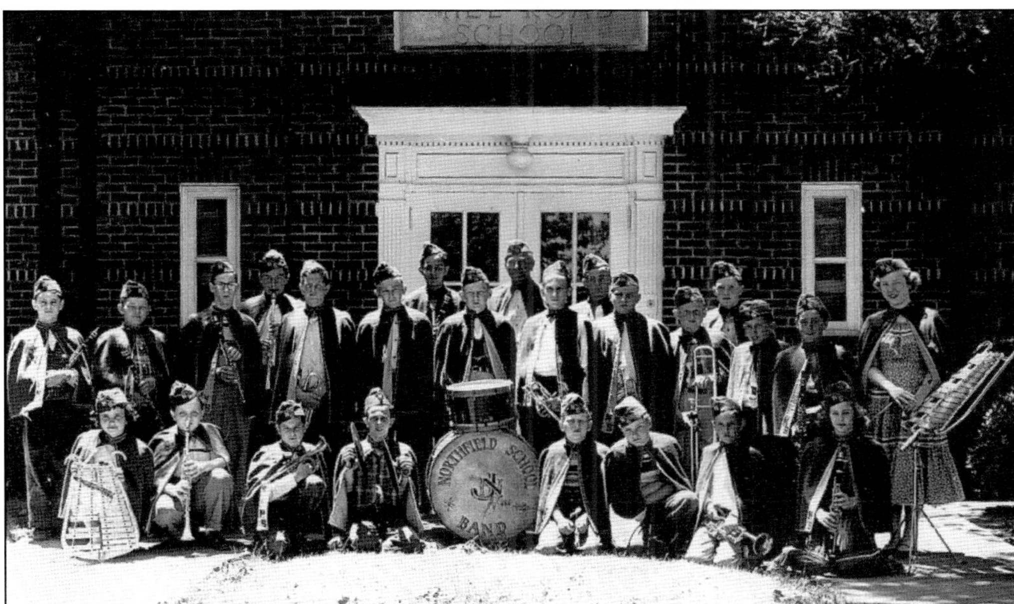

This photograph of the Mill Road School band, taken on June 18, 1954, includes, from left to right, the following: (first row) Betsy Slaybaugh, Ricky English, Bruce Breunig, Billy Hudson, Pat Dargis, Donald McCormick, John Doerr, and Ruth Ann Zimmerman; (second row) Matthew Jacobs, George Malinasky, Mark Jacobs, Wilmer Sharpe, Billy Geisel, Glenn Weeks, Pete English, Carl Scull, Herman Fiedler (band director), Corky Olson, Charles Hundertmark, Peter Pispisa, Gary Allen, Bruce Allen, Wesley Morton, Mitchell Mathot, and Jane Haley.

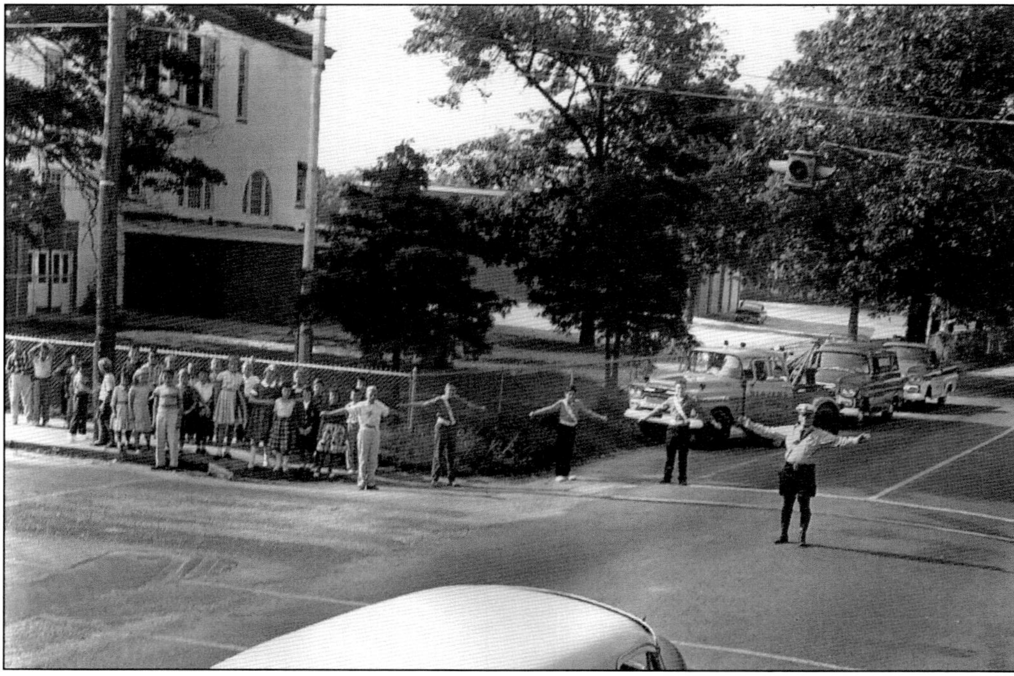

These students are crossing New Road (Route 9) and Mill Road on their way to the Mill Road School in 1959. Police Sgt. Howard Chambers, assisted by a student safety patrol, directs traffic. This intersection had a blinking light. The school is on the southeast corner of the intersection. This photograph was taken by Tom Wolcott, standing on a ladder.

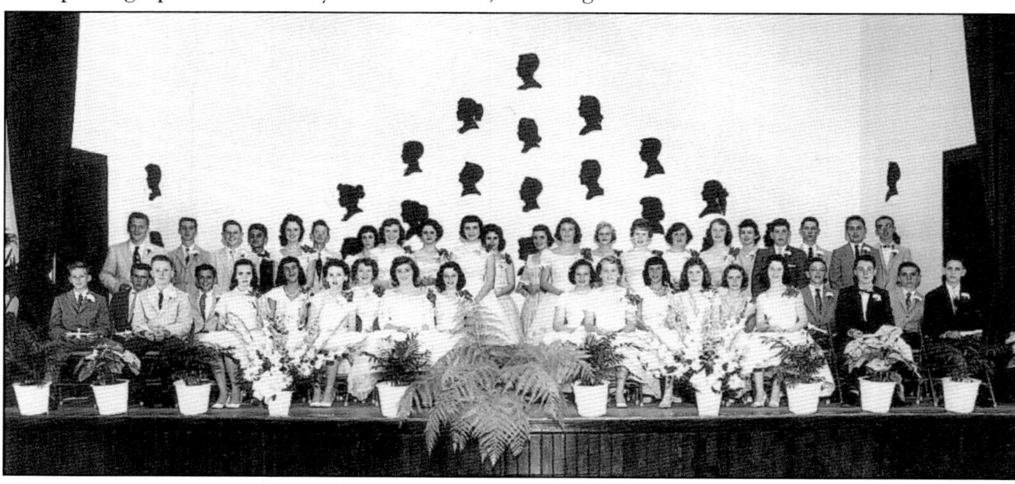

The members of the Mill Road Class of 1957 are Beatrice Appenzeller, Darylene Bell, Barbara Bew, Barbara M. Bew, Diane M. Bew, June Buxton, Alice Carmen, Robert Chester, George Collett, Judy Downs, Lawrence Faust, Bonnie Fraser, Harry Fulton, Marion Garr, Ruth Garrison, Carole Gaskill, Patricia Gillen, David Gunning, Mildred Harvey, Anthony Herda, Thelma Hundertmark, Martha Ireland, Mary Jane Karkella, Donna Landis, Kathleen Leap, James Lehman, David Leopardi, Daniel Littlefield, Betty Ann Lovett, Robert Maholland, Philip Male, Joseph McFarland, Linda Murphy, Patricia Murphy, Frank Pogue, Christine Purro, Daniel Reda, David Schenck, Betsy Slaybaugh, Carolyn Steer, Gary Steer, and Lee Woods.

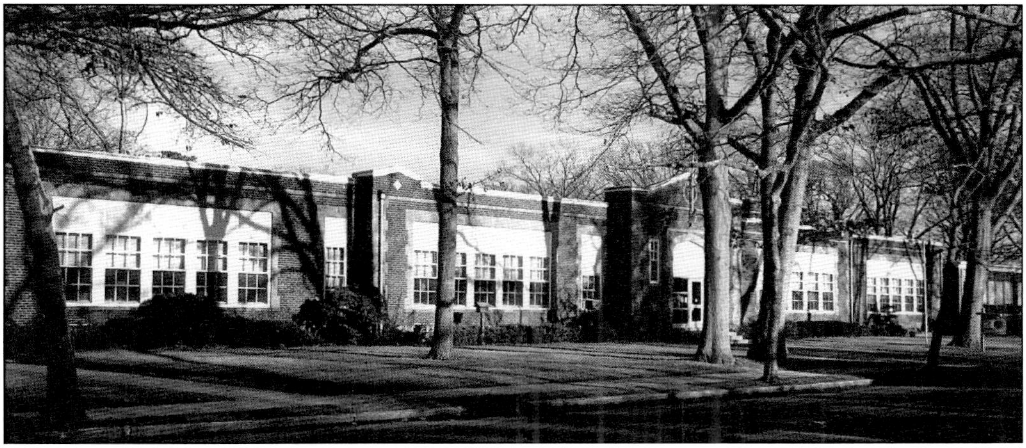

The Mount Vernon Avenue School was built in 1924. Records indicate that it originally had four rooms and that additions were built in 1956 and 1958. It was originally called the Parker Avenue School because that was the original name of the street. When the street was renamed Mount Vernon Avenue, so was the school. Still later, it was given yet another name, the Donald J. Adams School. The school, which housed classes from kindergarten through second grade, closed in 1998, when the four Northfield schools were replaced by the Northfield Community School.

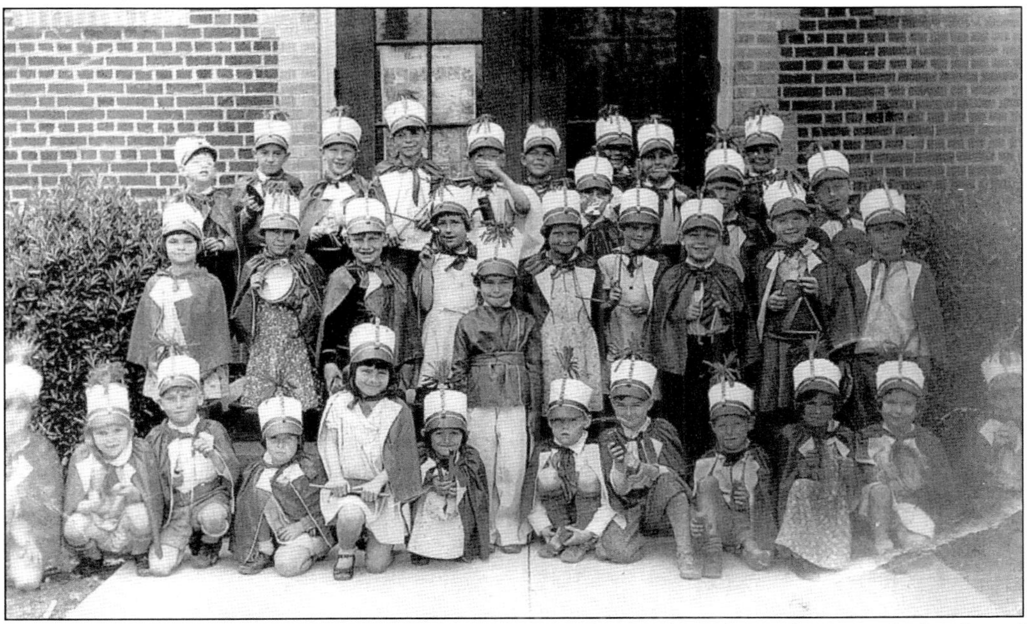

This is the Mount Vernon Avenue School band, with members from the second, third, and fourth grades, *c.* 1931. From left to right are the following: (first row) unidentified, Irene Powers, Buckie Lee, unidentified, Regina Dalman, unidentified, Doris Balestrieri (standing), Richard Snyder, Al Chambers, Ed Crowne, unidentified, Jane Balestrieri, and unidentified; (second row) unidentified, Marjorie Lawrence, Lloyd Southard, unidentified, Margaret Hollenbeck, Leila Crawford, unidentified, Agnes Drysdale, and Ray Schoenleber; (third row) John Fritchie, Earl Applegate, Stan Williams, Bill Eble, Bill Riley, Stan Carney, Jim Ervin, Norm Stapleton, Pat Haughey, Bill Linder, and Bill Wilkinson. (Courtesy of Ed Crowne.)

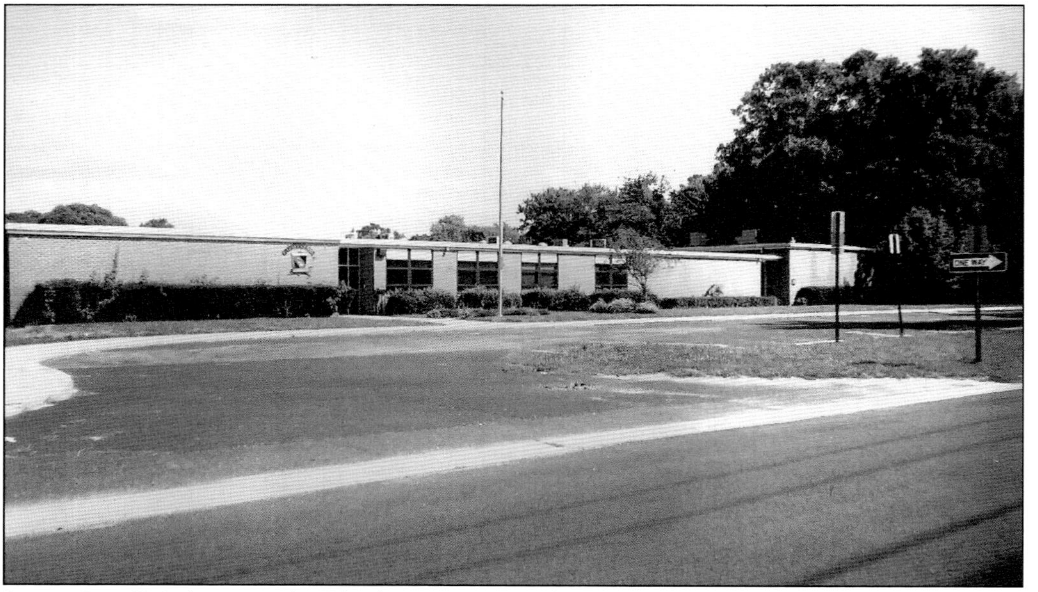

Located on Oak Avenue, the Charles M. Kresge School was named for its longtime teacher and principal. Originally from Pennsylvania, Charles Kresge came to Northfield in 1923 as a teaching principal at Mill Road. He was superintendent of Northfield schools for many years until his retirement in 1958. The school was dedicated on November 22, 1969. It held kindergarten through second grade at the time it closed, in 1998, when the four Northfield schools were replaced by the Northfield Community School.

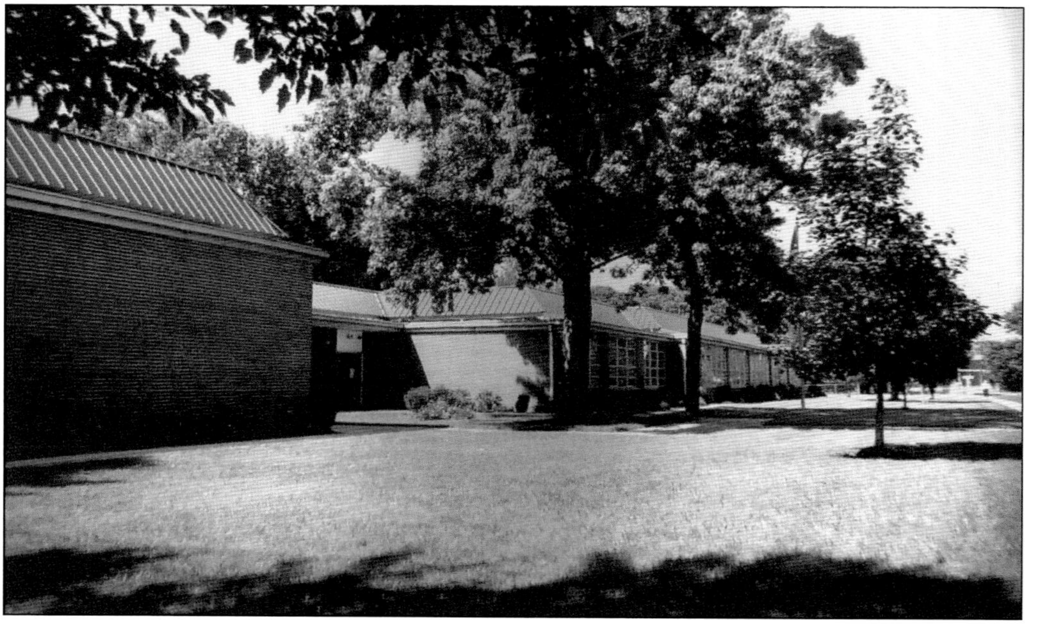

James E. Locuson was president of the Northfield Board of Education for many years. The Locuson School was located on Burton Avenue. It held grades three through five at the time it closed, in 1998, when the four Northfield schools were replaced by the Northfield Community School.

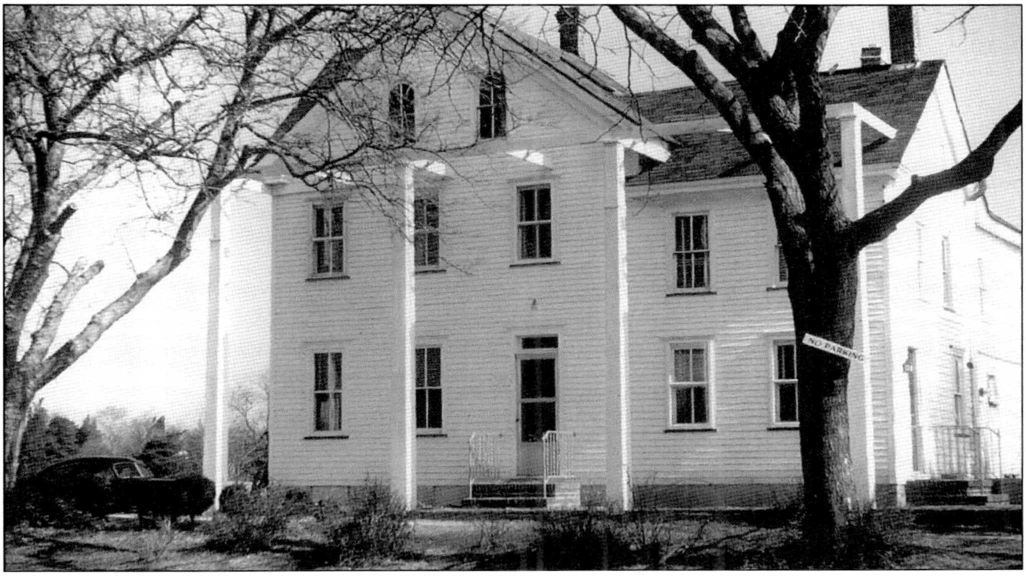

The Bayside School building, on Mill Road, had been a private home belonging to the Steelmans until Dr. Norwood Band converted it into a private school in the 1940s. It became a private home once again in 1996. Frederick Steelman Sr. built the first house on the site c. 1746. The original portions of the current house were built by David L. Steelman on the foundation of the first house.

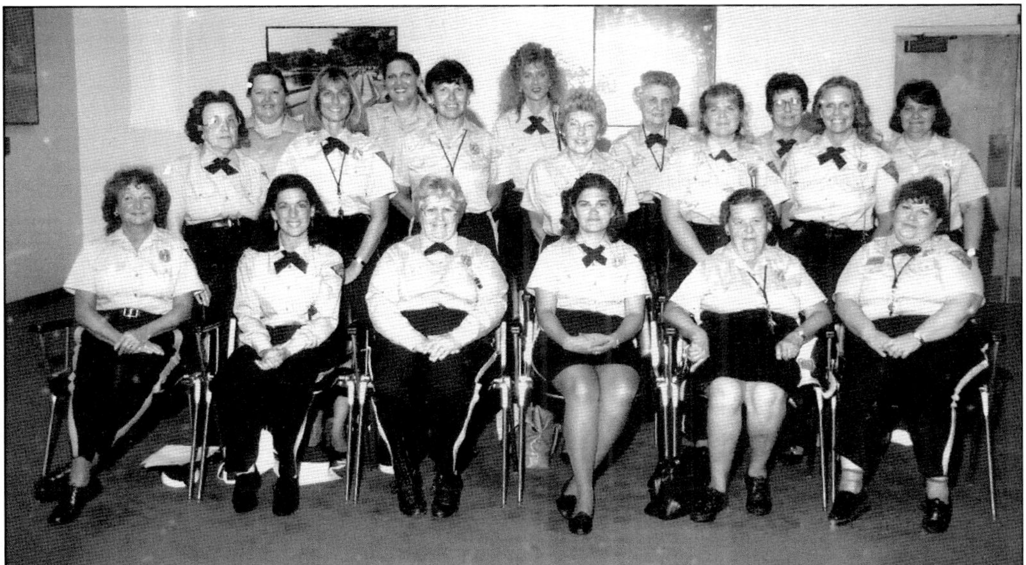

As traffic volume increased on the main roads, Northfield began using crossing guards at key intersections so that students could walk to school safely. This photograph of the crossing guards was taken c. 1990. From left to right are the following: (first row) Ann Newman, Mickie Nugent, Millie Mossman, Cindy Kern (supervisor), Beatrice Helder, and Carol Sturgis; (second row) Marge Banning, Lynn Crook, Barbara Yankuski, Phyllis Kyle, Lynn Victor, and Pat Parker; (third row) Ruth Roseburg, Debbie Doherty, Patricia Friel, Theresa Meloney, Lorraine Dixon, and Eileen Pantalena.

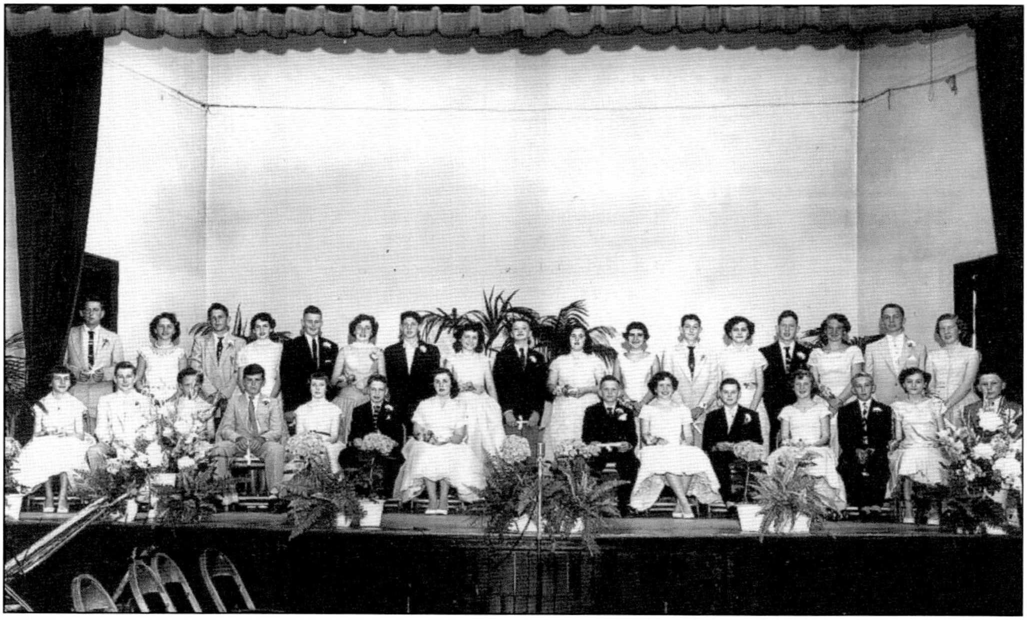

This Mill Road School class graduated in 1955, the year Northfield celebrated its 50th birthday. From left to right are the following: (first row) Susan Schwartz, Bob Cressey, Jeanette Arthur, Ralph Mulholland, Suzanne Myers, Gordon Pearson, Barbara Wilkinson, Bob Cordner, Betsy Bew, Bruce Breunig, Dianne Glenn, Glenn Weeks, Joan Whitehead, and Carl Scull; (second row) Alfred Davis, Geraldine DeVinney, John Moffett, Lillian Starn, Robert Morrow, Gloria DeFreitas, Michael Malin, Patricia Ridell, Richard King, Barbara Knorr, Dorothy English, Ralph Quicksall, Grace Whitehead, Thomas Guion, Madeline Levin, Bill McFarland, and Jane Haley.

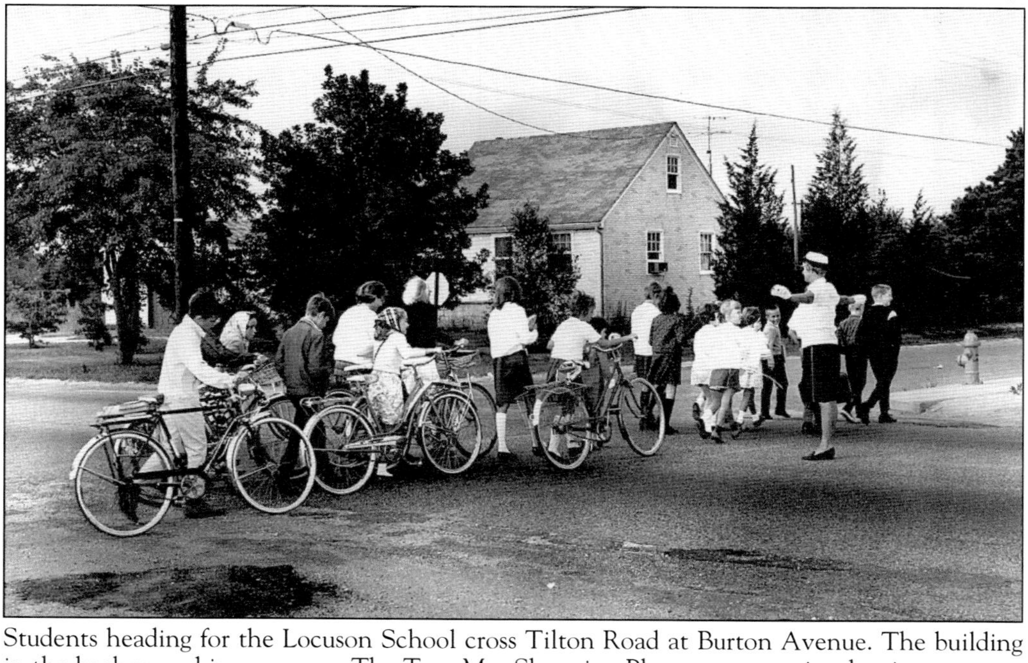

Students heading for the Locuson School cross Tilton Road at Burton Avenue. The building in the background is now gone. The TerraMar Shopping Plaza now occupies the site.

Five

Trolleys, Trains, and Trails

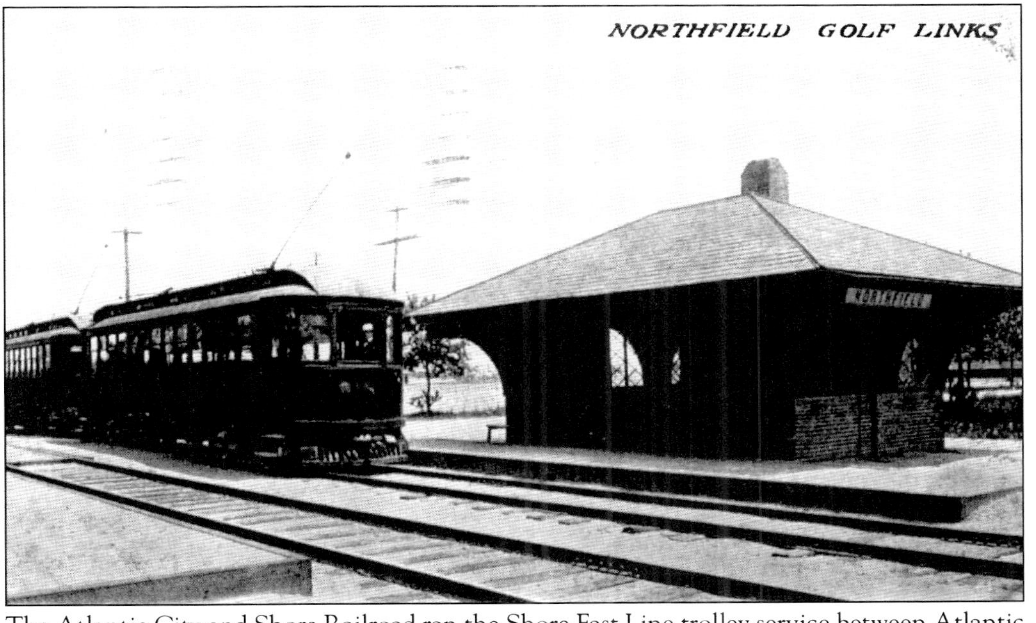

The Atlantic City and Shore Railroad ran the Shore Fast Line trolley service between Atlantic City and Ocean City. A 1931 timetable lists the Northfield stations as Dolphin, Northfield, Zion Road, Bakersville, and Oak Crest [*sic*]. Some residents who used the line as youngsters remember that there was once also a stop for Tudor Terrace. This photograph shows the Jackson Avenue Station, which was used by people heading for the Atlantic City Golf Course. The trolley tracks for this line were located one block west of Broad Street (now the location of the bike path). When Mary Muller Kosch and George Muller, son and daughter of longtime city clerk George Muller, were interviewed by Northfield's Cultural Committee, they remembered this as a beautiful station with a fireplace.

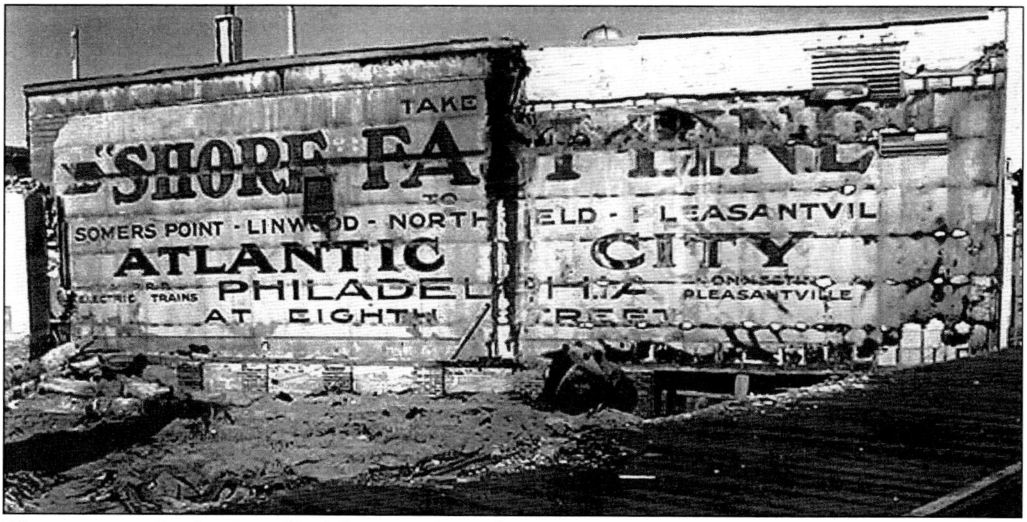

This sign, on the brick wall of the Moorlyn Theater in Ocean City, was found by construction crews as they were demolishing the building in 2002. Painted on tin, the sign survived because it was protected by the wall of the adjoining building. It has been removed by the Ocean City Historical Society and will eventually be placed where all can see it. The Shore Fast Line, started in 1906, was one of the trolley lines that ran through Northfield for many years.

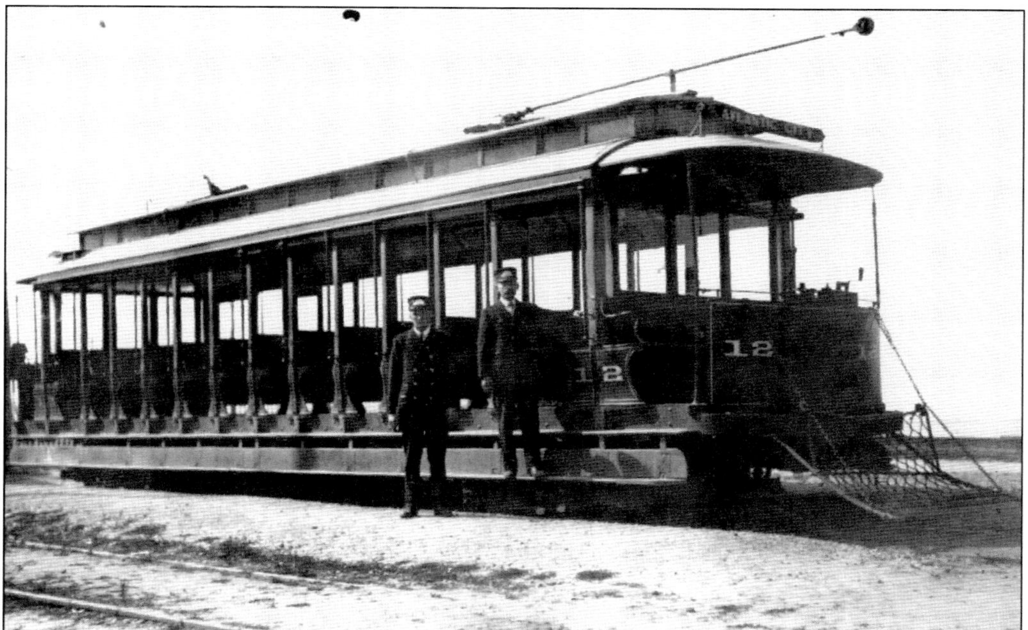

This is a photograph of a Suburban Line trolley and two conductors. This line ran down Shore Road between Atlantic City and Somers Point. It was often referred to as the "Toonerville Trolley." It operated for a few decades early in the 20th century.

Ralph Doerr Jr. stands next to one of the last cars used by the Shore Fast trolley line in 1948. The trolley is at the Northfield siding, Roosevelt Avenue.

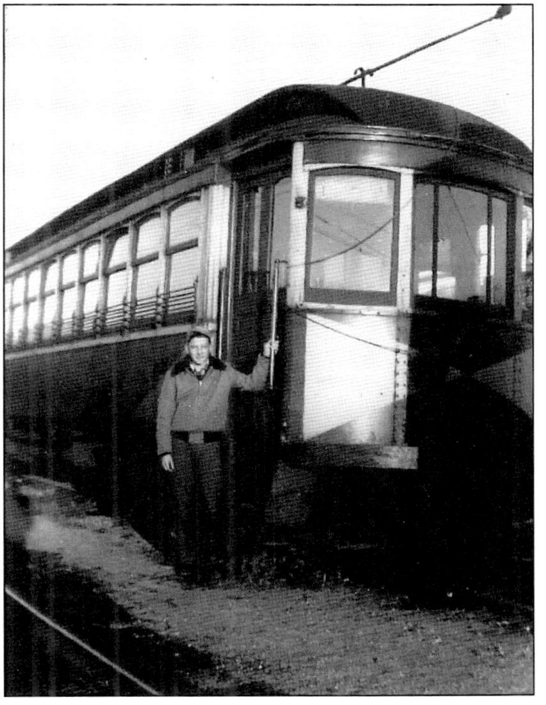

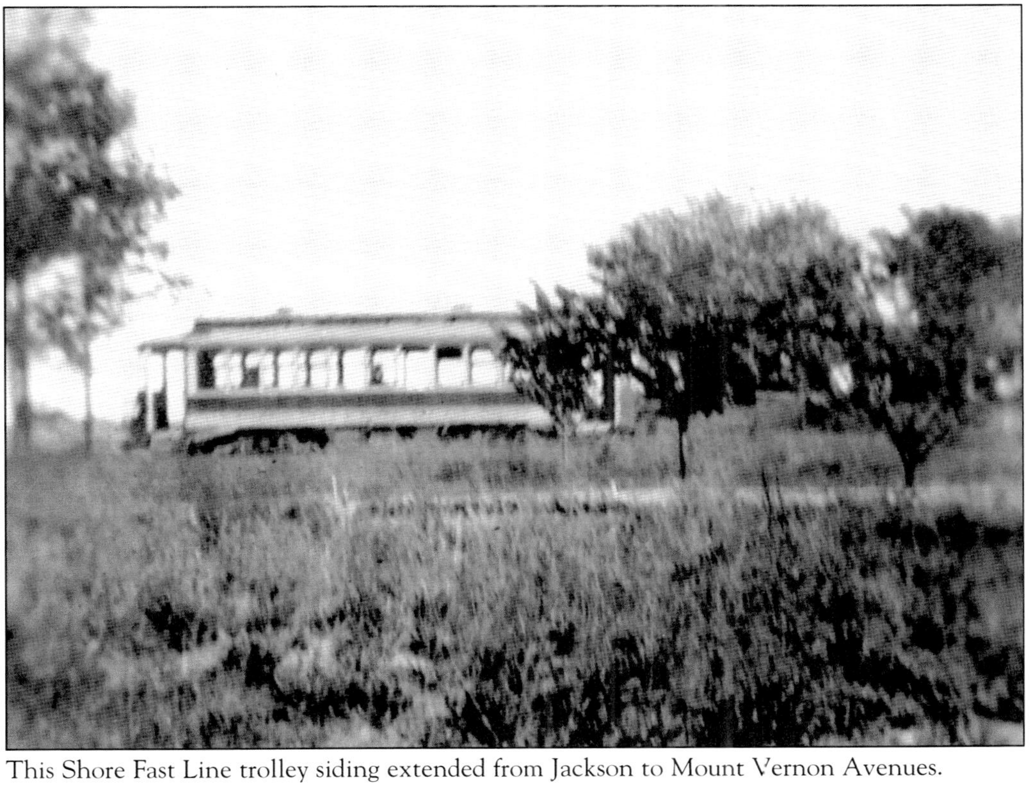

This Shore Fast Line trolley siding extended from Jackson to Mount Vernon Avenues.

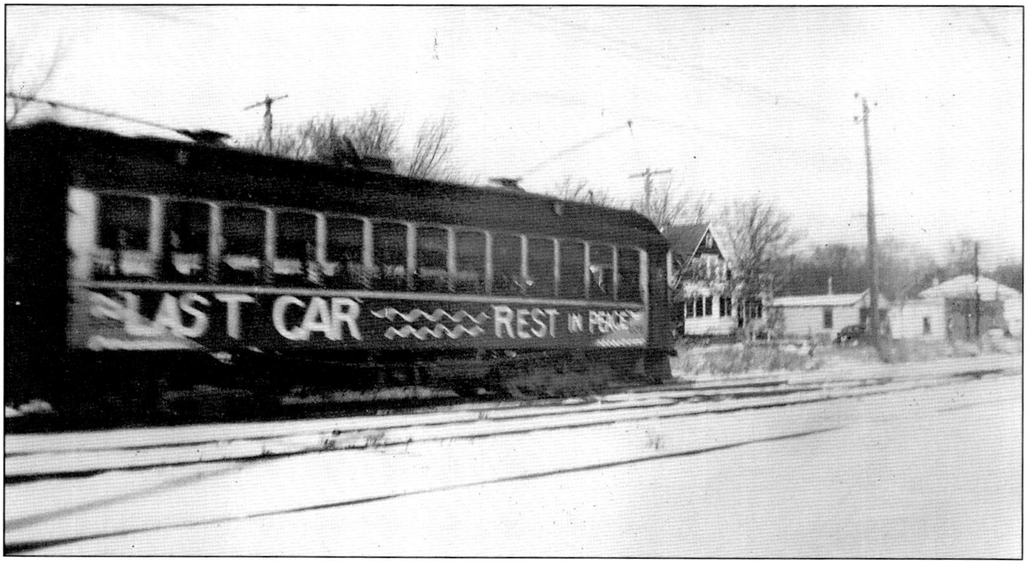

On January 18, 1948, the Shore Fast Line trolley made its last official run. This photograph was taken looking east from Roosevelt Avenue as the car left Northfield station on its return to Atlantic City. The messages painted on the side read "Last Car" and "Rest in Peace."

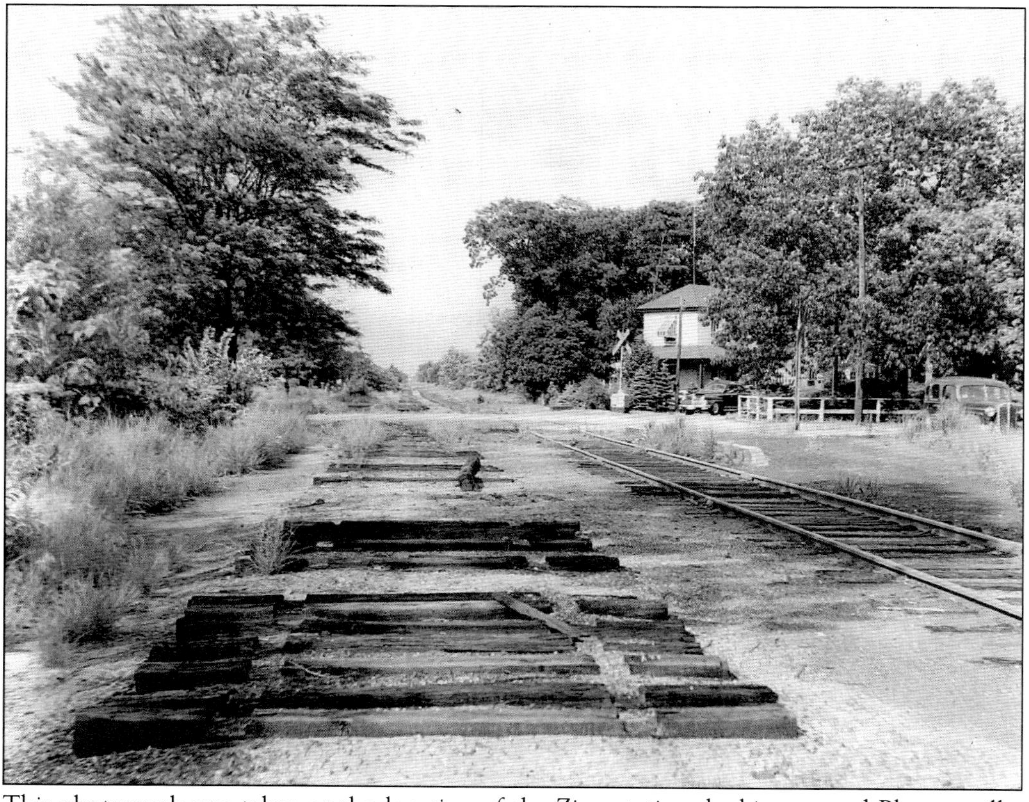

This photograph was taken at the location of the Zion station, looking toward Pleasantville, after 1948. Notice that both tracks are visible in the photograph.

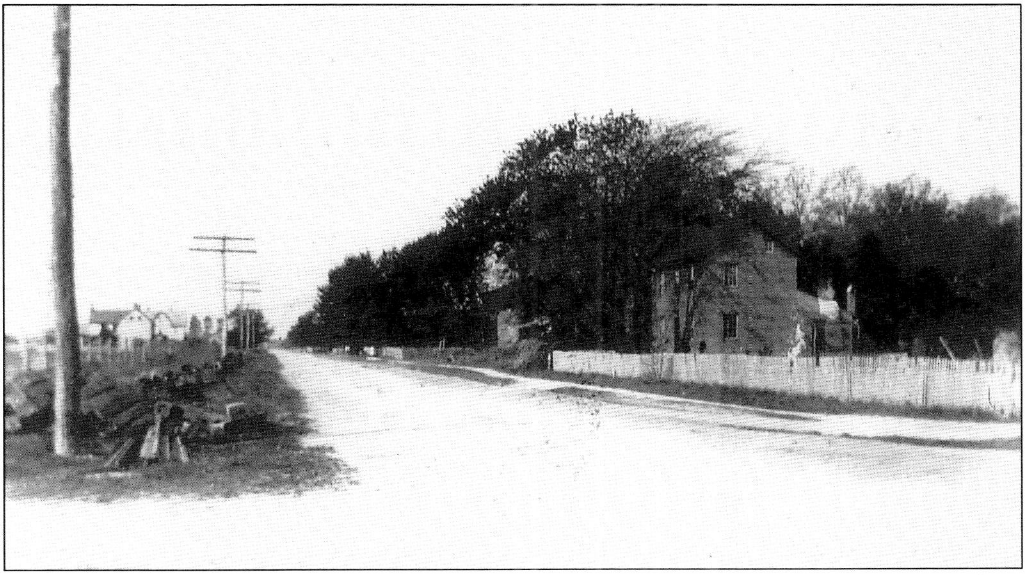

Shore Road was one of the first public roads in Atlantic County and one of the first roads in Northfield, possibly its earliest, although Tilton Road also follows an old Native American trail. The original Shore Road was laid out in 1716 and extended from Port Republic to Somers Point. Records indicate that it was resurveyed and moved slightly east of its former location to ground that was drier and easier to travel. The upper photograph was taken in the early 1900s, looking south on Shore Road at the intersection of Mill, Tilton, and Shore Roads. The lower photograph was taken looking north on Shore Road.

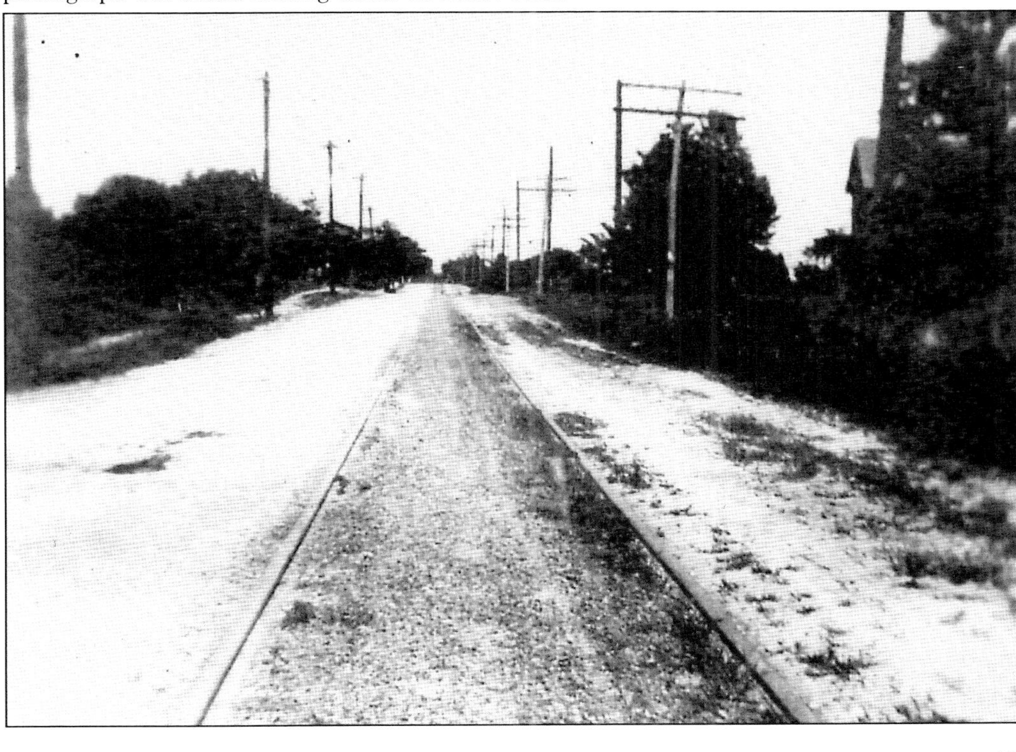

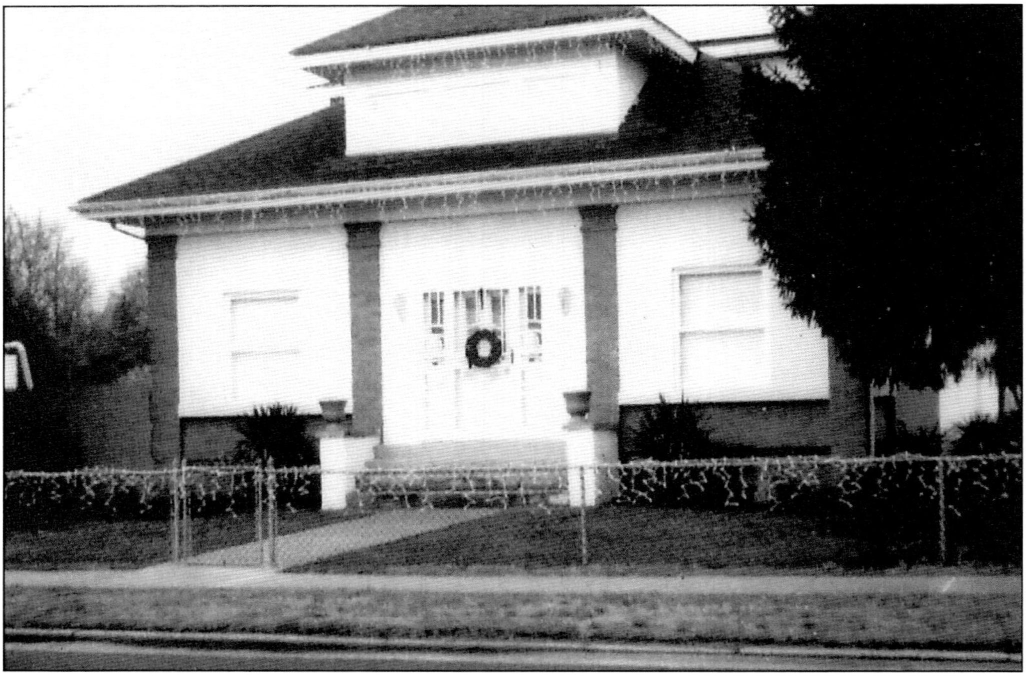

During the early 20th century, Shore Road was the commercial and professional center of Northfield. The building at 1401 Shore Road held the private hospital run by Dr. G. L. Infield and B. M. Lawther. Pauline Surpless remembers taking her son there to have his tonsils removed in 1945. Babies were born there, and stitches were sewn on cuts big and small. Everett Jesse Lever, son of Police Chief Bud Lever, was born there in 1943 (the delivery and hospitalization charge was $100). Optometrist Dr. Roy Soloff, who practiced in the area for many years, set up his first office in the basement of the private hospital.

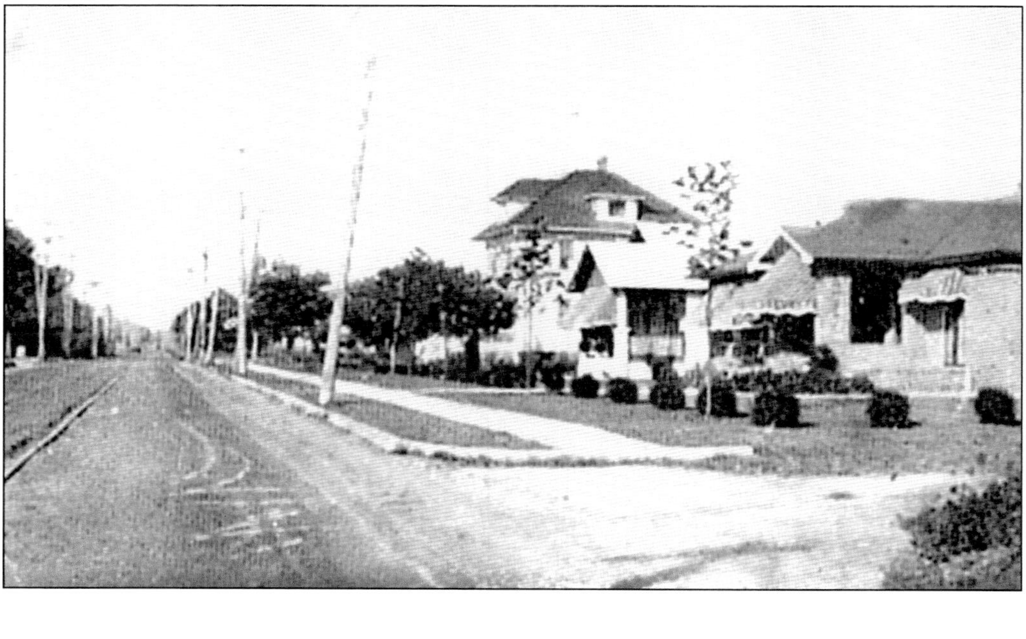

This very early shot shows Henry Price *boating* at Tilton, Shore, and Mill Roads—now one of the busiest intersections in Atlantic County—after a heavy rain. Fishing was one of Price's hobbies. For years after he retired, he gave out candy to children at Clark's Esso, located at this intersection.

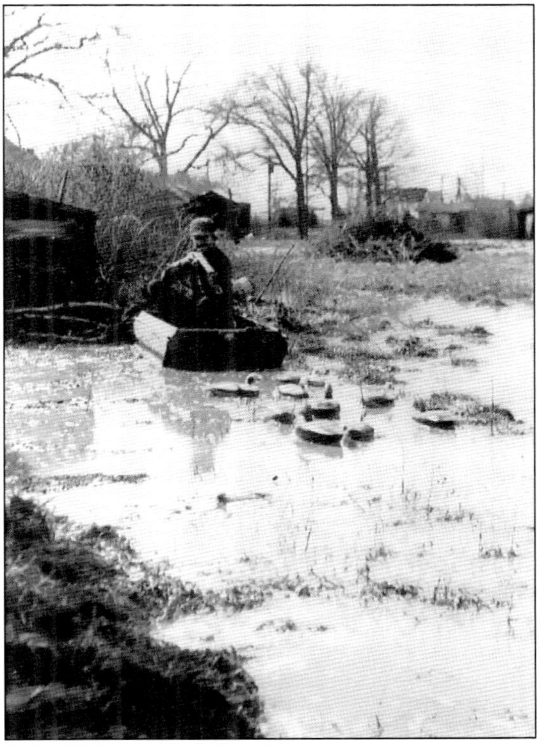

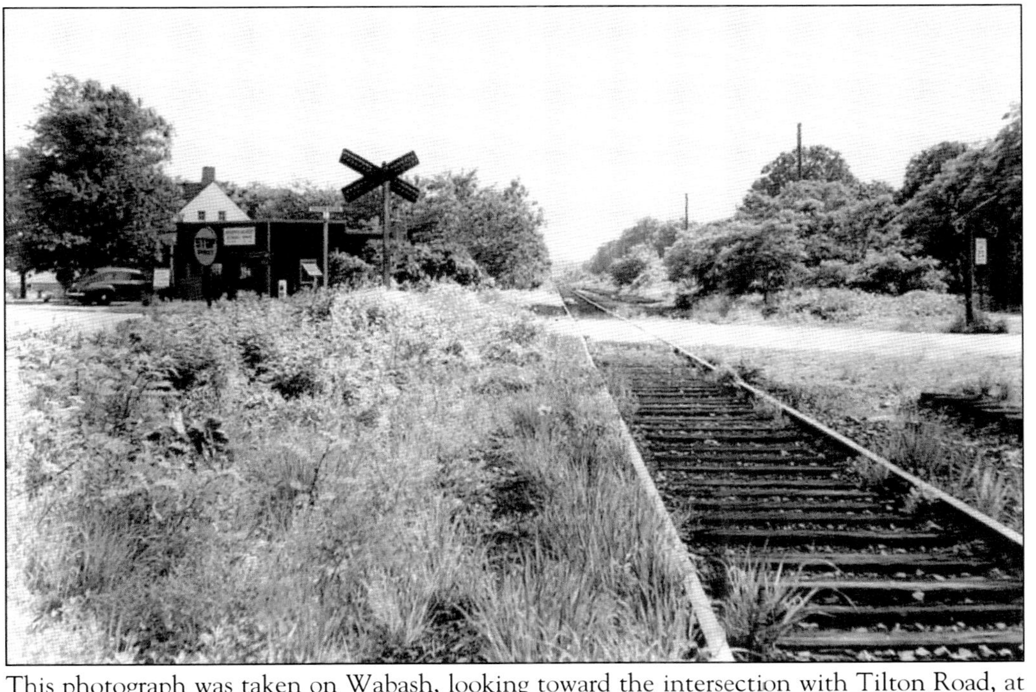

This photograph was taken on Wabash, looking toward the intersection with Tilton Road, at a time when the trolley tracks were still in limited use by Dee Lumber cf Linwood. The building on the left is Gilbert's Auto Repair (now Bruce's Auto Repair).

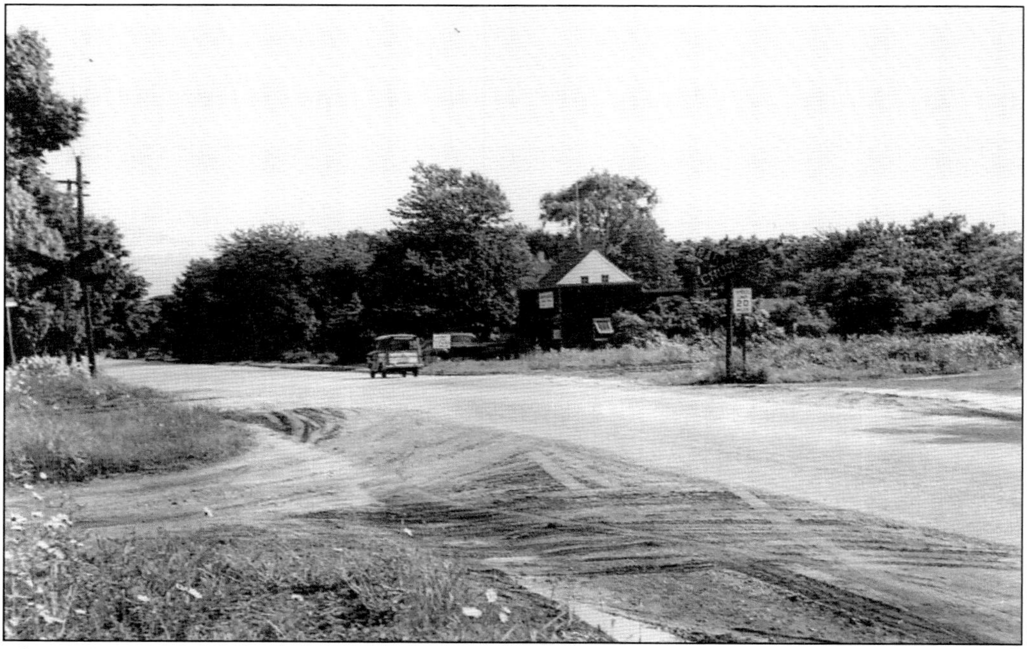

This is the intersection of Tilton Road and Wabash Avenue *c.* 1954, after one set of tracks had been removed. Tub Street (also called Tubb Street) was the original name for the easternmost part of Tilton Road. According to Carol A. Patrick, writing in *Historic Houses of Northfield*, it was so named because "the local women kept their washtubs on their front porches and on washday carried the tubs to the pumps at the tracks to wash their family's clothing. Tub Street ended its graveled way at the tracks except for a path through the woods."

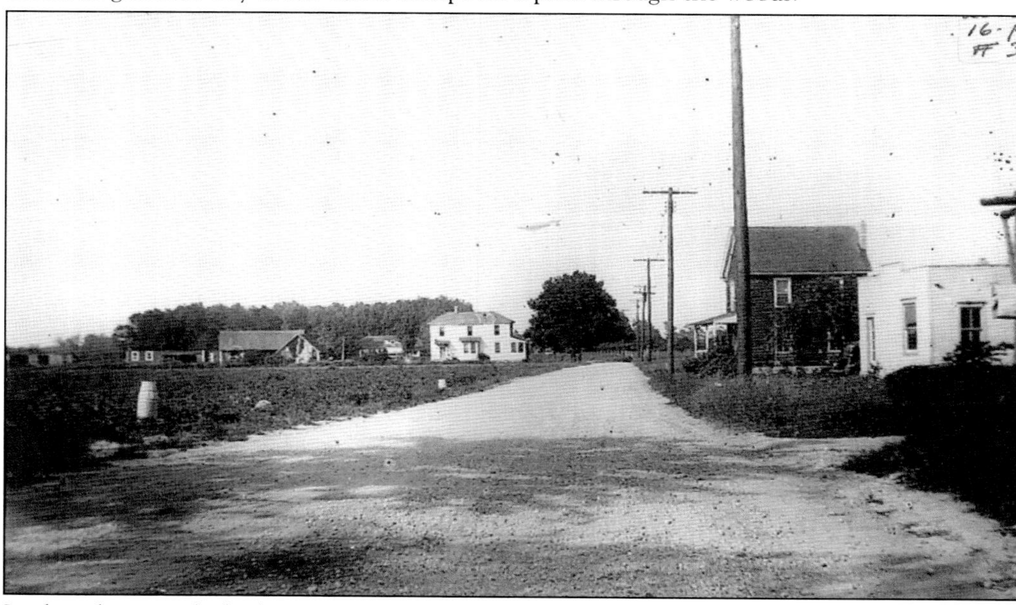

In this photograph, looking north on Sutton Avenue, the house on the left was the home of Marion and Richard Sutton. Their farm surrounds the house and barn, which can be seen behind the house. The house on the right was the home of James Scheck.

Jim Dickinson, one of the pilots with the Atlantic City Air College in the 1930s, and his wife, Flora (Thau), lived on Mill Road for 50 years. They had four children: James, Patricia, Andrea, and Thomas. Many of those who visited Birch Grove Park over the years have warm memories of Flora Dickinson—that is, unless they encountered her while they were flouting a park regulation. A longtime member of the Birch Grove Park Advisory Board, she made many contributions, including development of the Memory Garden.

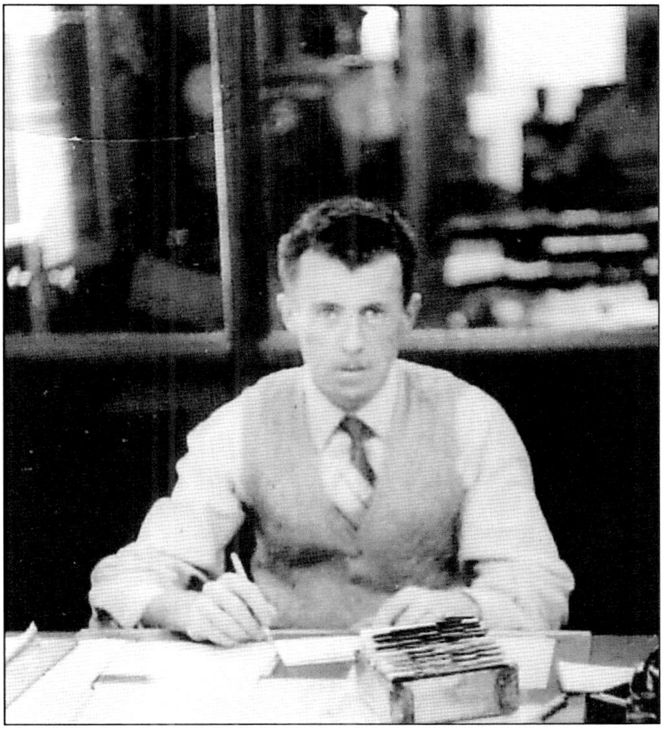

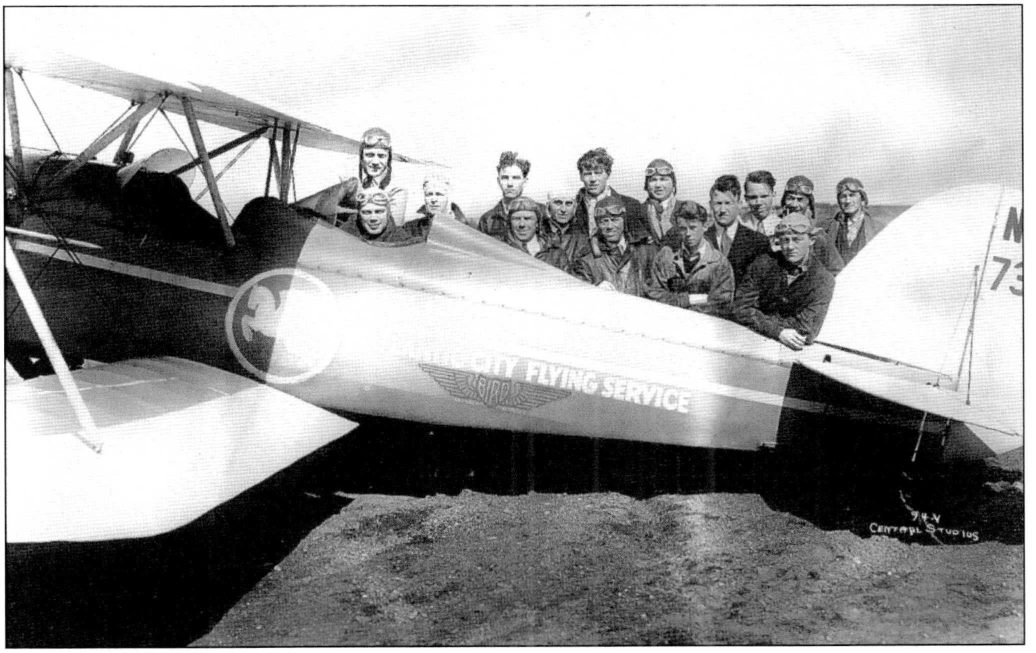

This 1931 photograph shows the Atlantic City Air College-Atlantic City Flying Service pilots. From left to right are Bev Baldwin, Ed Fay, Bob Hunt, Jim Eckman, Ross Seely, Charlie Paxson, Jim Dickinson (from Northfield), Bob Andrews, Sam Schwartz, Bill Johnson, Harry Nordheim, Charles Fulmer, Arthur Haguy, Bill (Whitey) Thomas, and John Johnson.

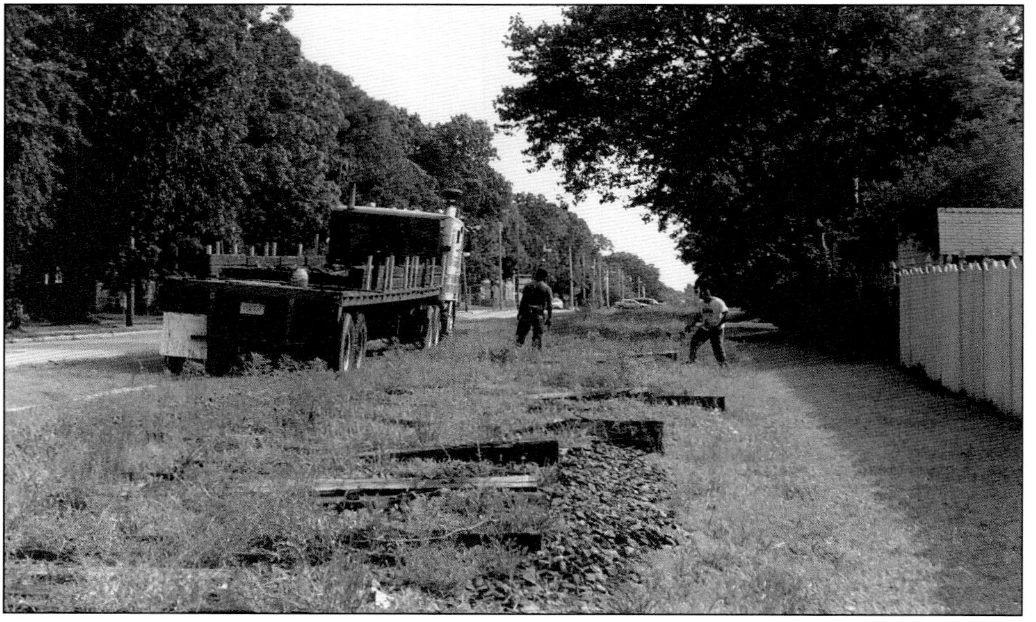

This 1996 photograph, taken looking north on Fuae Avenue at Davis Avenue, shows workmen removing Shore Fast Line tracks during construction of the bike path. Today, the bike path extends the entire length of the city, from the Pleasantville to the Linwood borders.

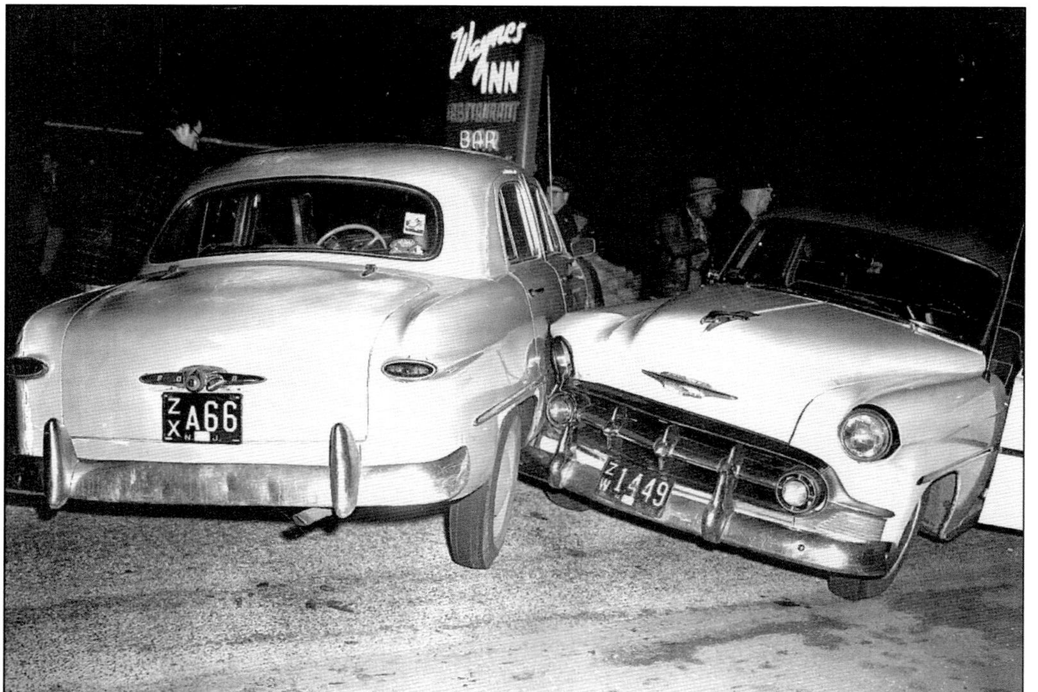

Visible in the background of this photograph is the sign for Wayne's Inn, which was located where the Owl Tree is today. This accident took place on New Road, near Merritt Drive.

Six

People Who Served Our City

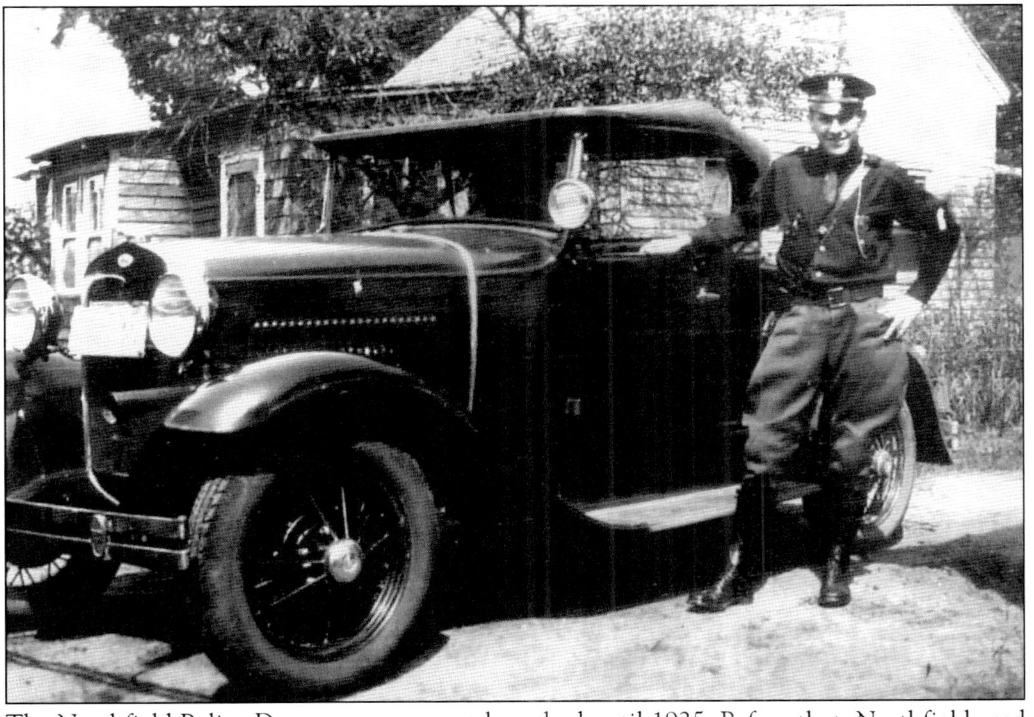

The Northfield Police Department was not launched until 1925. Before that, Northfield used county constables and marshals when needed. Records indicate that there were four police chiefs from 1925 through 1929: William Ritz, Constant "Connie" Adams, Walfred Harper, and John P. "Phin" Wilson. Pictured is W. Everett "Bud" Lever, who joined the police department in 1927 as night patrolman and was made police chief in December 1929, when Phin Wilson was hit by a car and killed. Chief Lever was issued a Model T Ford and a motorcycle, but he had to provide his own weapon, handcuffs, and flashlight. He served as chief of police until his retirement in 1961.

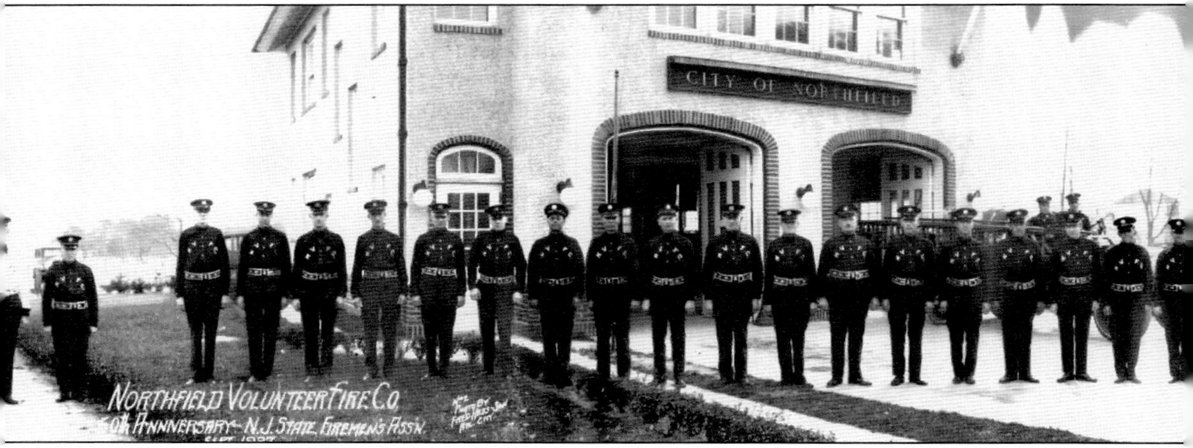

Northfield's volunteer fire department was formed in 1924 as Northfield City Fire Company No. 1. William Stokes was elected to serve as chairman of the fire company, Harry Braddock was the first fire chief, and there were 29 charter members. Seen here, from left to right, are Chief Harry Braddock, John Howell, Earl Booye, Joseph Rodgers, unidentified, Jim English, unidentified, W. Everett "Bud" Lever, George Banning, unidentified, Victor Keller, Constant "Connie" Adams, Charles Fenton, Gustav Carlson, unidentified, Howard Blazer, Miah "Mike" Banning, unidentified, George Barrett Jr., Walter Block, and Bud Keller. On the truck are Lenny Wescott and Robert Himelrich.

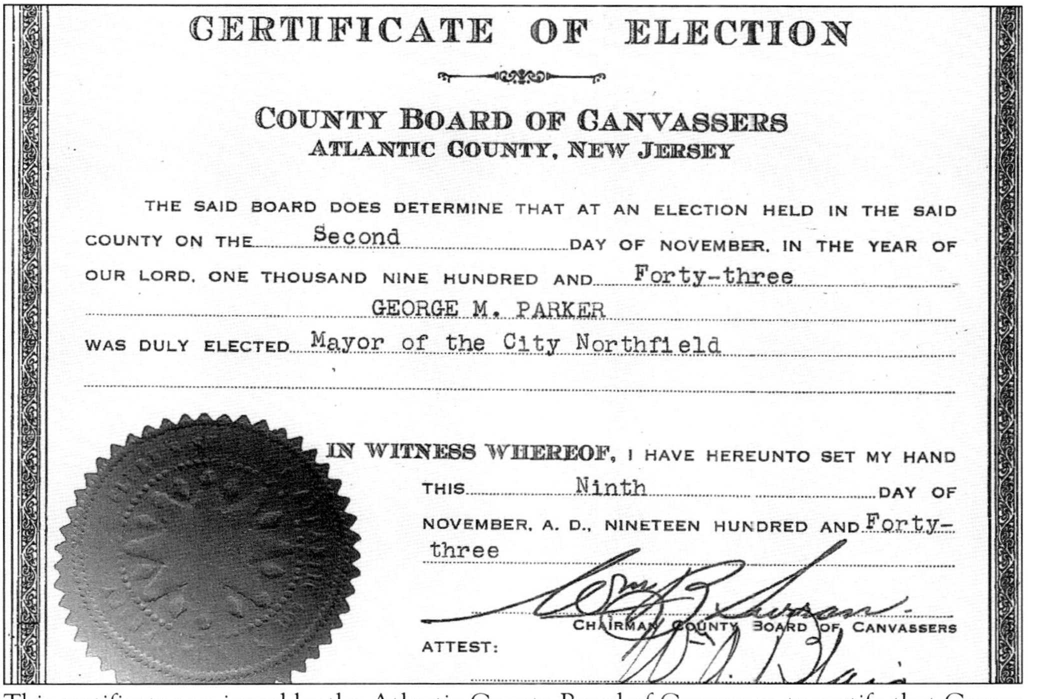

CERTIFICATE OF ELECTION

COUNTY BOARD OF CANVASSERS
ATLANTIC COUNTY, NEW JERSEY

THE SAID BOARD DOES DETERMINE THAT AT AN ELECTION HELD IN THE SAID COUNTY ON THE Second DAY OF NOVEMBER, IN THE YEAR OF OUR LORD, ONE THOUSAND NINE HUNDRED AND Forty-three

GEORGE M. PARKER

WAS DULY ELECTED Mayor of the City Northfield

IN WITNESS WHEREOF, I HAVE HEREUNTO SET MY HAND THIS Ninth DAY OF NOVEMBER, A. D., NINETEEN HUNDRED AND Forty-three

CHAIRMAN COUNTY BOARD OF CANVASSERS

ATTEST:

This certificate was issued by the Atlantic County Board of Canvassers to certify that George M. Parker was elected mayor in the 1943 election. Northfield, to date, has had 18 mayors: George Fifield (1905–1907), William Boice (1908–1909 and 1912–1920), Joseph Rass (1910–1911), Walter Yates (1921–1923), Eugene Swilkey (1924–1927), William B. Stokes (1928–1929), Andrew K. Littlefield (1930–1942), George M. Parker (1943–1947), Gerald L. Infield, M.D. (1948–1957), Englebert Breunig (1958–1959), Raphael K. Feeney (1960–1964), Jim Smith (1964), Otto Bruyns (1965–1975), Nicholas Kuchova (1976–1979), Arthur Faden (1980–1982), William M. Felton Jr. (1983–1986), Philip S. Munafo (1986–1995), and Frank Perri (1996–present).

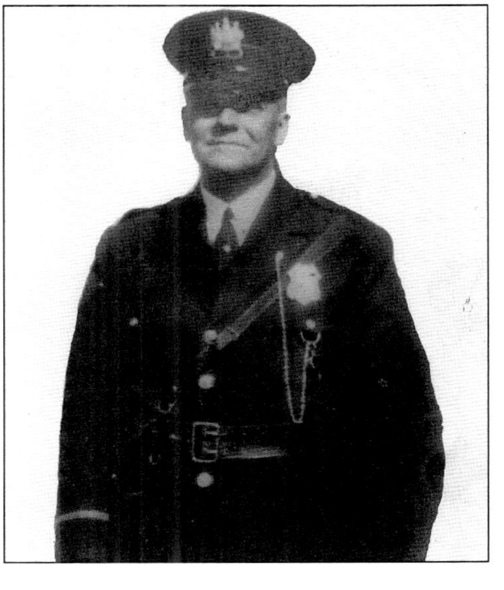

Northfield's fourth chief of police was John Phineas Wilson, who served from January 1927 until December 9, 1929, when he was struck and killed by a car as he was crossing Shore Road in front of city hall. (Courtesy of Pat Stephanik.)

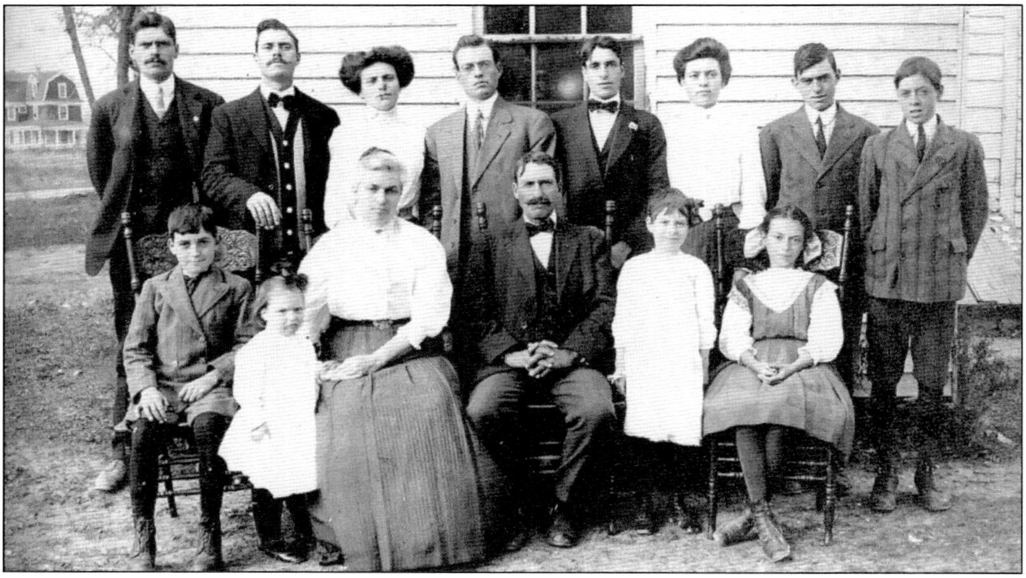

Mary Elizabeth and Jeremiah Banning (front center) are pictured with their family. Originally from Delaware, they purchased and lived on a farm in Northfield. Over the years, this family has served the city in many civic and political capacities. Miah Banning (front left) first worked in the road department and then became a fireman and, after that, one of Northfield's first police officers. Others pictured with the mother and father are, from left to right, as follows: (first row) Estelle (Lindner), Mary (Lee), and Emma (Kershaw); (second row) Bill, Herman, Lizzie (Burroughs), Luther, Chat (John Chapman), Abbie (Hinmon), Dan, and George.

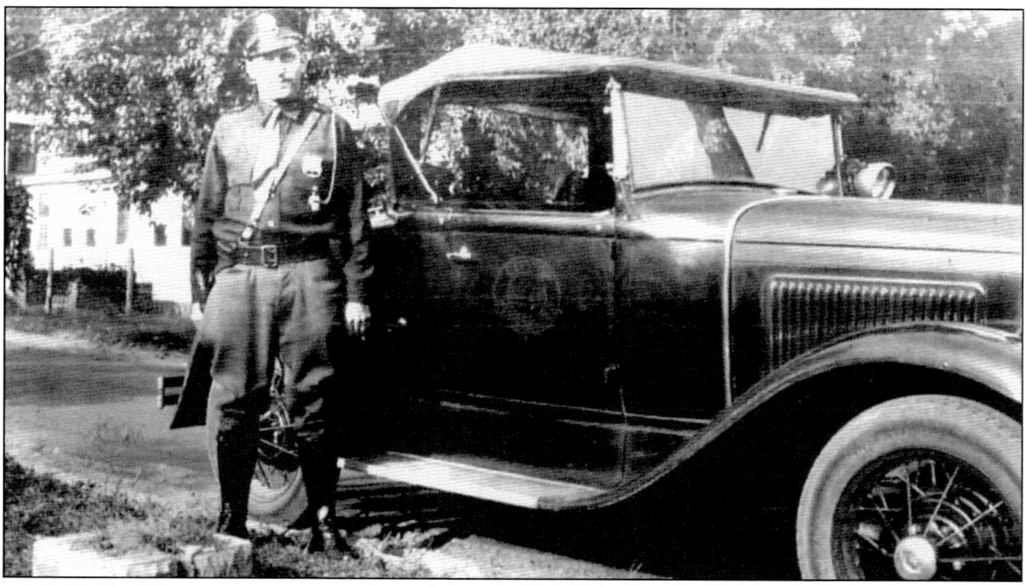

Miah "Mike" Banning was a member of the Northfield Police Department from 1929 until his death in 1946. When he joined, just two men made up the entire force: he and police chief Bud Lever. He began as a volunteer with the fire department when it was first organized, in 1923, and, in 1925, became the city's first paid firefighter.

Ralph English served as a relief officer for the Northfield Police Department. A 1930s newspaper article reported: "Chief of Police Everett Lever and Officer Miah Banning are having their vacation this week during the gunning season. They will spend several days in Virginia and other Southern states on a motor trip. Howard Arthur and Ralph English are acting as their substitutes during their absence."

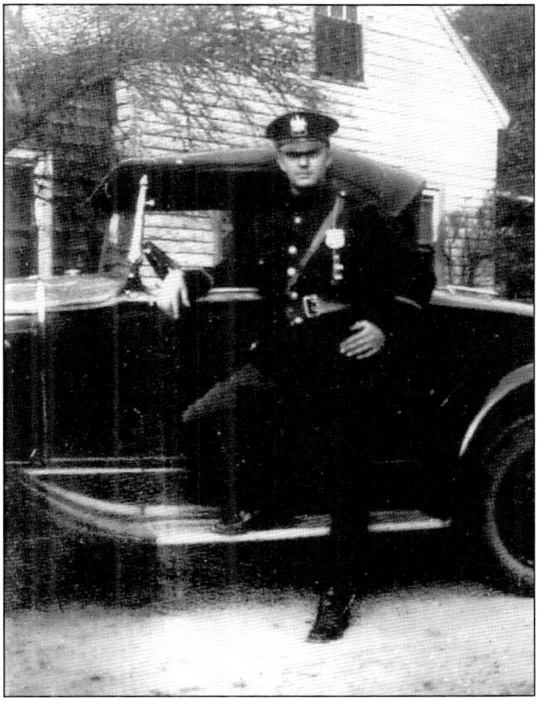

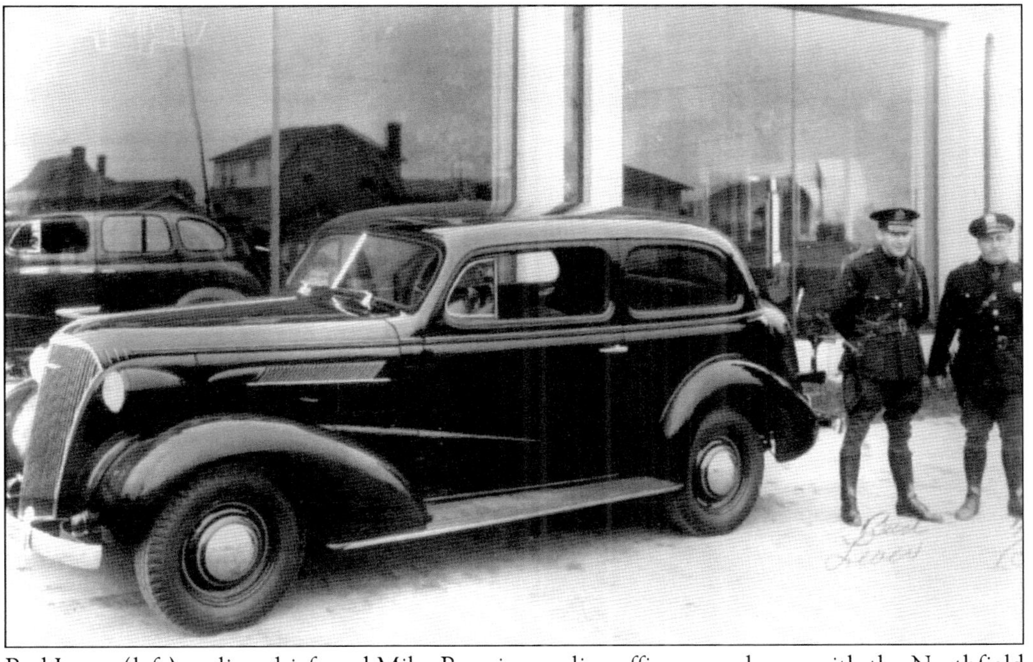

Bud Lever (left), police chief, and Mike Banning, police officer, are shown with the Northfield Police Department's 1937 Chevrolet at the car dealership in West Atlantic City. Until the mid-1930s, these two men were the entire Northfield Police Department. One patrolled from 8:00 a.m. to 6:00 p.m. and the other from 6:00 p.m. until 8:00 a.m. In 1936, a relief officer was hired to give each of them a day off, and in 1940, the department hired another full-time officer.

If you know of the disposition of three (3) Canadian Geese, apparently taken from Birch Grove, please advise.

Police Chief
EVERETT LEVER,
Northfield City Hall

Once upon a time, it was alarming when geese disappeared from Birch Grove Park. . . .

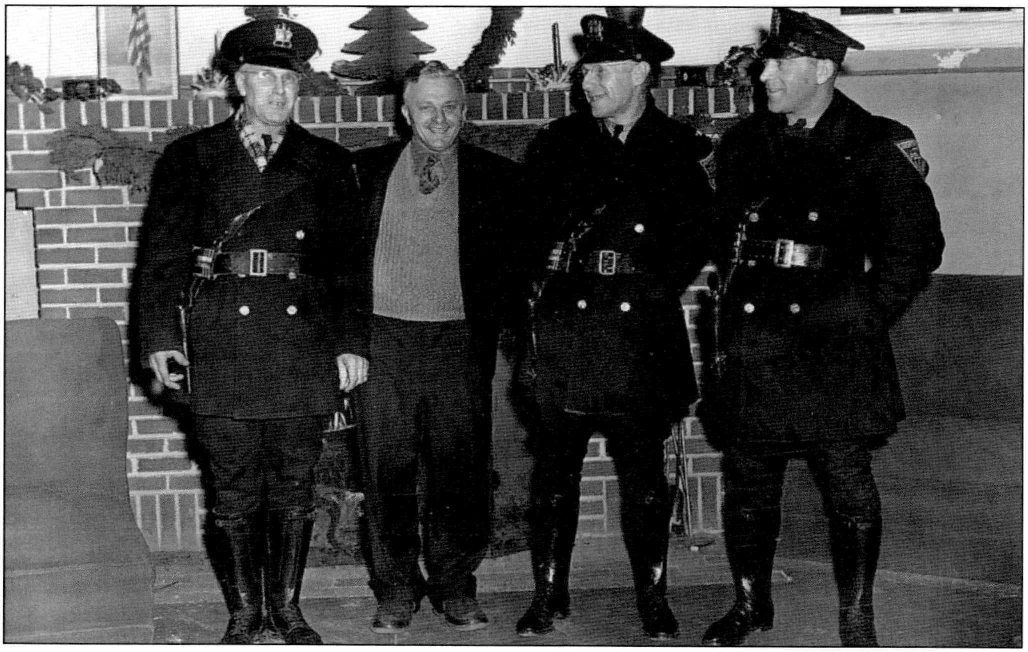

Photographed inside the Northfield Recreation Lodge are, from left to right, Harry Gant, Dave Leopardi, Chief Bud Lever, and Howard Chambers. In 1948, Lever concluded that the regular police and reserves in the department needed systematic firearms training. An outdoor range that was set up at the old brickyard was often unusable because of inclement weather, so an indoor range was constructed at the Northfield Recreation Lodge. The range was in operation for practice on Monday nights from 1950 until 1970.

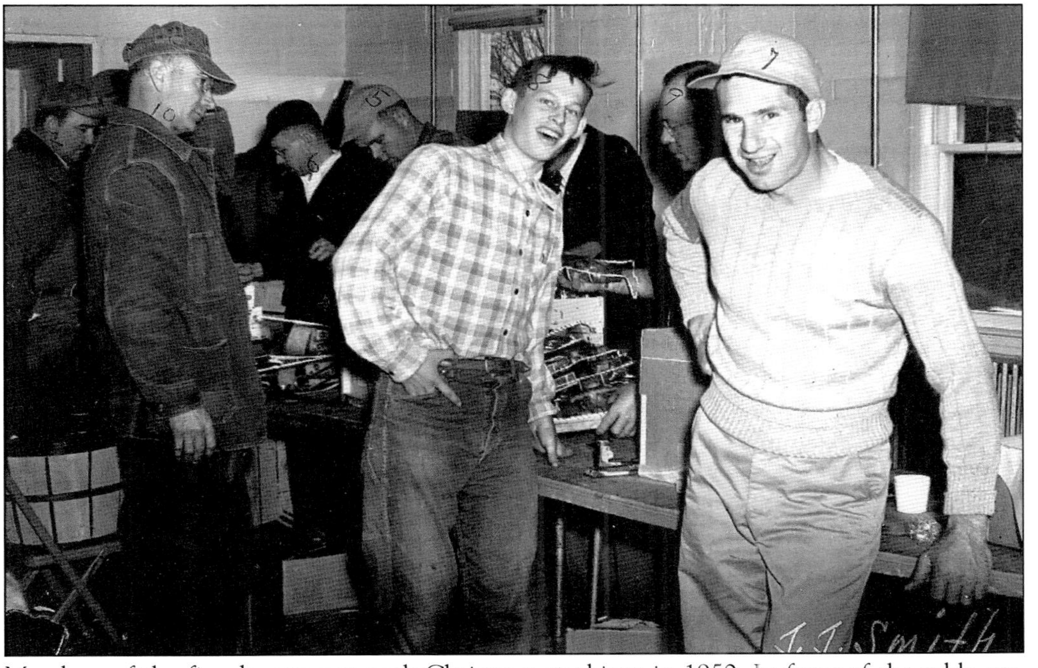

Members of the fire department pack Christmas stockings in 1950. In front of the table are, from left to right, Milt Dailey, Ray Wilson, and Sam Mazza. In back are, from left to right, Inky Breunig, Mike Mazza, and Bill Merrigan. For many years the fire and police departments had a tradition of distributing gifts to Northfield children at Christmas. According to one newspaper article c. 1938, "The Northfield firemen and police appreciate the cooperation they received from many who made it possible for them to visit seventy-five homes and bring Christmas cheer, with toys and gifts for about 250 children. Dolls were dressed and given by the Girl Scouts and the fire company purchased a number of new toys."

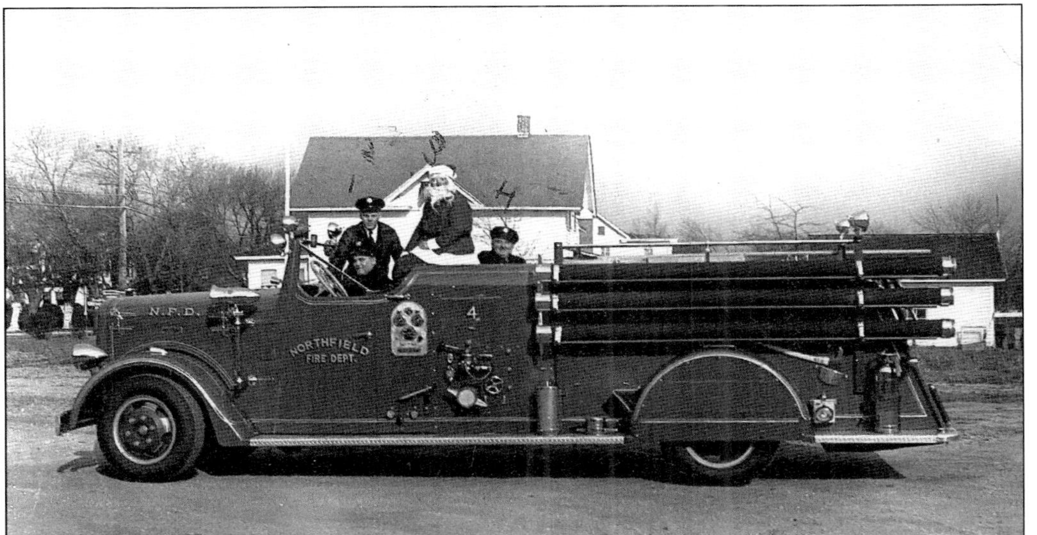

In 1951, the fire department brings Santa Claus to Northfield. From left to right are Ed Pyott, Bill Carney, Santa Claus, and Bill Moody.

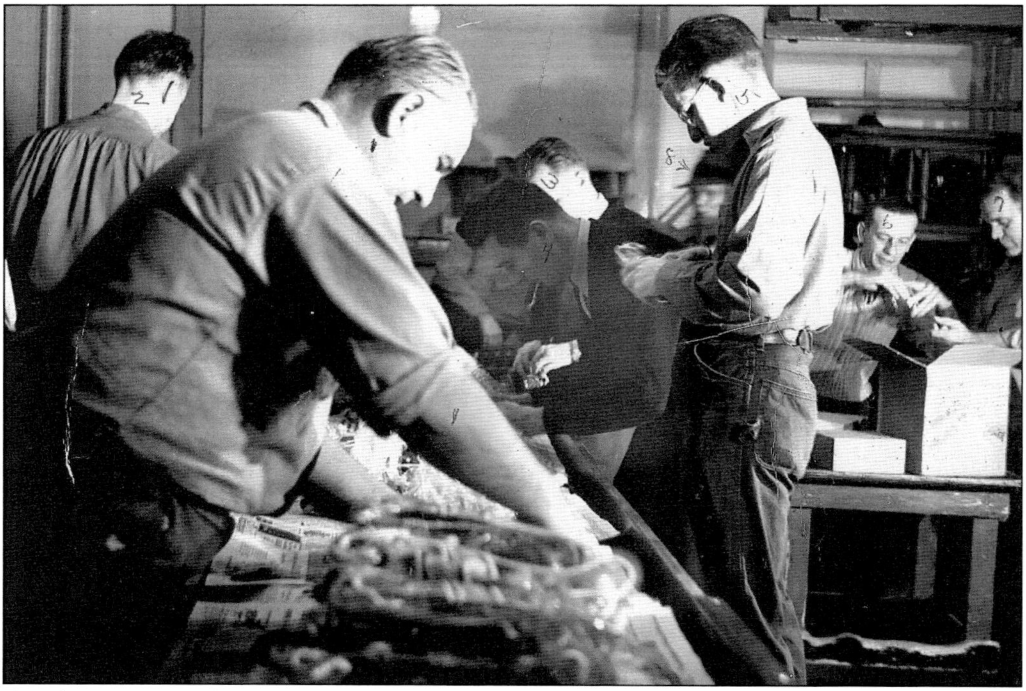

Fire department volunteers pack Christmas gifts. On the left side of the table are Bill Moody and Inky Breunig (back to camera). To the right of the table are, from left to right, Si Littlefield, Milt Dailey, and Jimmy Ryon. In the back are, from left to right, Dan Snyder, Marty Zimmerman, and Ed Pyott.

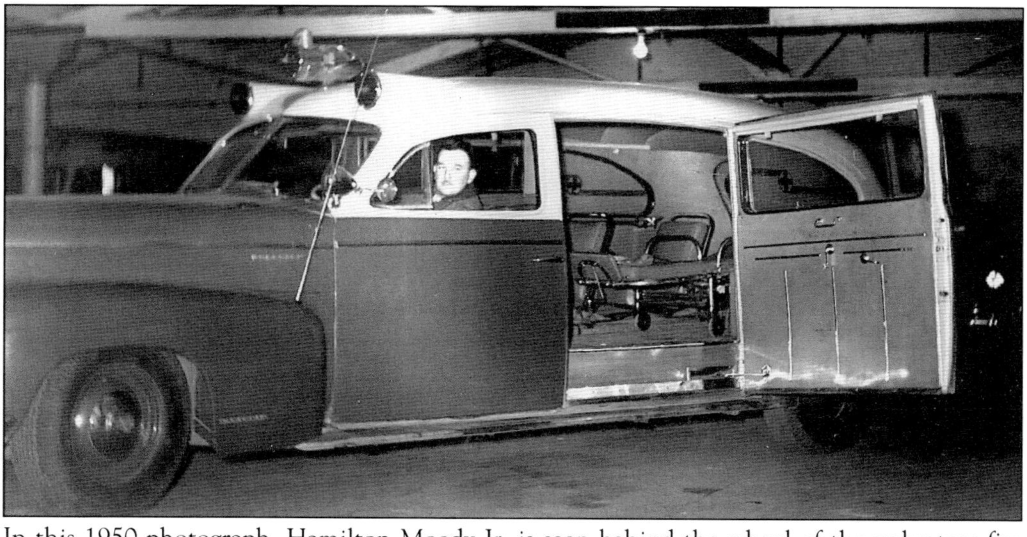

In this 1950 photograph, Hamilton Moody Jr. is seen behind the wheel of the volunteer fire department's 1948 Cadillac ambulance. The program booklet for one fund-raising event included this note under a picture of the ambulance: "We are proud to say that this vehicle has answered approximately 500 calls in 2 1/2 years of service. We need assistance in securing a more modern one to still serve YOU better." The ambulance was replaced in 1954 with a new Cadillac ambulance.

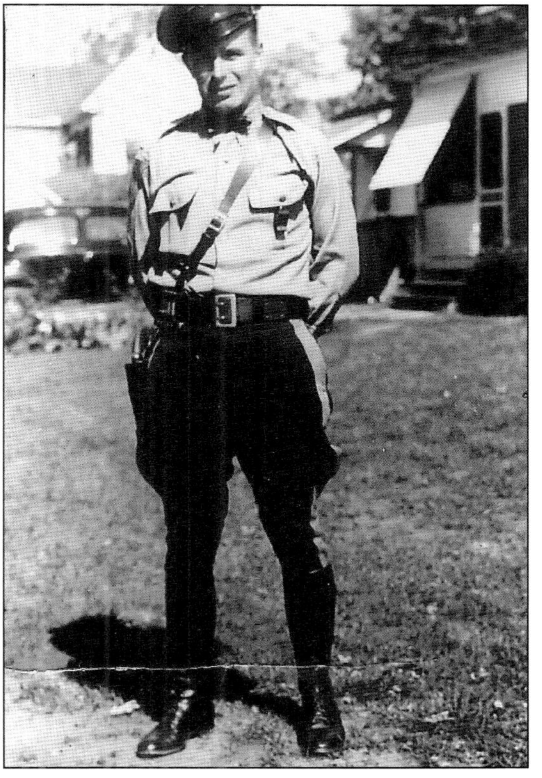

These photographs are of New Jersey State Police Capt. Theodore F. Schmidt. A Northfield resident, he was the first Atlantic County trooper to attain the rank of captain. Schmidt was in charge of the Garden State Parkway and commanded the state police during the Newark riots. He was instrumental in getting the traffic light installed at New and Tilton Roads. He was also president of the Acacia Club. He was descended from the Stuber family, longtime residents of Linwood. His daughter, Lynn, was a teacher in the area for many years and is the wife of Roy Clark, curator of the Northfield Museum.

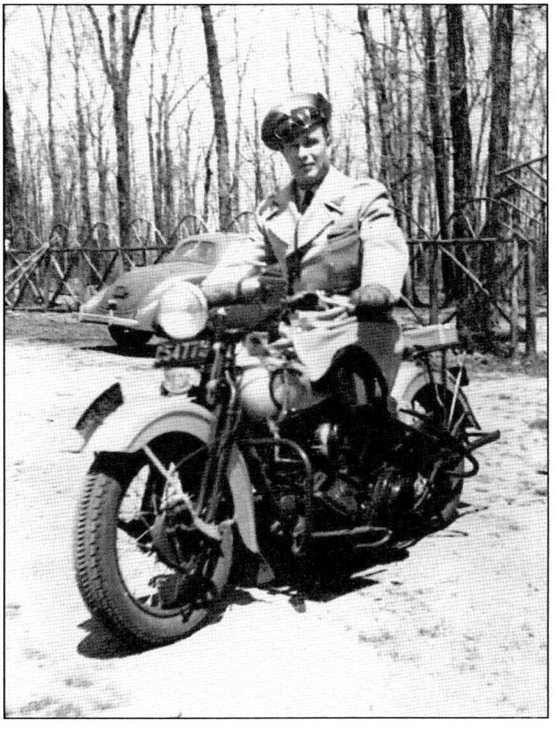

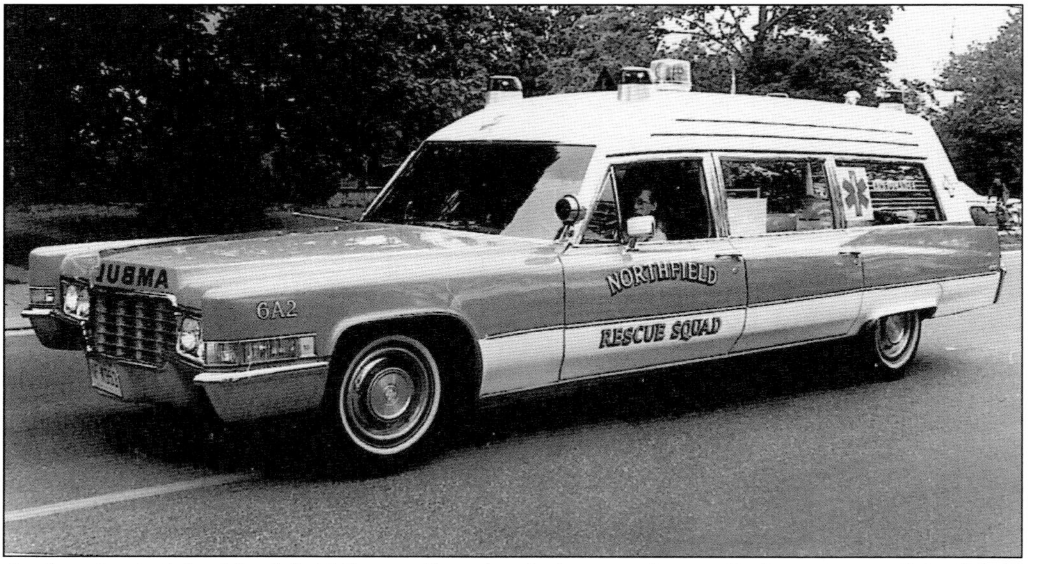

At the wheel of this Northfield Rescue Squad ambulance is George Parker, mayor of Northfield from 1943 to 1947.

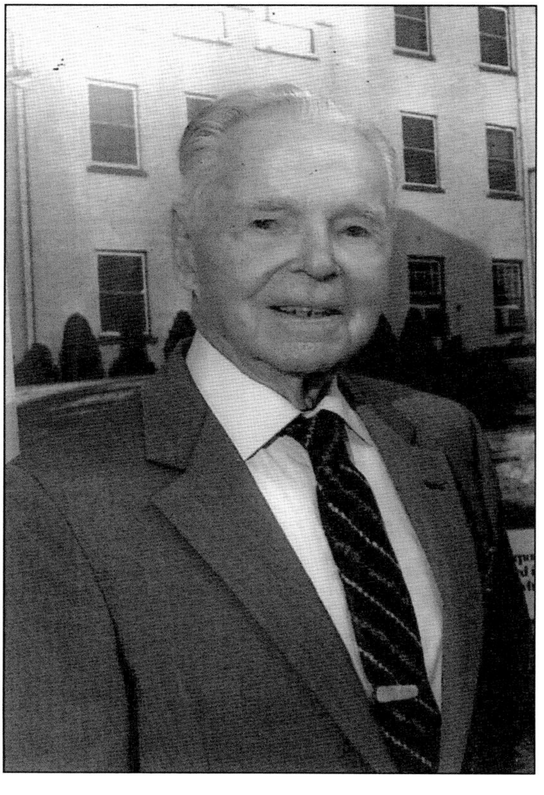

Dr. Peter H. Marvel served as physician to many Northfield residents for more than 50 years. He was hired in 1933 as the first resident physician at the Atlantic Shores Hospital in Somers Point, where he served as house physician until 1935. After opening a private practice in Northfield, Marvel spearheaded a public fund-raising effort to convert the privately held institution into a community hospital. It was formally incorporated as the not-for-profit Shore Memorial Hospital in 1940.

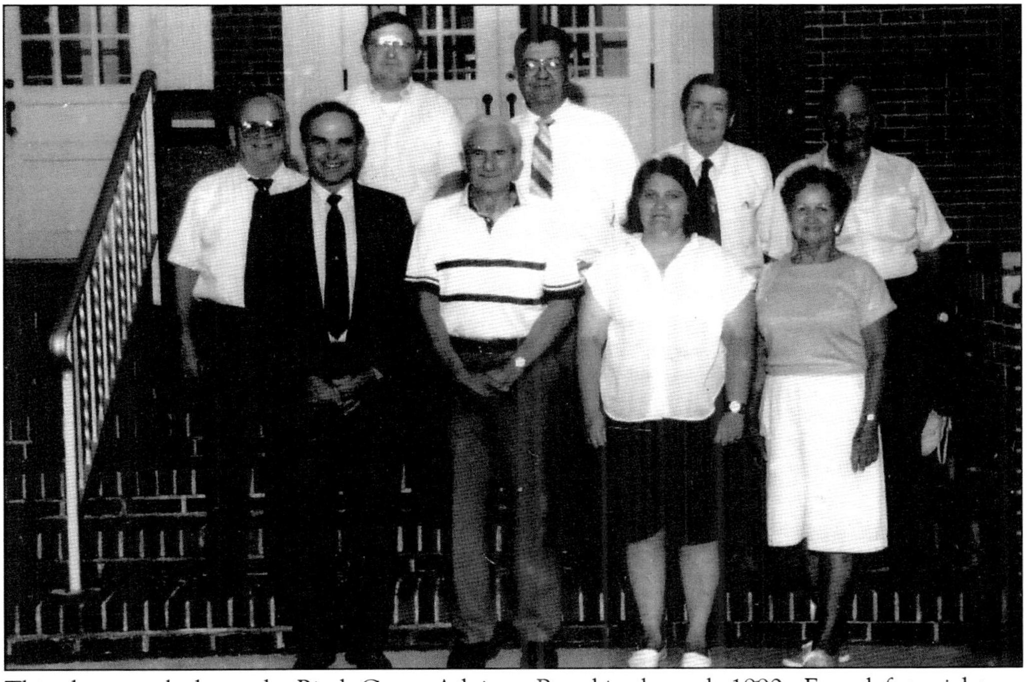

This photograph shows the Birch Grove Advisory Board in the early 1990s. From left to right are the following: (first row) Gene Compton, Sam Mazza, Eileen Pantalena, and Flora Dickinson; (second row) Dick Warren, William Shaw, Jack Hafner, Dan Lawless, and Ed Klingener.

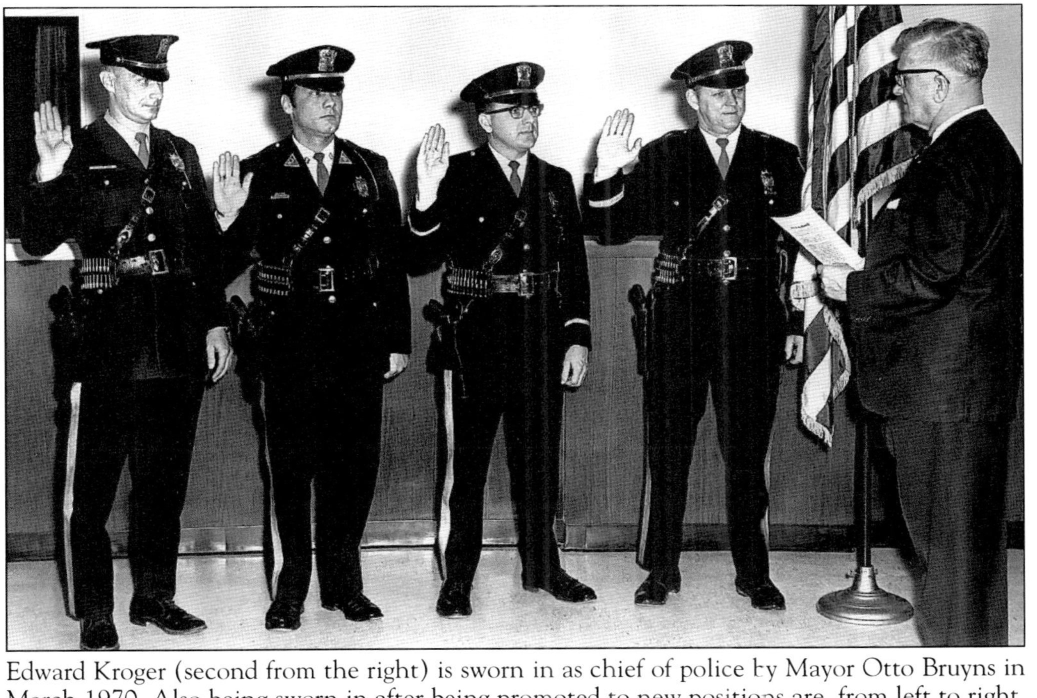

Edward Kroger (second from the right) is sworn in as chief of police by Mayor Otto Bruyns in March 1970. Also being sworn in after being promoted to new positions are, from left to right, Bob Shaw, Bill Cressman, and Tom Wolcott.

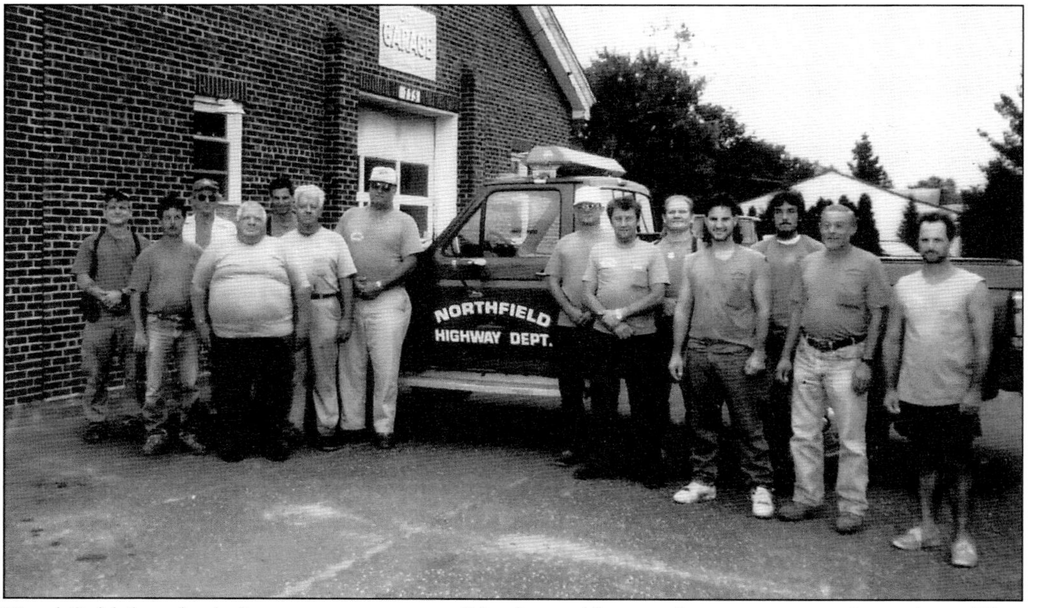

Northfield has had departments responsible for public works since its earliest days. This photograph shows the members of the Northfield Public Works Department *c.* 1990. From left to right are William Ritcher, John Thornewell, Pete Foster, George "Buddy" Rogers (supervisor), John Ayres, Tom Webb, Ray Ford, Jewel Jones (mechanic), Joe Axelson (assistant supervisor), Art Axelson, Mike Balesteri, Pete Clark, Ed Pritchard, and Mark Balesteri.

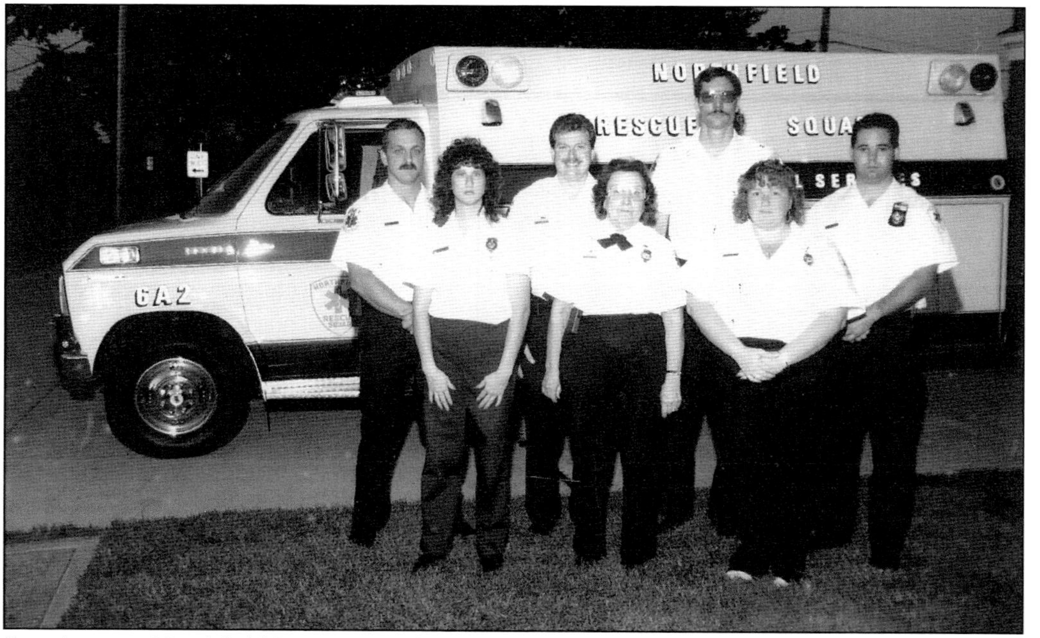

Seen here are Northfield Rescue Squad officers in the early 1990s. From left to right are Thomas Corona (chief), Kim Price (vice president), Richard Collinson (assistant chief), Marjorie Banning (president), Kevin Fehr (captain), Teresa Powers (secretary), and Richard Solkin (lieutenant). Not pictured are Charles Lippincott (treasurer) and Esther Fries (chaplain).

Seven

Places That Served Our City

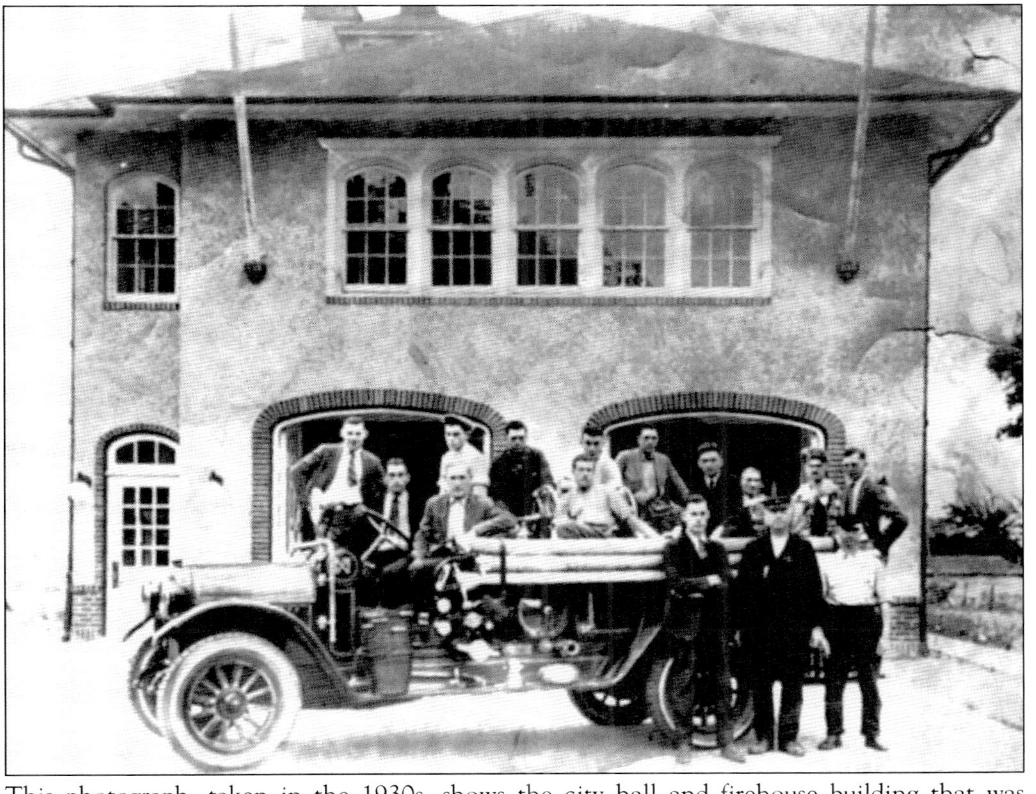

This photograph, taken in the 1930s, shows the city hall and firehouse building that was dedicated on September 12, 1924, National Defense Day. Eugene Swilkey was the mayor at that time. Howard A. Stout Sr. was the architect; Charles S. Corson was the builder. The public library was in the mayor's office, on the second floor. This building was later taken down and replaced with the current city hall building, which was dedicated in 1970.

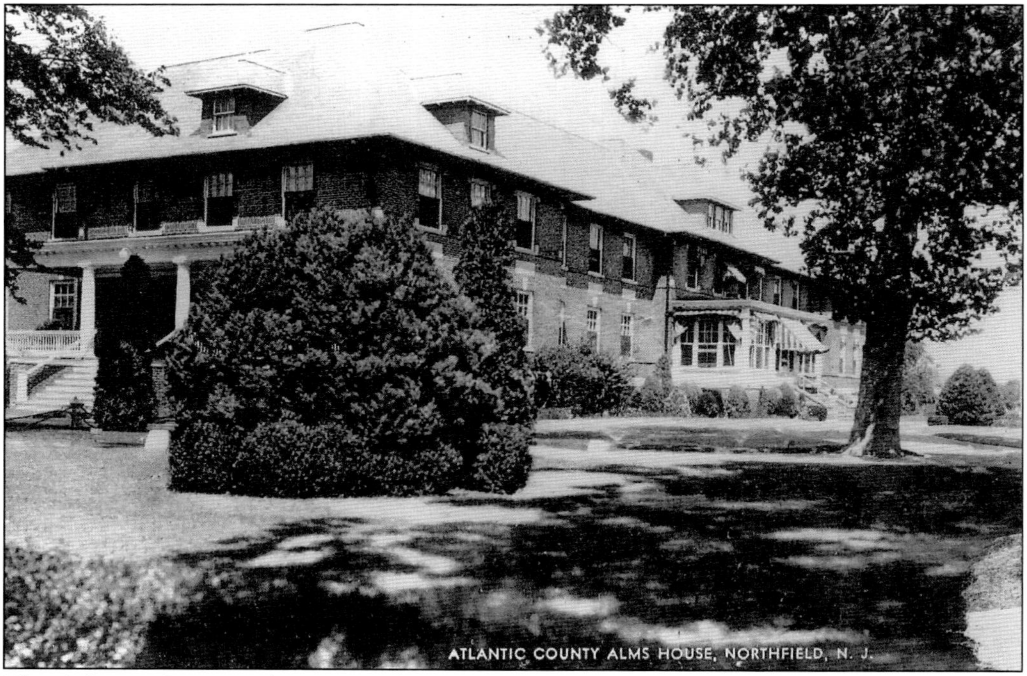

The Atlantic County Alms House, located at 191 Shore Road, next to the Atlantic County Insane Asylum, was built in 1913 as a home for the area's indigent. In 1957, it was converted into the Home for the Chronically Ill and Aged. The other county building that was located in Northfield was the Hospital for Tuberculosis Diseases, Clyde M. Fish Memorial. It was built in 1940–1941 to replace the dilapidated Pine Rest Tuberculosis Sanatorium.

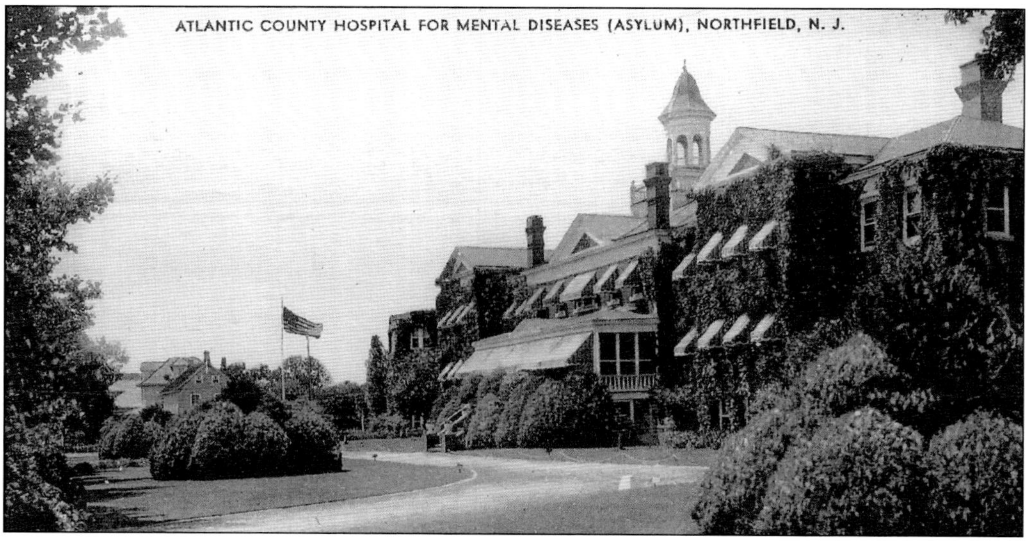

Atlantic County Insane Asylum, also known as the Atlantic County Hospital for Mental Diseases, was established in 1895. This was also the place where Northfield residents were required to apply for marriage licenses. Dr. Edward Guion, M.D., the asylum's medical director, was also Northfield's registrar of vital statistics. He was the only person permitted to issue marriage licenses, and he did so at his only office, which was at the asylum.

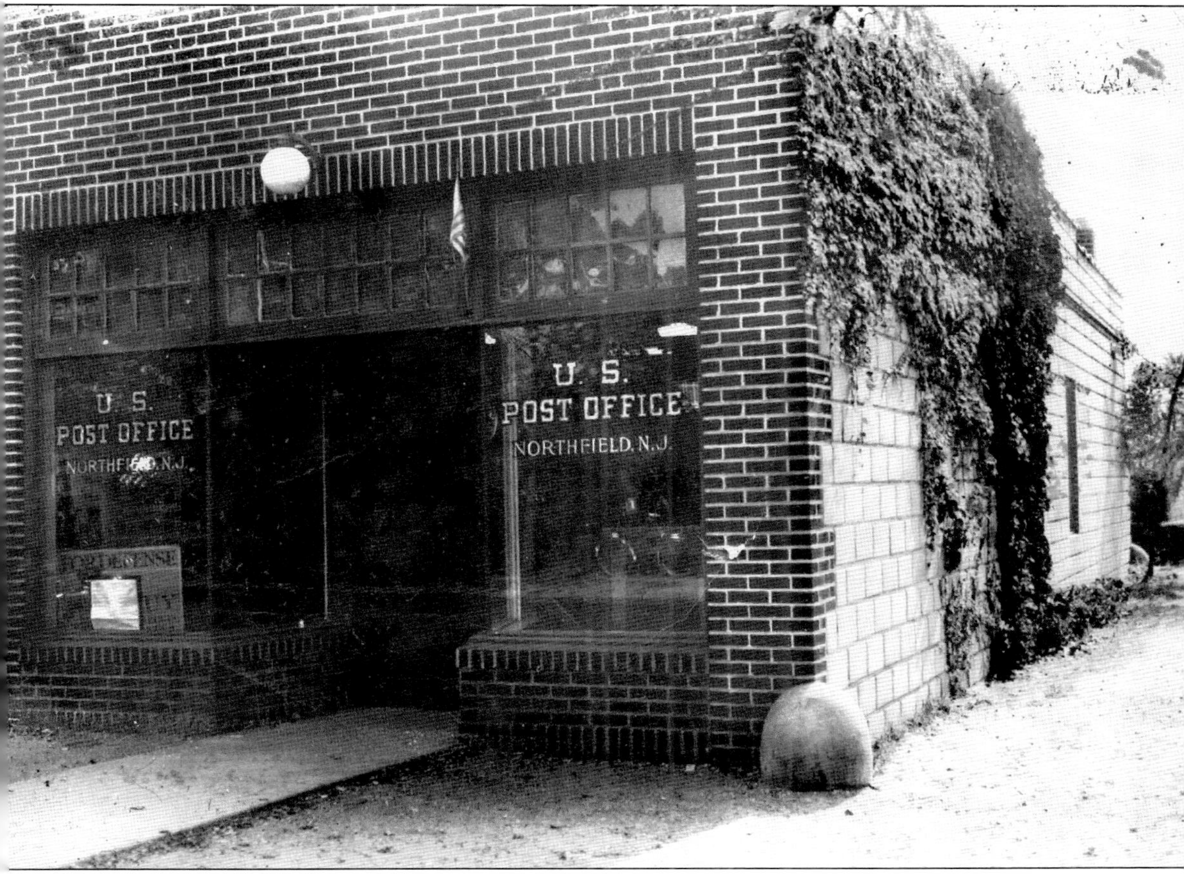

The first post office was on Shore Road in Ryon's General Store, next to the Ryon homestead. The next location for the post office was the space at the south end of the commercial building on the east side of Shore Road, across from Fifield Avenue. A separate building was constructed c. 1954 adjacent to this one; the post office was there until the building on New Road was constructed. Several newspaper articles dated August 22, 1938, reported that an unsuccessful attempt had been made on the previous Sunday to blast open the Northfield post office safe, probably with nitroglycerine. The attempt was discovered by William Casto, who was employed to carry mail between the post office and the Shore Fast Line station. Dr. G. L. Infield, who lived just across the road from the post office, at 1401 Shore Road, reported that he had been awakened by an explosion at 1:30 a.m. and had heard an automobile drive away.

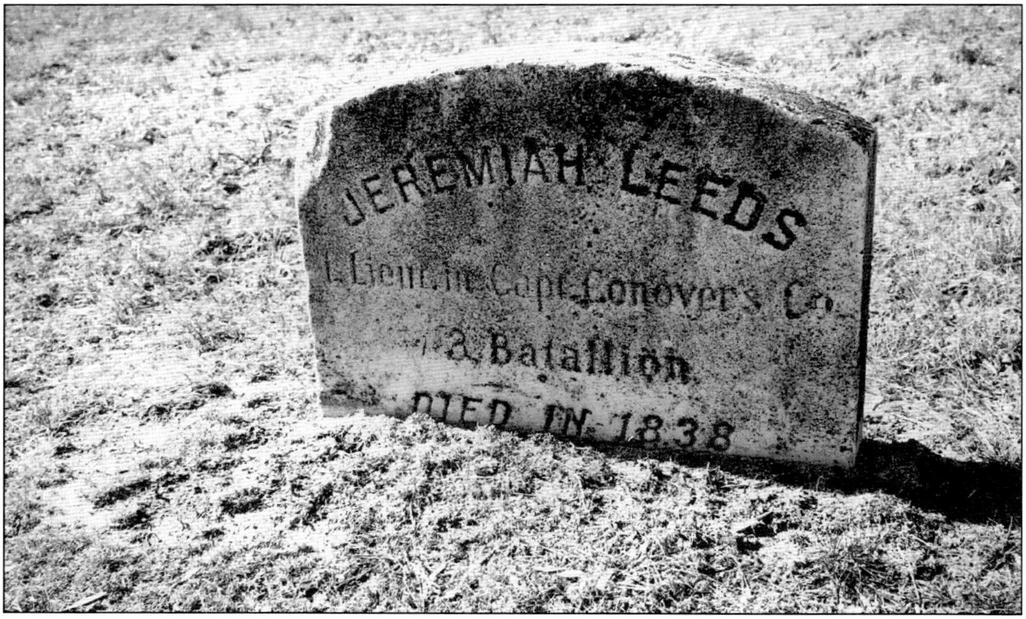

Jeremiah Leeds, the first settler in Atlantic City, was originally buried in Atlantic City. His remains were later moved to the Steelman family cemetery, located on the knoll between what is now Steelman Avenue and Oxford Circle. At some point, the original cemetery was demolished. Area residents, dismayed to realize that the cemetery no longer existed, enlisted the support of the Daughters of the American Revolution, which then placed the four memorial stones in the current location. There are stones for Jeremiah Leeds, Frederick Steelman, his daughter Rachel, and her husband, Peter.

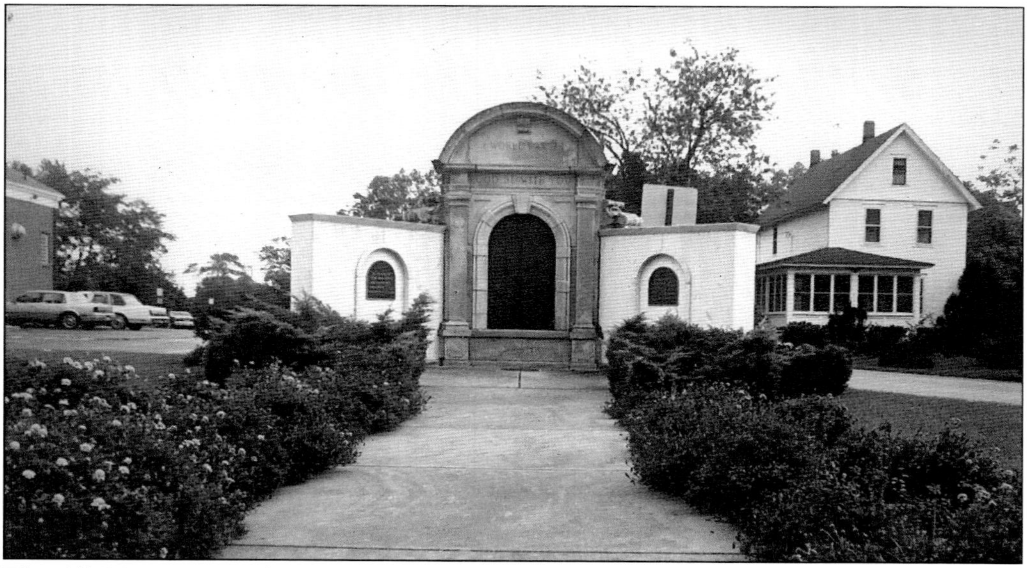

The All Wars Memorial, in front of city hall, was dedicated on June 18, 1944, during Mayor George Parker's administration. The names of 266 men and women in the armed services and five men in the merchant marine were listed. Seward G. Dobbins was the architect, Angelo Vespertino was the builder, and A. E. Stone did the cement work.

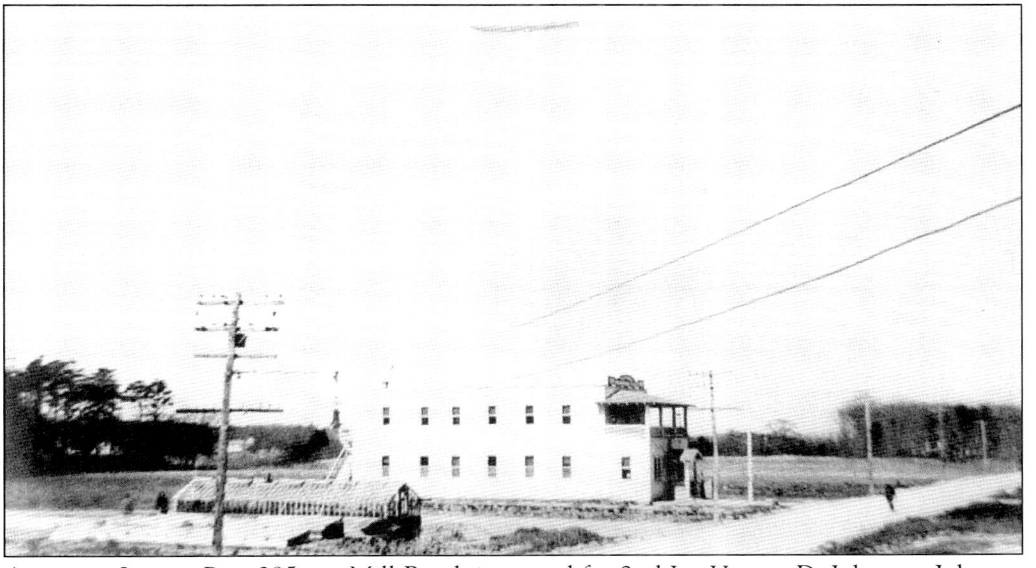

American Legion Post 295, on Mill Road, is named for 2nd Lt. Harvey D. Johnson. Johnson died in a plane crash in London, England, but heroically managed to avoid a populated area. The building, erected in 1925, for a short time was the Roseland dance hall, according to some longtime residents. It then became the Progressive League Hall. In this photograph, taken by Lee W. Herrick Jr., it is shown as it looked in 1927. The German-built dirigible overhead, the *Los Angeles-ZE-3*, was received as part of World War I reparations. (Courtesy of American Legion Post 295.)

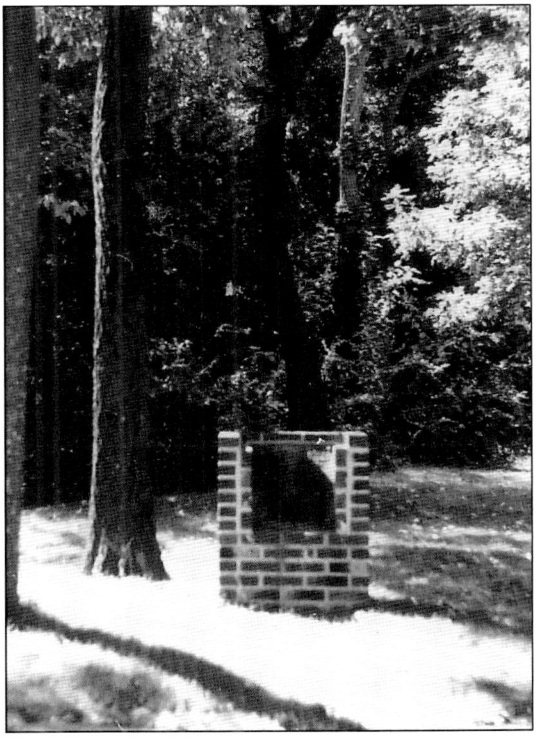

Northfield Bird Sanctuary, located south of Mill Road behind Cove and Rosedale Avenues, is a wooded area situated between a residential area and saltwater marshland. The sanctuary is a 25.3-acre preserve that was obtained through two acquisitions, in 1973 and 1979, from the Frank H. Stewart Trust Committee.

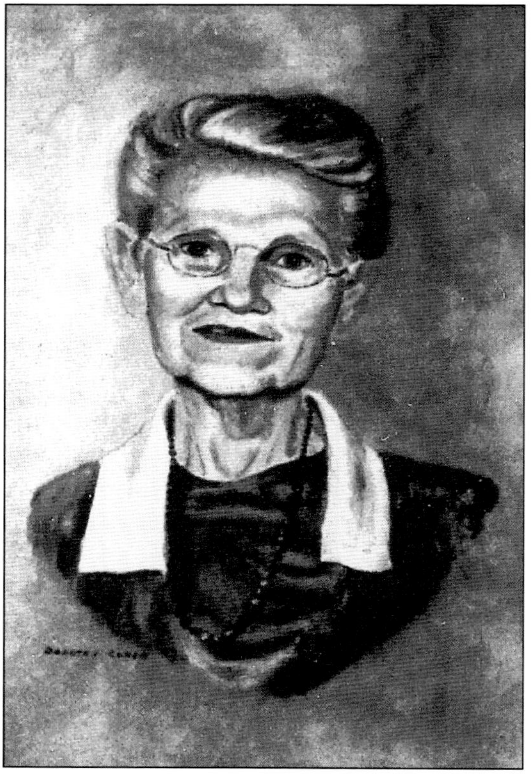

The Otto Bruyns Public Library, on Mill Road, was dedicated on August 26, 1983. Northfield's first public library was opened in November 1926, with 150 books shelved in front of Mayor Eugene Swilkey's desk; within a year, the council chamber was lined with bookcases. Lizzie J. Price, depicted here in a portrait that hangs in the Otto Bruyns Library, was appointed the first librarian in 1926 and served for more than 20 years. In 1928, the library was moved to a room on the second floor of the house across Shore Road, and in December 1938, it was moved to a small city-owned building next to city hall. This latter building had been purchased by the city, moved from its original location in the 1930s, and remodeled as a Works Progress Administration (WPA) project. This building is now part of the Northfield Museum. In late 1969, the library was moved inside the new city hall, where it stayed until the Otto Bruyns Public Library on Mill Road was built. (Courtesy of the Northfield Public Library Association.)

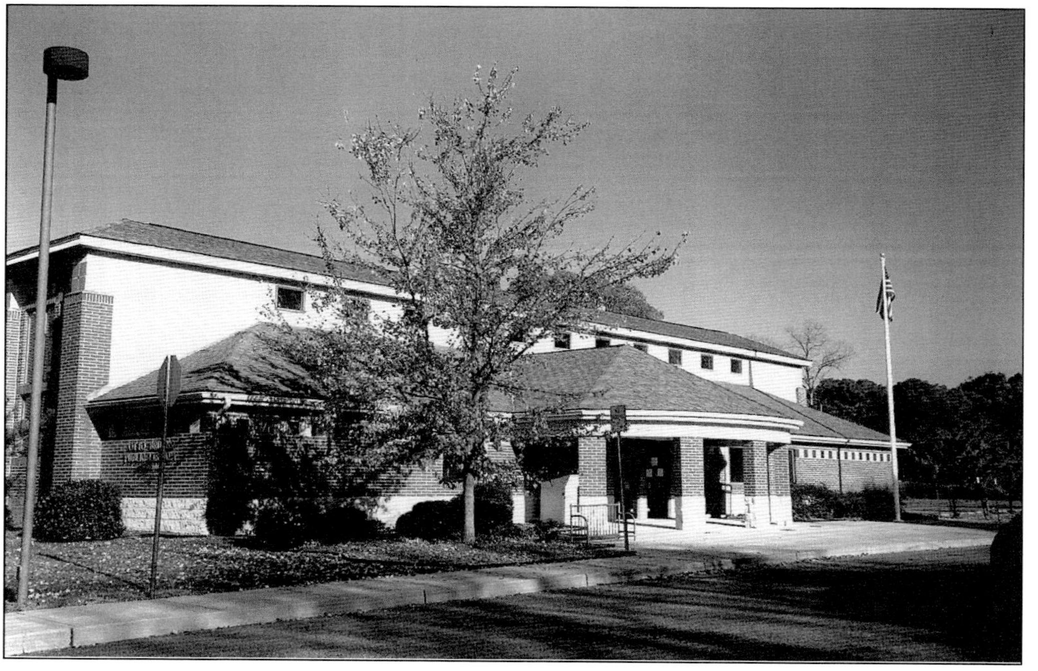

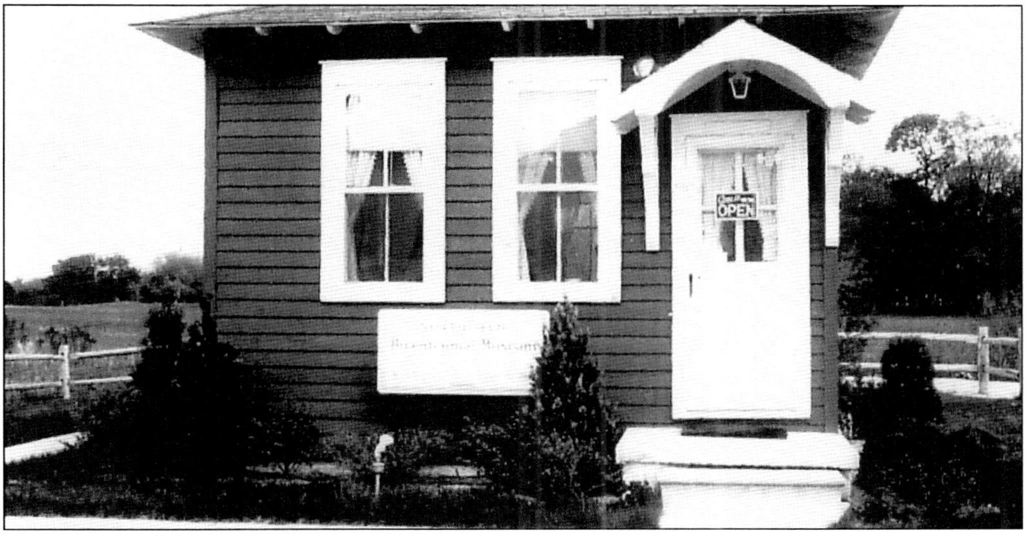

This building, purchased by Northfield in the 1930s, was first used as an office and then as a polling place. In 1938, it became Northfield's first freestanding public library. When the library was moved inside the new city hall, the former library building was moved behind it. The building was later used for storage at the city garage until 1976, when it was moved behind city hall, renovated by the Northfield Bicentennial Committee, and opened as the Northfield Museum. In the mid-1980s, the building was again moved, this time to its present site in Birch Grove Park, where it is now one wing of the museum.

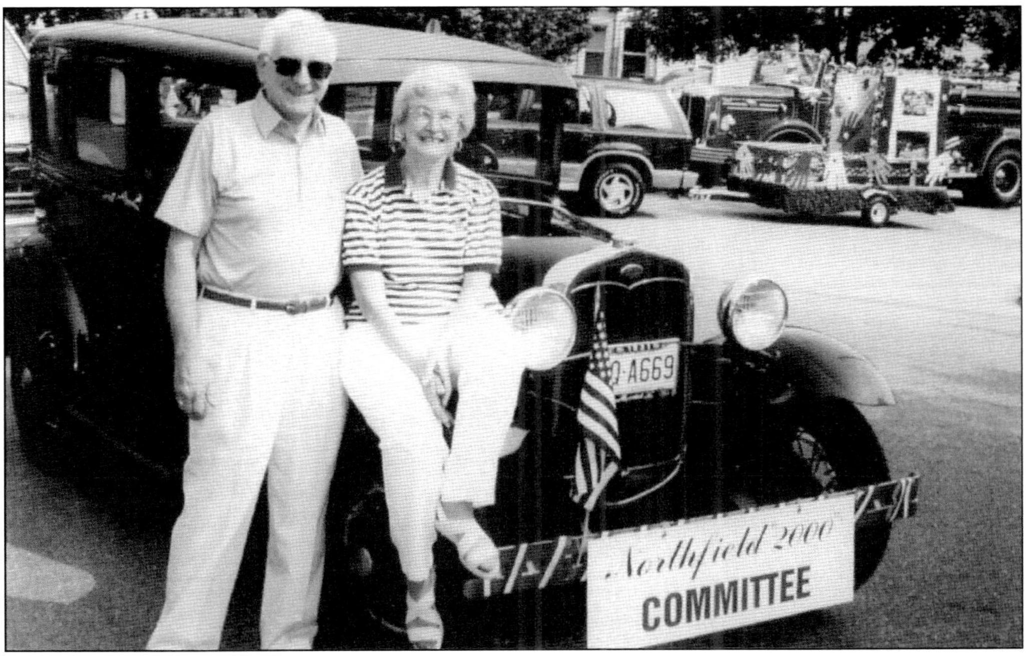

Northfield celebrated the arrival of the year 2000 with a yearlong series of community events, coordinated by the volunteers of the Year 2000 Committee and sponsored by many local organizations. The photograph shows Marge Milone, committee chairperson, and her husband, Lou, just before the start of the Memorial Day Parade in May 2000.

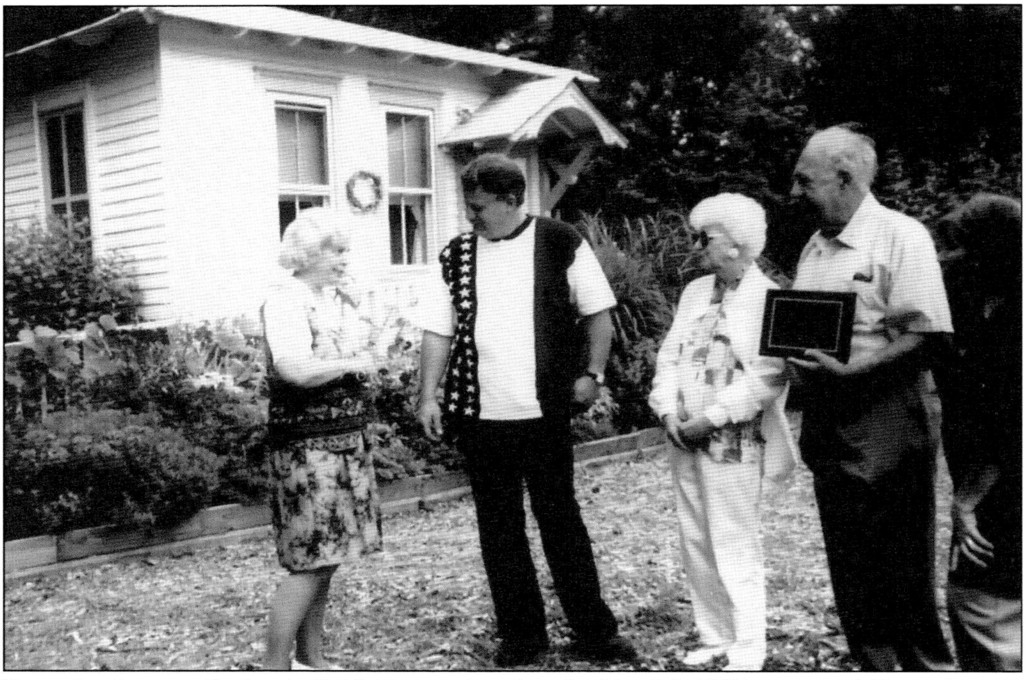

From the dreams of a few individuals appointed as the Northfield Bicentennial Committee in the early 1970s, the Casto House and Northfield Museum evolved into a museum that effectively displays Northfield's multifaceted history. The first museum, the Northfield Bicentennial Museum, commenced operations in 1976; it was located behind city hall in the building shown in the photograph on the previous page. In 1996, Charles and Mary Doerr very generously donated the 150-year-old Casto House to Northfield, with the stipulation that it be moved from its New Road location. In August 1996, the house was moved to its new location next to the Northfield Museum, in Birch Grove Park. After four years of planning, construction, exhibit development, and renovation, the greatly enlarged and revamped Casto House and Northfield Museum reopened on June 23, 2000. The photograph at the top shows, from left to right, Patricia Doerr Parker, Mayor Frank Perri, Mary and Charles Doerr, and Carol Patrick, chairperson of the Northfield Cultural Committee, which manages the museum.

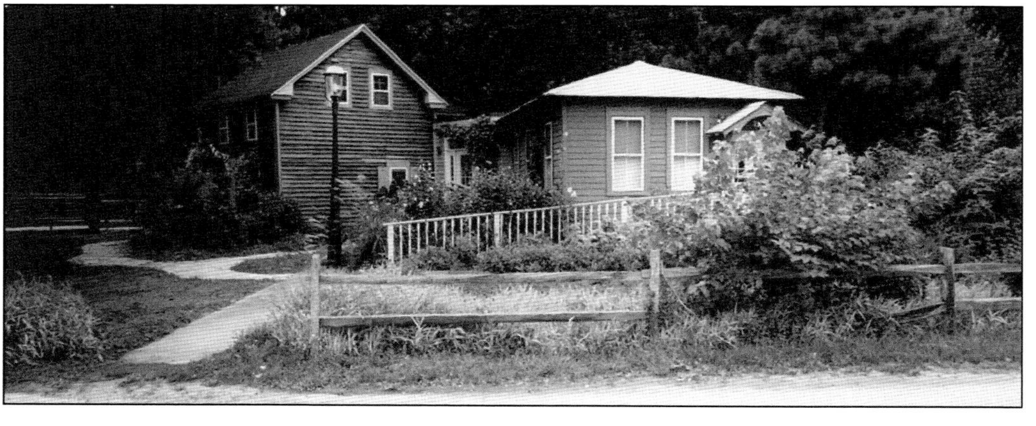

Eight
Playing and Praying

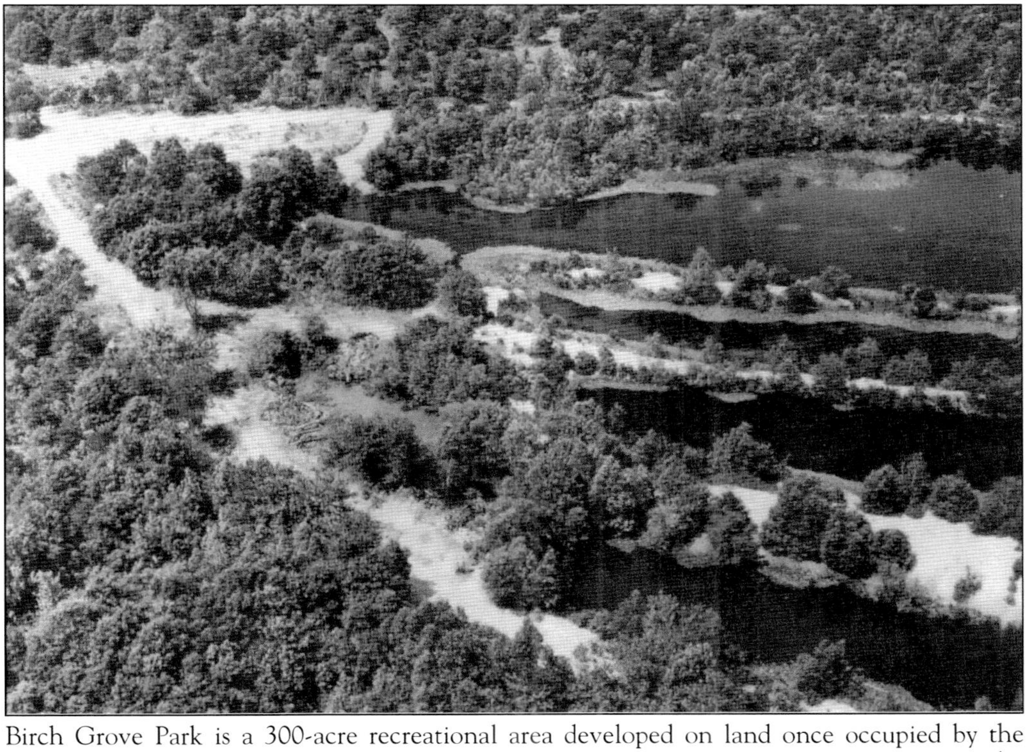

Birch Grove Park is a 300-acre recreational area developed on land once occupied by the Somers Brick Company. Sometime after the brickyard closed during the Depression, the property was turned over to the city. Engelbert "Inky" Breunig spearheaded the project of converting the brickyard into what would become Birch Grove Park. Local business groups, civic organizations, and private individuals worked together as a community, donating time and money to transform the brickyard into a park. The site was dedicated as a city park on August 7, 1951, and the park opened in March 1952. A citywide contest held to choose a name for this new area was won by Claire Kreutz (Moyer). Birch Grove Park has developed into a sports, historical, and cultural complex, while retaining its natural beauty. The park has trails that meander throughout it and natural areas that attract wildlife. It originally had 29 lakes, but several were filled in over the years. At one time boating and swimming were permitted, but they were discontinued because of insurance costs.

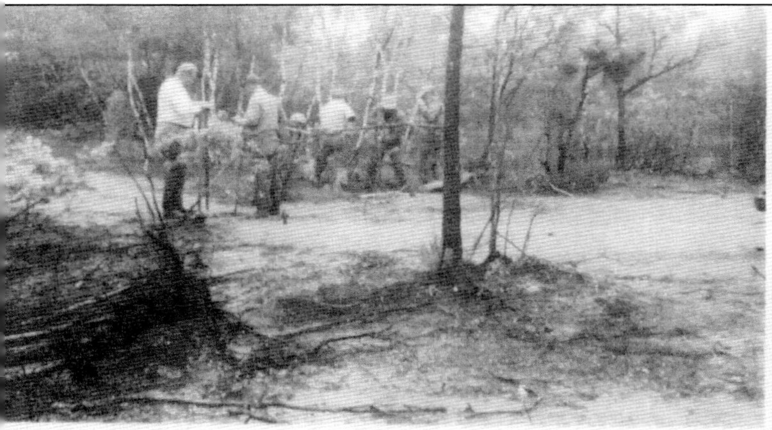

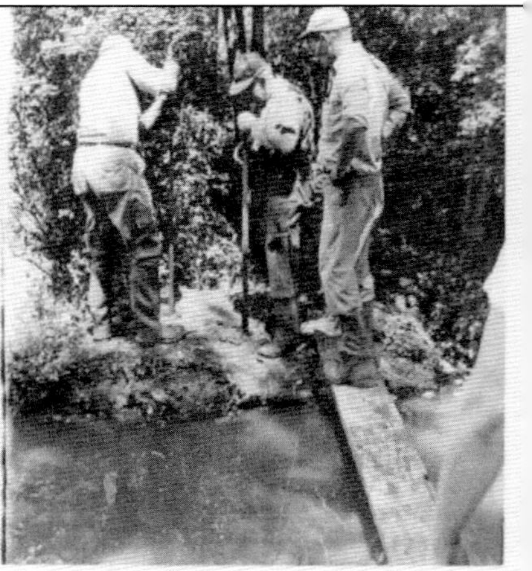

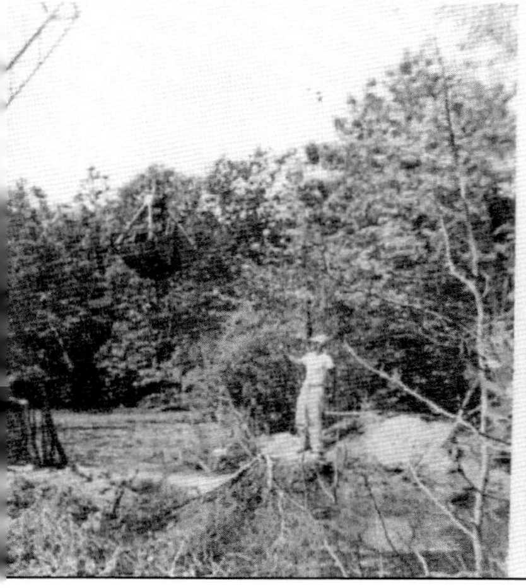

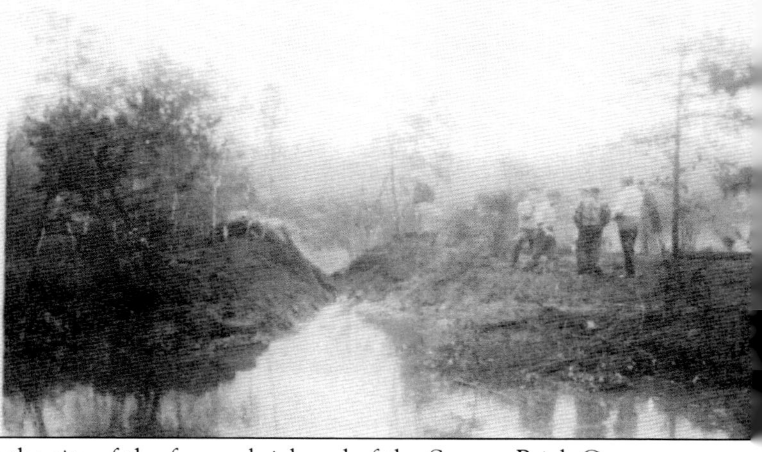

Inky Breunig had a vision that the site of the former brickyard of the Somers Brick Company could be transformed into a park. The transformation began in 1951. All expenses were met through membership drives, picnics, and other fund-raising efforts. Everything was done by local volunteers, some of whom are seen in these 1951 and 1952 photographs. Many of them put in long weekend hours of effort, clearing brush, creating trails, building boardwalks, and making ponds accessible—just a few of the jobs that the volunteers tackled as they developed the park.

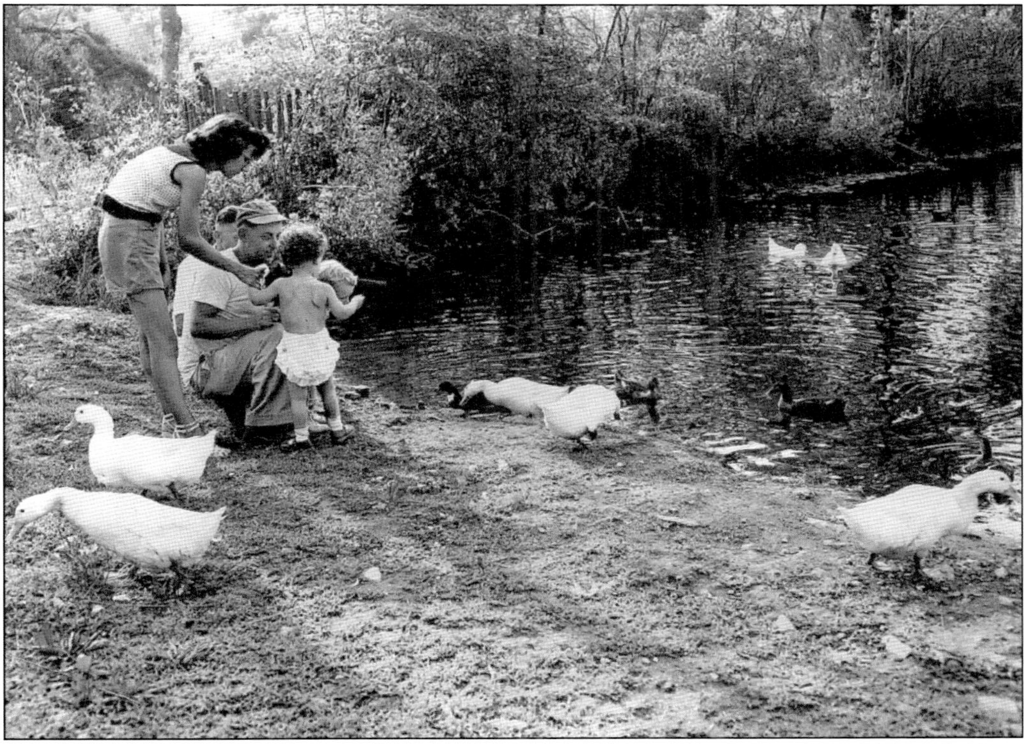

A family visits one of the 25 ponds in Birch Grove Park in 1954. Since the park's early days, ducks of all varieties have made the park their home. For many years the park has had a covered bridge, which can be seen in the back of the pond.

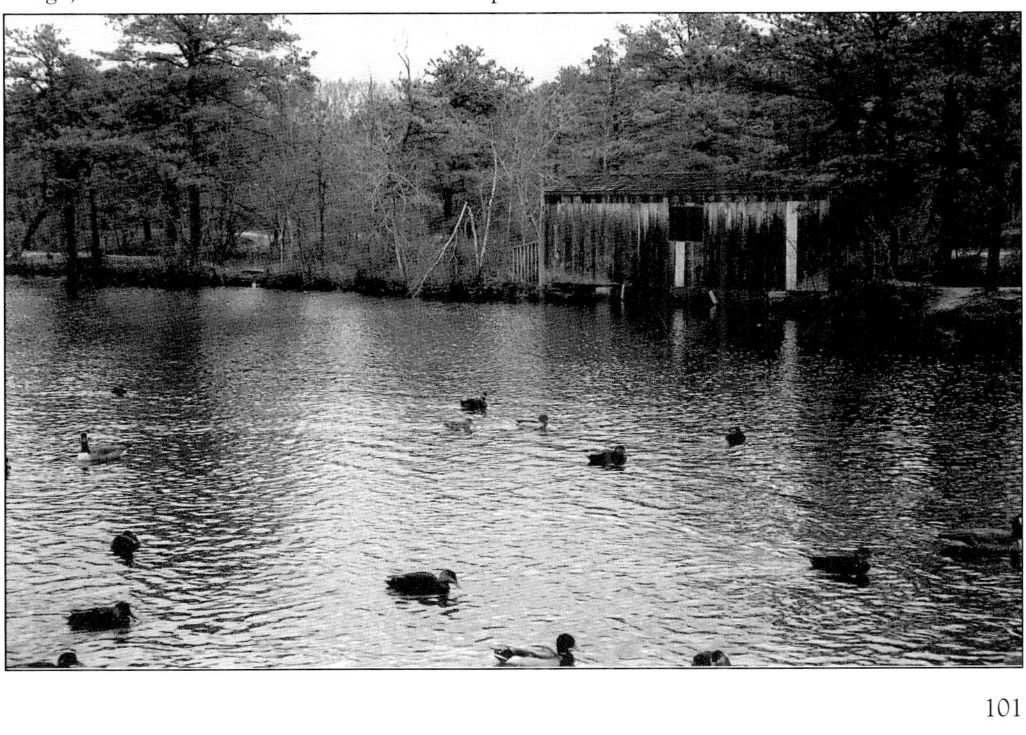

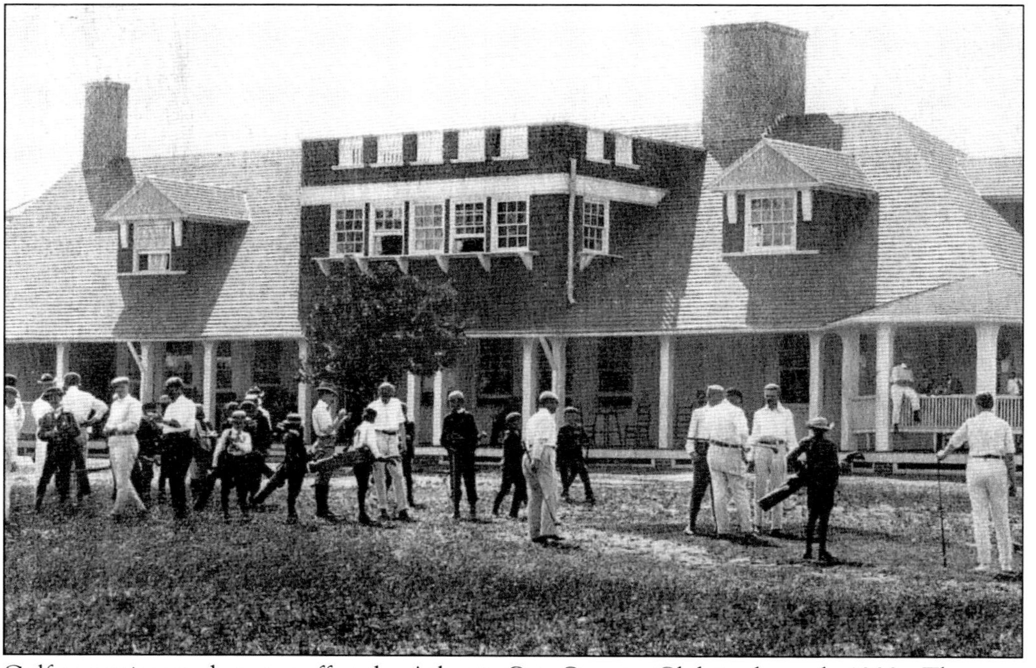

Golfers getting ready to tee off at the Atlantic City Country Club in the early 1900s. The term birdie (one under par) was coined on the 12th hole in 1903. The Atlantic City Country Club, a private course established in 1895, is one of the country's oldest. Listed as one of the finest golf courses in the United States, it has hosted many tournaments and world-famous golfers.

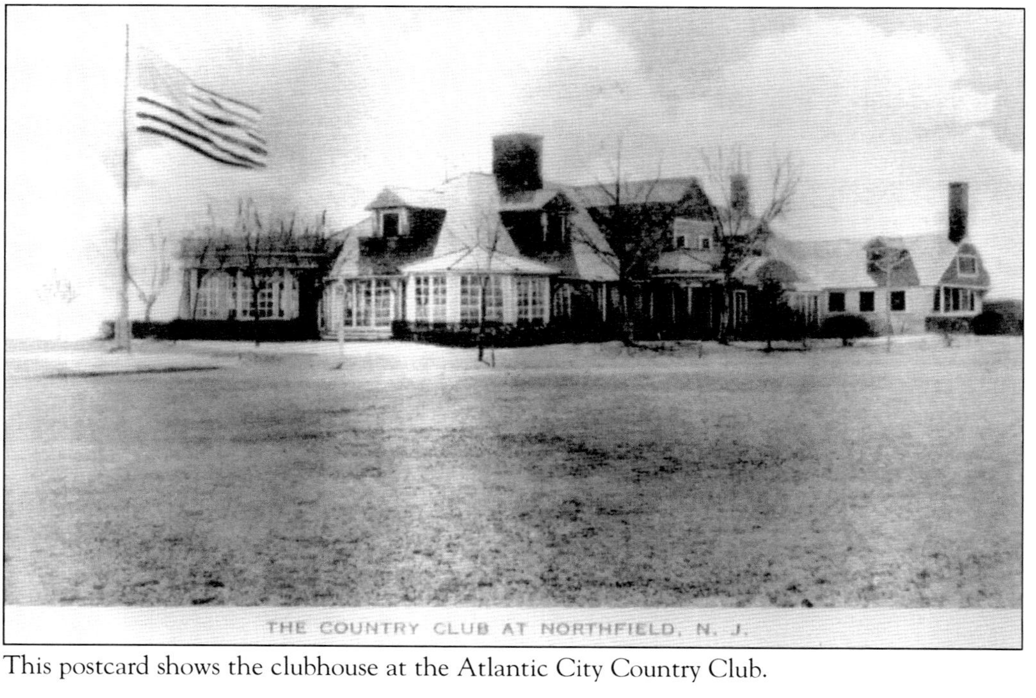

This postcard shows the clubhouse at the Atlantic City Country Club.

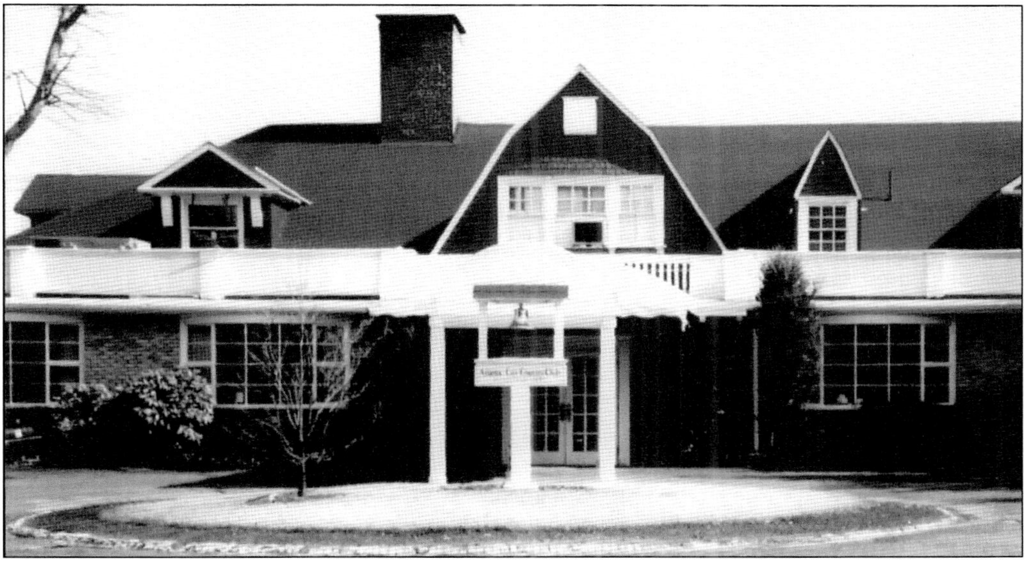

The Atlantic City Country Club was originally envisioned by hotel owners as a means to attract the carriage trade who played golf in Philadelphia but had no place to do so in Atlantic City. These hotel owners chose to build a golf course in what was then known as Bakersville. The club was incorporated in 1897, with J. H. Lippincott as its first president, and officially opened on June 18, 1898. The large bell that still hangs in the circle in front of the club entrance was rung to remind golfers that the day's last trolley from the club to Atlantic City was leaving. The fare was 7¢. The golf course was considered one of the finest in the country; major tournaments were held at the Atlantic City Country Club, major names in golf played there, and celebrities were not uncommon. In 1998, the Fraser family sold the club to Bally Park Place.

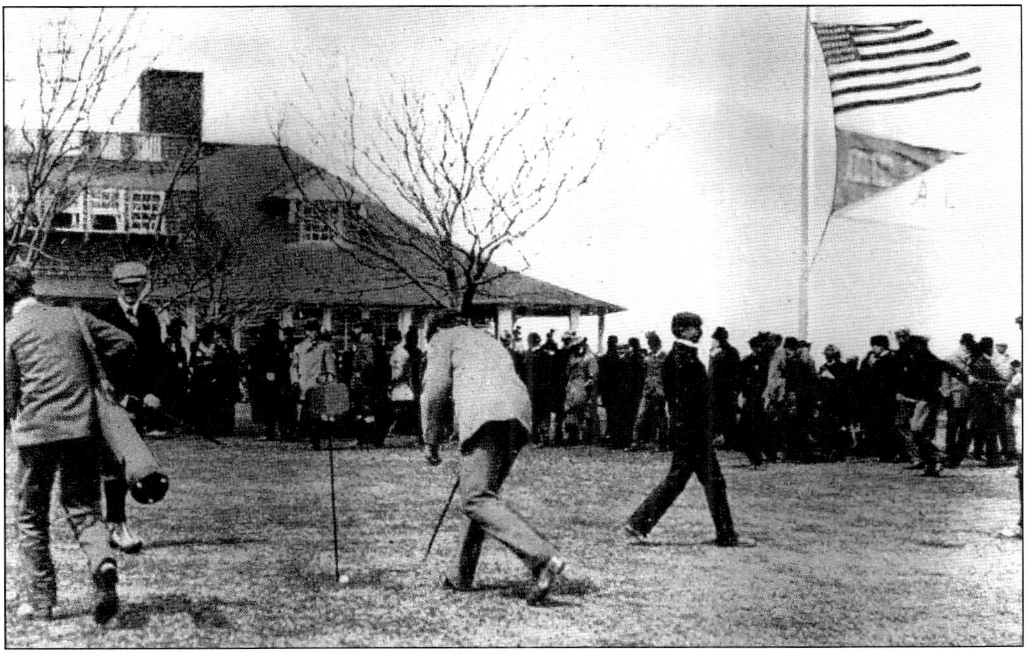

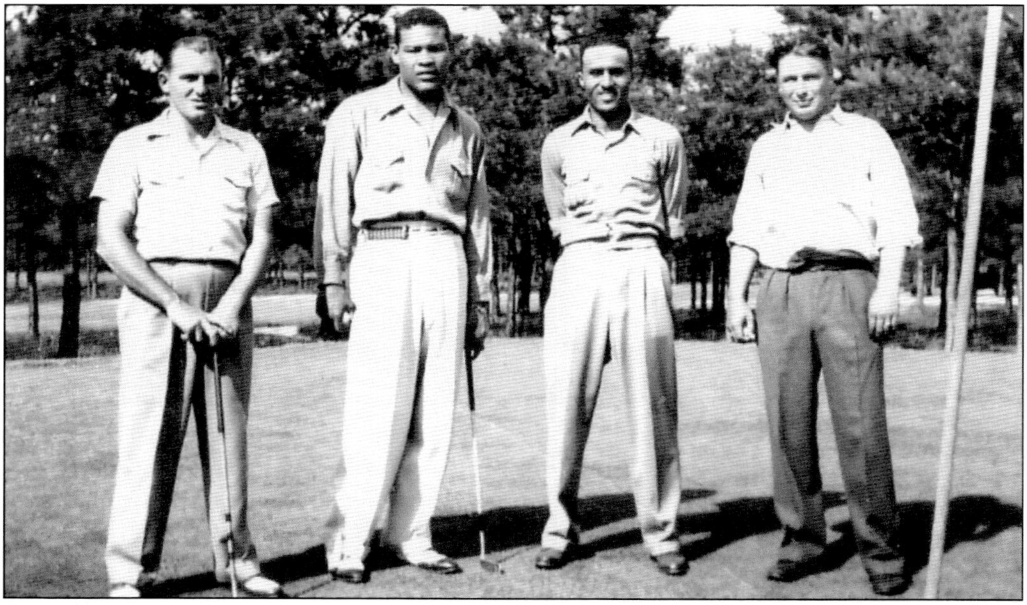

One of boxing's most extraordinary athletes, Joe Lewis—nicknamed "the Brown Bomber"—was the heavyweight champion of the world for 12 years, beginning in 1937. This photograph, taken at the Atlantic City Country Club *c.* 1950, shows, from left to right, Bud Traynor, Joe Lewis, unidentified, and Capt. T. F. Schmidt. Traynor and Schmidt were New Jersey State Police officers.

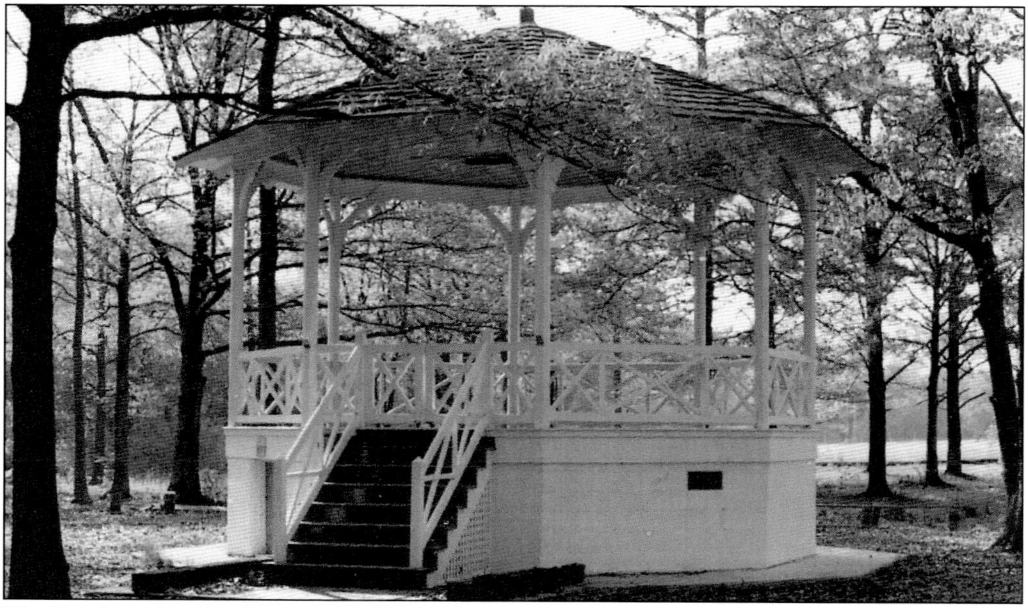

The bandstand in Birch Grove Park, erected in 1976, was built by John and Emmet English and designed by Howard A. Stout Jr. Free concerts are presented there every Tuesday evening in July and August. The bandstand is also used for events such as weddings. In 2003, it was moved to a new location within the park to make room for soccer fields. This photograph was taken by local photographer Dan Cox.

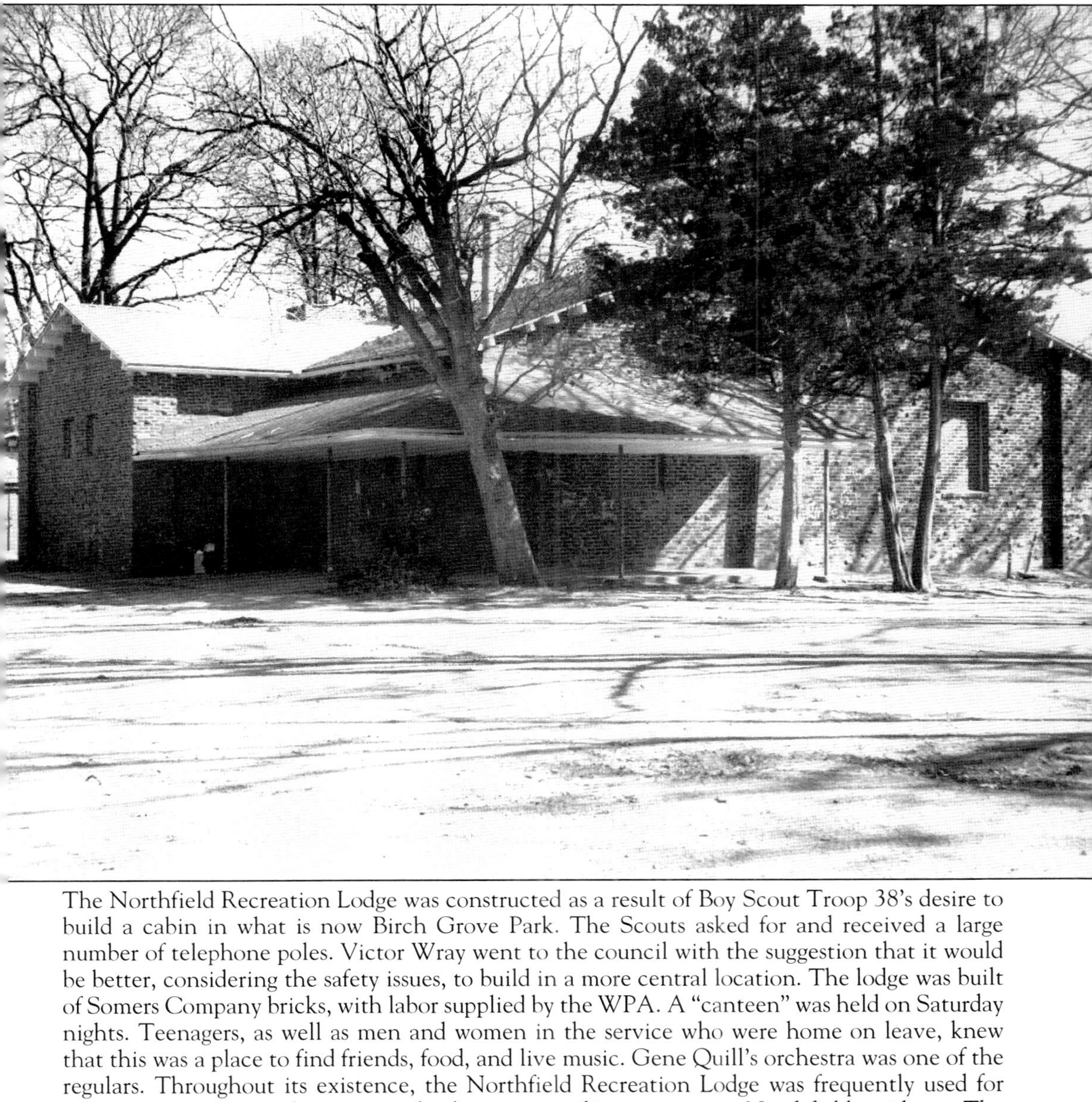

The Northfield Recreation Lodge was constructed as a result of Boy Scout Troop 38's desire to build a cabin in what is now Birch Grove Park. The Scouts asked for and received a large number of telephone poles. Victor Wray went to the council with the suggestion that it would be better, considering the safety issues, to build in a more central location. The lodge was built of Somers Company bricks, with labor supplied by the WPA. A "canteen" was held on Saturday nights. Teenagers, as well as men and women in the service who were home on leave, knew that this was a place to find friends, food, and live music. Gene Quill's orchestra was one of the regulars. Throughout its existence, the Northfield Recreation Lodge was frequently used for meetings, games, social events, and other events of importance to Northfield residents. The building was demolished when the new community school was built. (Information courtesy of Fran K. Nugent.)

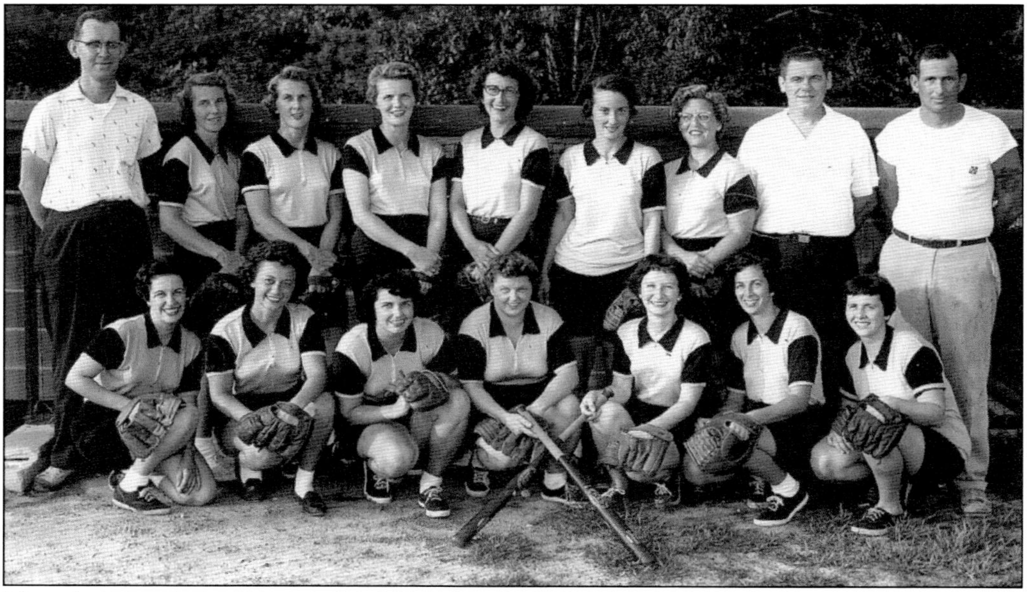

This photograph shows a Northfield Mothers League softball team. From left to right are the following: (first row) unidentified, Betty Fiori, Merion Perfect, Betty Stover, Jane Palmisano, Julia Greishaber, and Joan Stetzer; (second row) Bob Vogel (coach), Virginia Warner, Lois Daughenbaugh, Dorothy Horton, Ruth Vogel, Connie English, Esther Slota, Coach John Slota, and Bert Horton (coach).

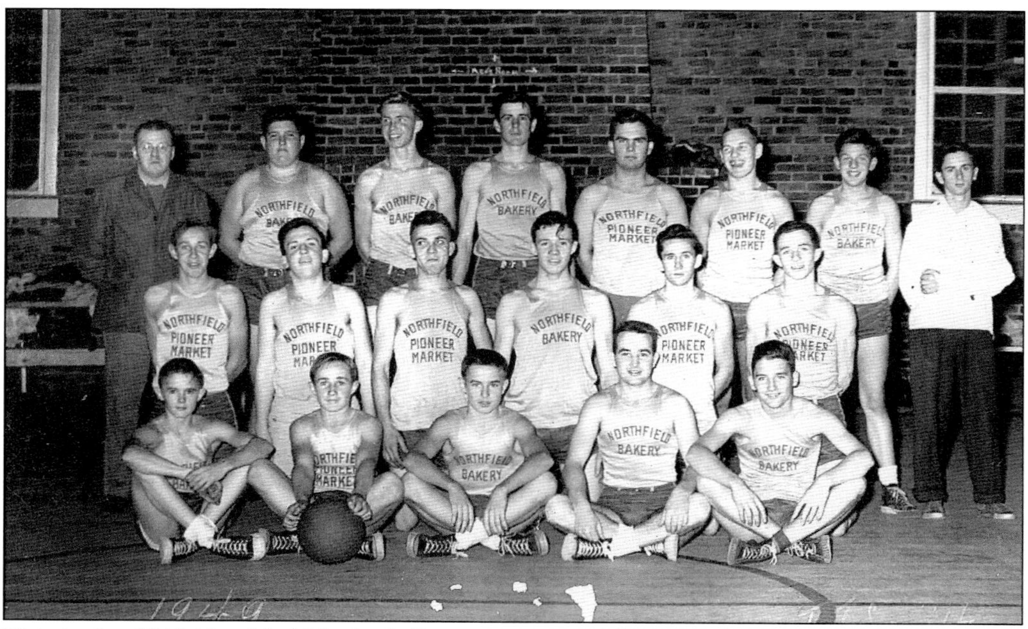

This is the 1949 Northfield basketball team sponsored by Northfield Bakery and Northfield Pioneer Market. From left to right are the following: (first row) Bill Horton, Walter Hampton, ? Blasko, Rich Cressy, and Ralph Doerr; (second row) Jerry Hampton, Ned Dixon, Dick Schultz, Alex Bryce, Les Carmen, and Tom Naughton; (third row) Quint Wyeth (coach), ? Teschler, Donald Perry, John Lupton, Bob Grist, ? Blasko, Ed DeMille, and Jimmie English.

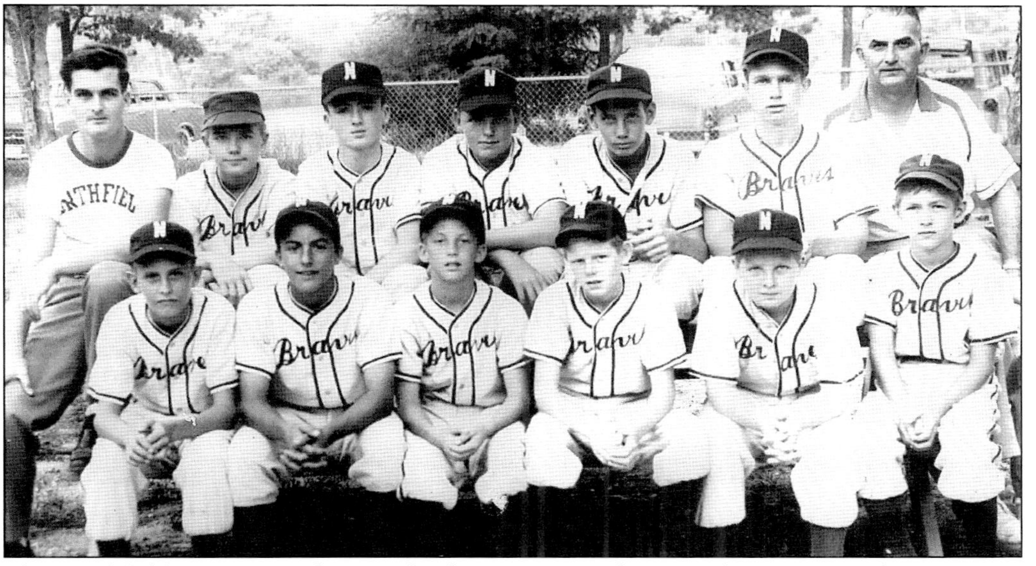

The Northfield Braves won the Mainland Pony League championship on September 12, 1961, when they defeated Ralston Drug of Linwood. From left to right are the following: (first row) Bill Westervelt, Charles Smith, Jeff Glenn, George Smith, and George Sutton; (second row) Rich Nichol (coach), Bill Shaw, Eddie Foy, Howard Thompson, Jack Ransom, Howie Layton, and H. W. Westervelt (assistant coach).

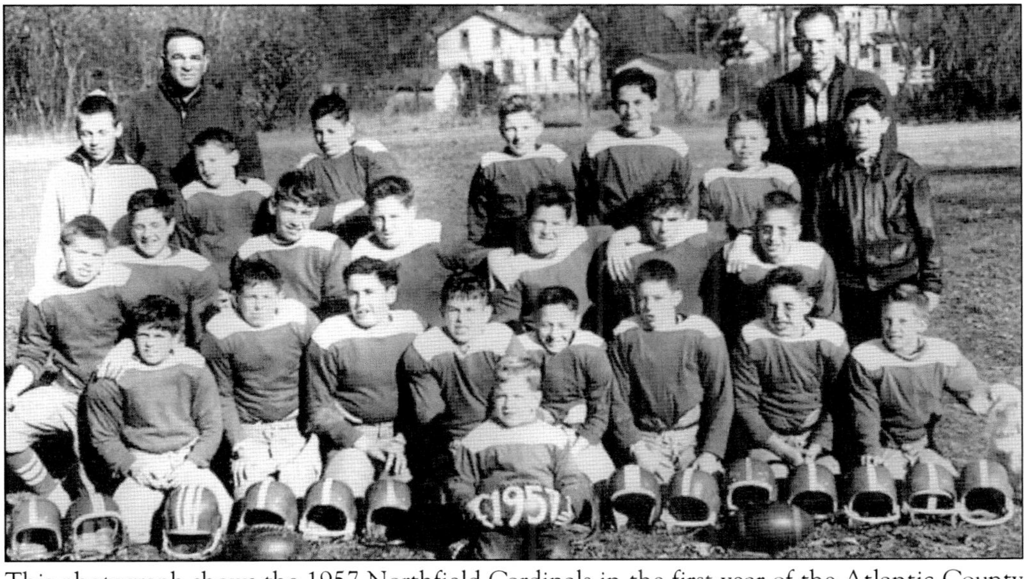

This photograph shows the 1957 Northfield Cardinals in the first year of the Atlantic County Football League. Dean Brewin, the mascot, is seen in front. Also shown are, from left to right, the following: (first row) Jim Care, Howard Martin, Bill Horton, Warren Slotterback, Pete Clark, Joe Brennan, Stan Carty, and Jeff Glenn; (second row) Dave Goodman, Joe Wilkinson, John Infield, John Landis, Butch Fried, Albert English, and Rick Wilson; (third row) Jeff St. John, Jim Fraser, Rick Dickerson, Bill Stevens, Clayton Thomas, Jim Daughenbaugh, and Greg Friedman (manager); (fourth row) Glen Brewin (coach and cofounder of the Atlantic County Junior Football League), and Bill Casto (assistant coach).

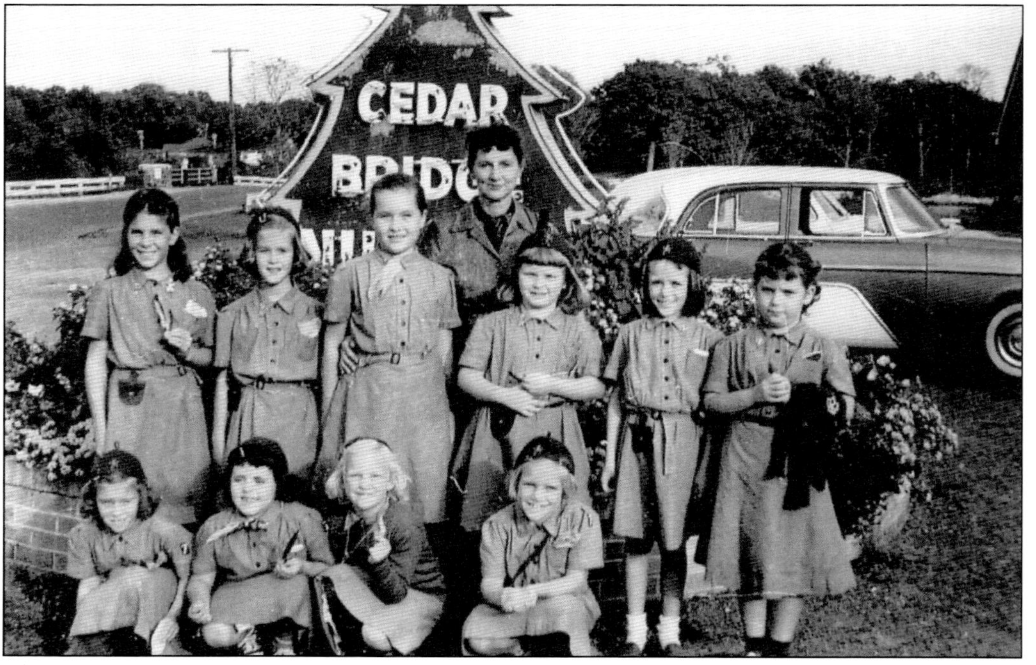

These Brownies were photographed in front of the sign for Cedar Bridge Nurseries & Greenhouses, which was located at Bargaintown and Zion Roads.

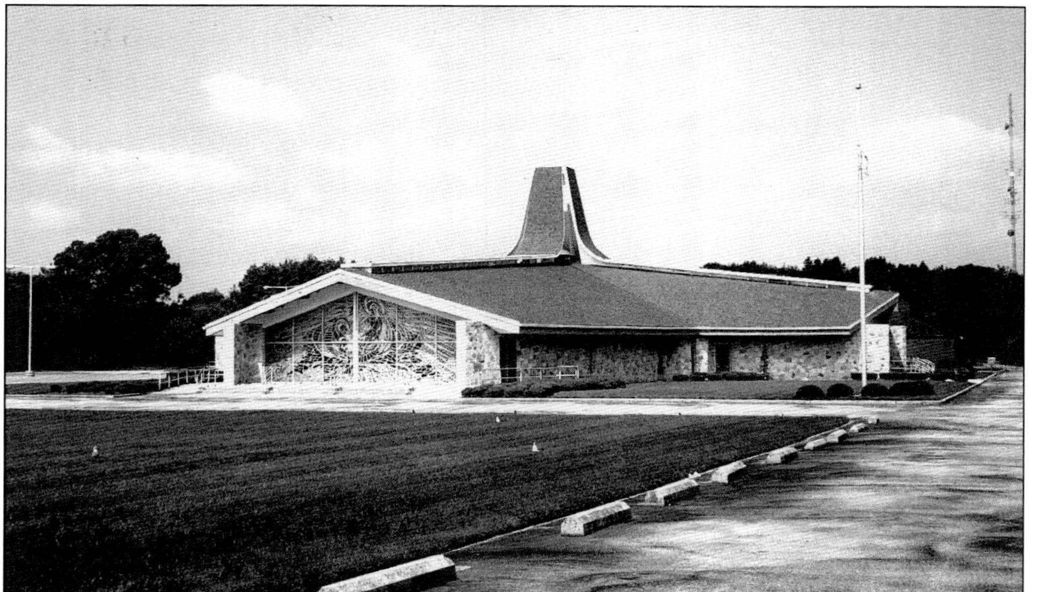

The Church of St. Bernadette, located at 1421 New Road, was dedicated in October 1969. The first Mass ever said in Northfield was offered at the home of William and Mary Nugent by Msgr. Charles C. Beausang, who was appointed as pastor on June 17, 1966. During construction of the new church buildings on New Road, services were held temporarily at the American Legion Hall, Harvey D. Johnson Post 295. The first Mass at the new church was said on Christmas 1968, although the building was not yet completed. This new parish had 900 families.

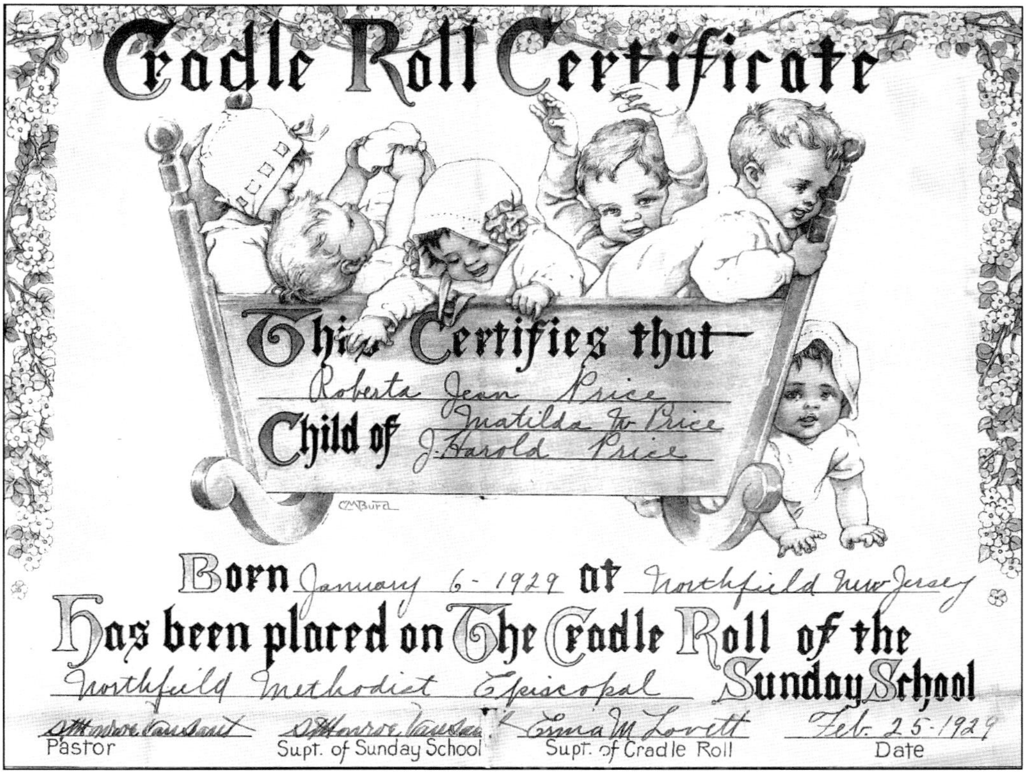
Cradle Roll Certificate

This Certifies that Roberta Jean Price

Child of Matilda W. Price J. Harold Price

Born January 6 - 1929 at Northfield New Jersey

Has been placed on The Cradle Roll of the Northfield Methodist Episcopal Sunday School

S. Monroe VanSant — Pastor | S. Monroe VanSant — Supt. of Sunday School | Erma M. Lovett — Supt. of Cradle Roll | Feb. 25-1929 — Date

This document certifies that Roberta Jean Price, daughter of Matilda and J. Harold Price, born on January 6, 1929, was placed on the Cradle Roll of the Northfield Methodist Episcopal Sunday School on February 25, 1929. S. Monroe VanSant was the pastor and superintendent of the Sunday school, and Erma M. Lovett was the superintendent of the Cradle Roll.

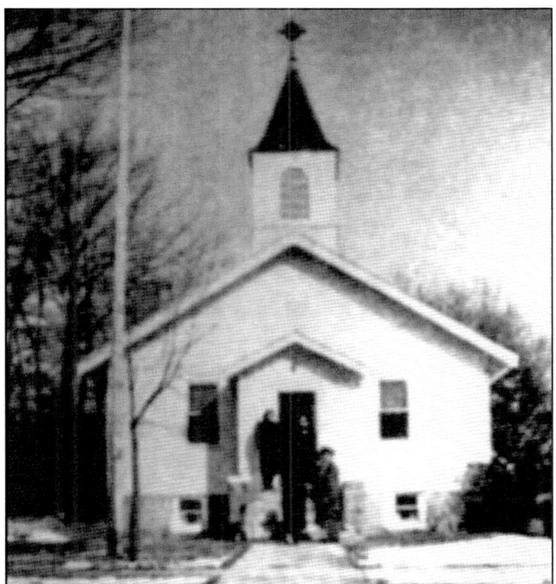

Northfield United Methodist Church was officially organized in 1923 with 36 charter members, under the direction of Dr. Corson. This photograph shows the original church building. The new church building was dedicated in 1956, and Fellowship Hall was added in 1969. In 1997, the congregation merged with the congregation of the Calvary United Methodist Church in Atlantic City to become Good Shepherd United Methodist Church, at the Northfield location.

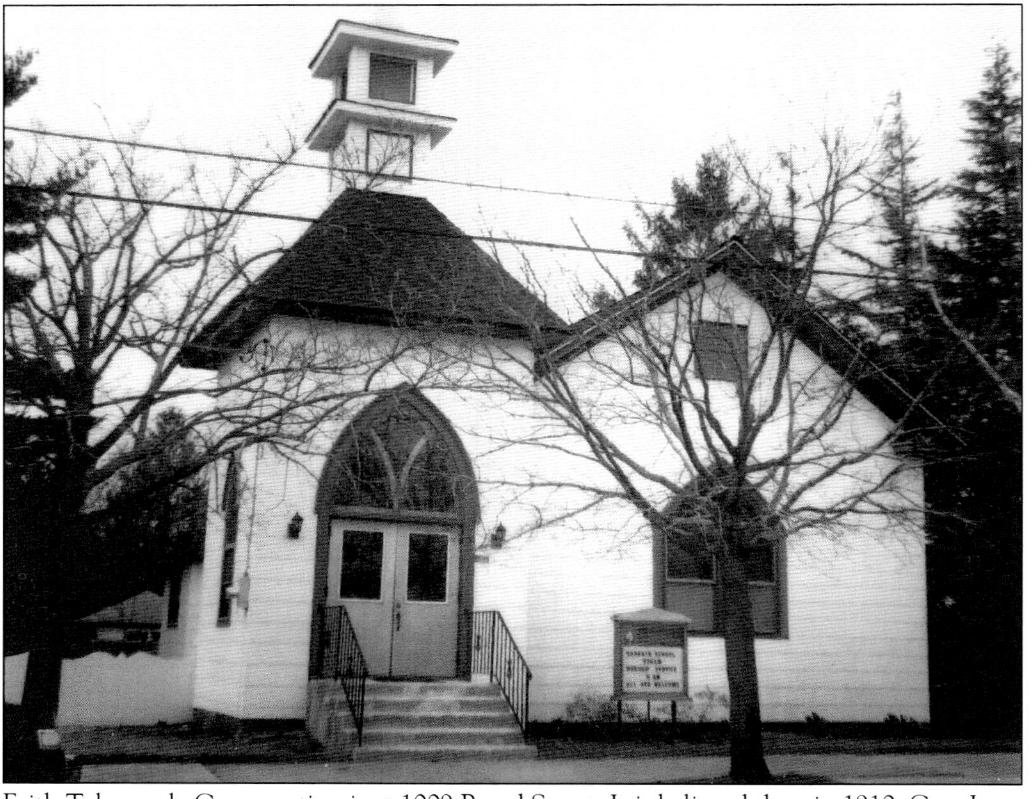

Faith Tabernacle Congregation is at 1009 Broad Street. It is believed that, in 1910, Cora Lane Ireland contacted the head office of this church and asked that they send a minister to Northfield. Initially, services were held in her home on Jackson Avenue, in the homes of other early members, and in a small shop on Roosevelt Avenue. In 1912, a small church on Broad Street was dedicated. This church was destroyed by fire in 1935, but another church was built on the same spot in 1936.

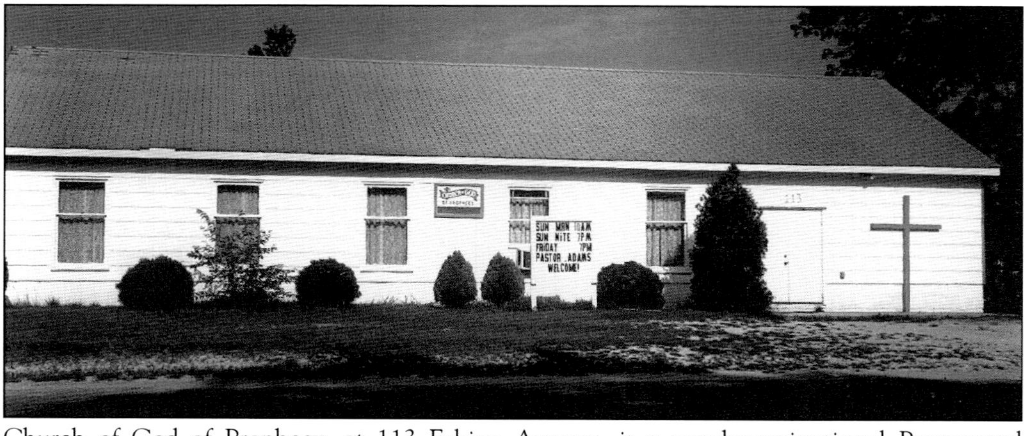

Church of God of Prophecy, at 113 Fabian Avenue, is a nondenominational Pentecostal Holiness church. The Reverend Walter Harvey was its first pastor, sent here *c.* 1950 by the church's headquarters to establish a congregation in this area. He constructed the original church building almost entirely by himself, with some assistance from members and friends.

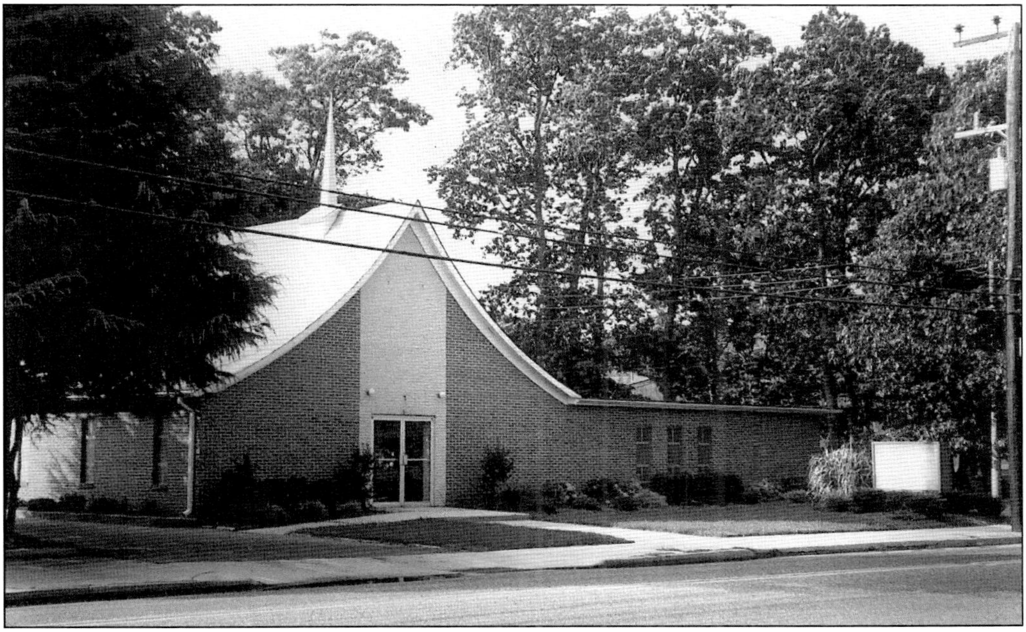

Church of Christ is at 2535 Shore Road, across from Revere Avenue, next to House & Garden department store. At first, from 1966 to 1972, the church was located in the former home of Dr. Richard Bew on Shore Road, known as the Bew Mansion. The home was then torn down to permit the construction of a new church building. While the new church was being built, services were held at the Northfield Recreation Lodge. The new church building was dedicated in late 1972.

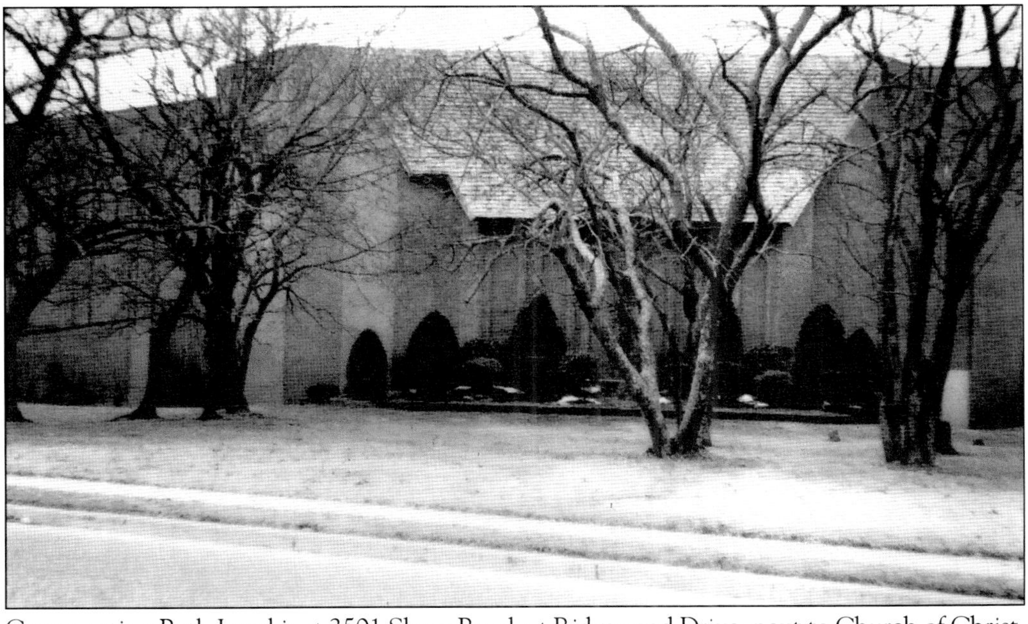

Congregation Beth Israel is at 2501 Shore Road, at Ridgewood Drive, next to Church of Christ. This Reform congregation moved to Northfield in 1987 from its previous location in Margate. The history of Beth Israel extends back to its 1889 origins in Atlantic City.

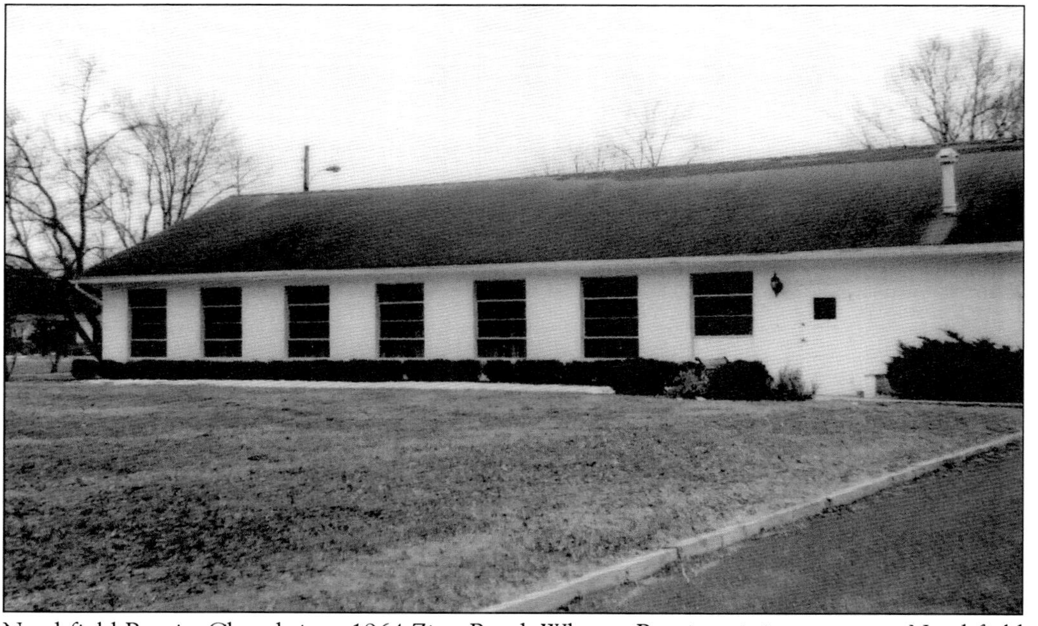

Northfield Baptist Church is at 1964 Zion Road. When a Baptist minister came to Northfield in 1963 to establish its first Baptist church, he held Bible classes at first in the Northfield Garden Club building in Birch Grove Park. Very soon, Sunday services were being held in a small building on Tilton Road. The growing congregation then decided to construct its own church building, which was dedicated in 1965.

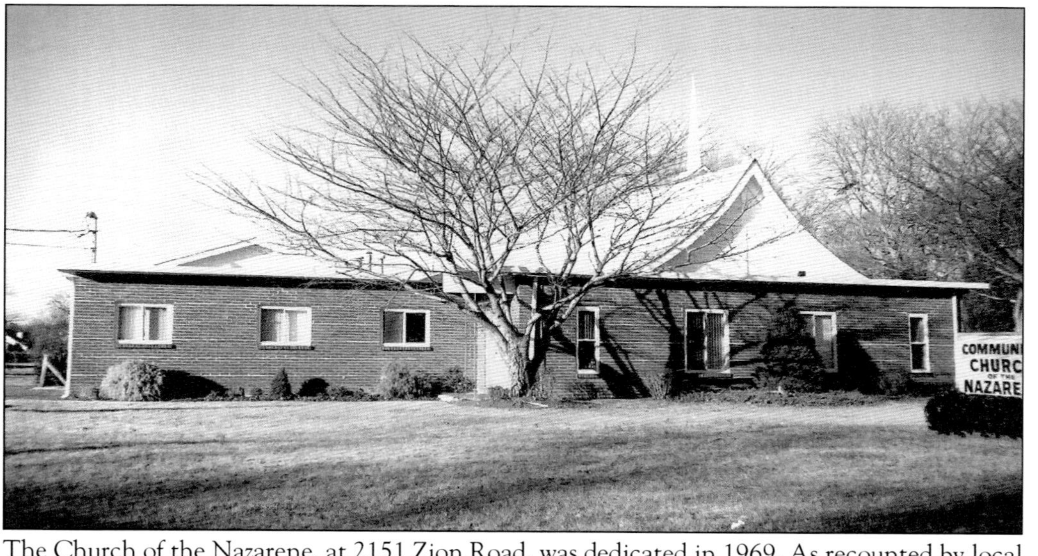

The Church of the Nazarene, at 2151 Zion Road, was dedicated in 1969. As recounted by local historian Josephine DiStefano Kapus in *The Churches of Northfield*, Joseph Causey, a barber, and his wife were asked to hold services on the Mainland. Organized in 1956, services at first were held at the Causeys' home and barbershop (which later became Max's Barber Shop). The former American grocery store, at Fuae and Jackson Avenues, was then purchased and converted into a church. During construction of the current church, the congregation met in the Northfield Recreation Lodge.

Nine
MEMORABLE MOMENTS

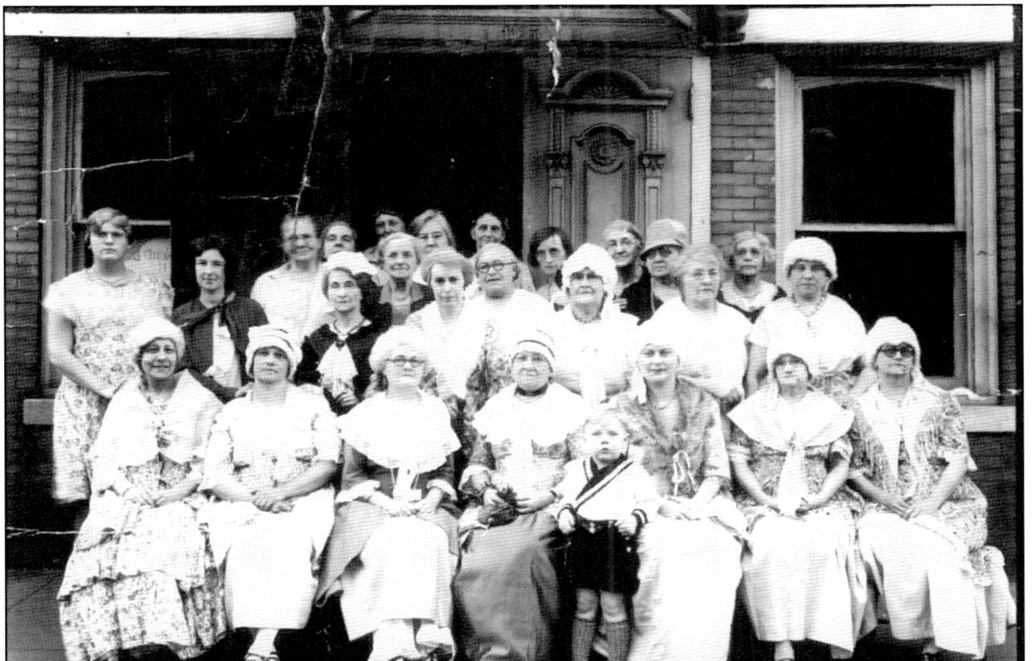

These local women, shown at a Martha Washington Tea, are, from left to right, as follows: (first row) Mrs. Brown, Estelle Ralston (Mrs. Darrington?), Mrs. Fehman, Mrs. A. L. Harris, Peg Merz-Benton Furrey, Carrie Stadler, and Mrs. Marg; (second row) unidentified, Ruth Fehman, Mrs. Henry Milk, Elsie Harris, Mrs. Thilda Gunn, unidentified, and Ethel Cunningham (Mrs. Harry Mason); (third row) Mrs. Walter Geary, Mrs. Craig, and Mrs. McCracken; (fourth row) Martha Bagley, Mrs. Harry Yates Sr., Mrs. Walkey, Mrs. Carey, and Mrs. George (Estelle Benson).

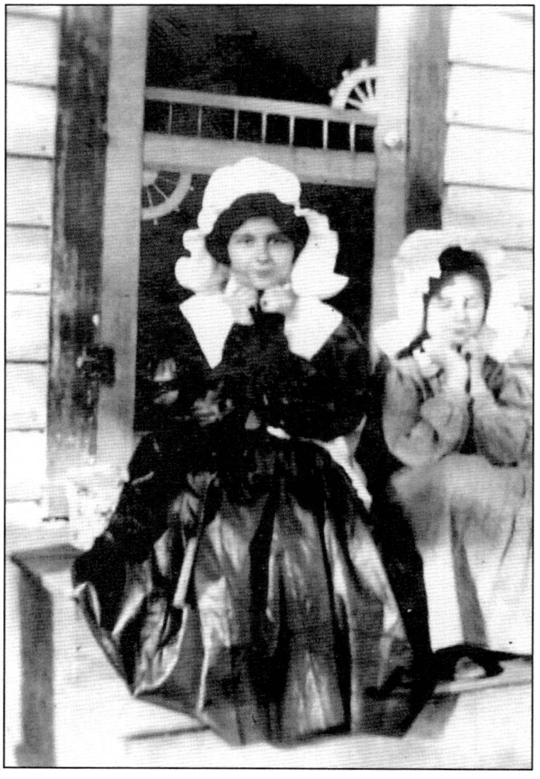

This photograph, labeled "The Sunbonnet Girls," was in an album donated to the museum by the estate of Sybilla Probst. Sybilla Probst, who grew up in Northfield and was the first curator of the Northfield Museum, served as Northfield's unofficial historian.

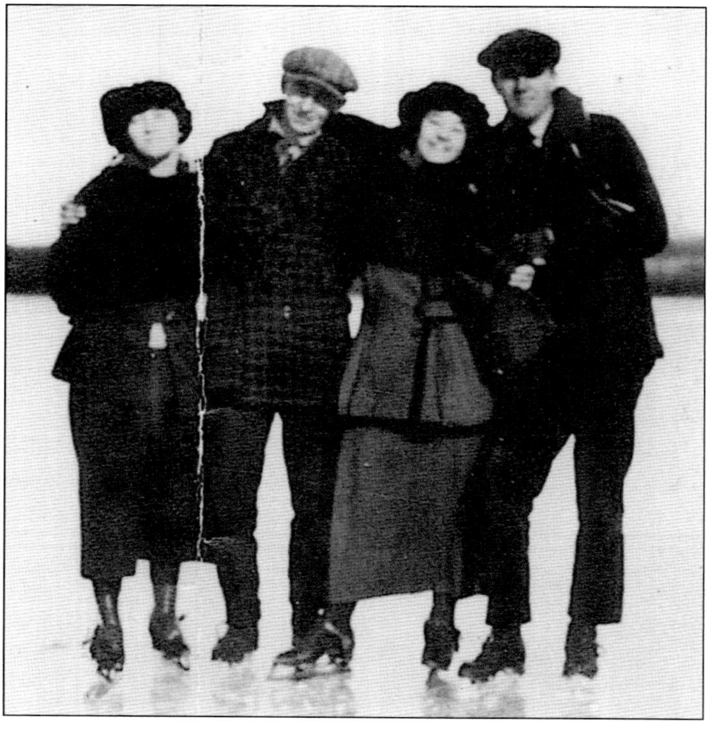

Two couples, Alex and Julia (Angerman) Forshaw (left) and Len and Gertrude (Angerman) Robinson, skate on Bargaintown Mill Pond *c.* 1920. This was a favorite skating place for many years. It was well lit at night during the winter, and hot dogs and other food items were available at the southwest end of the pond, just past the bridge. In the summer it was a delightful place to swim, with cool, clear water. Youngsters rode their bicycles from Northfield to get there. (Courtesy of L. W. Forshaw.)

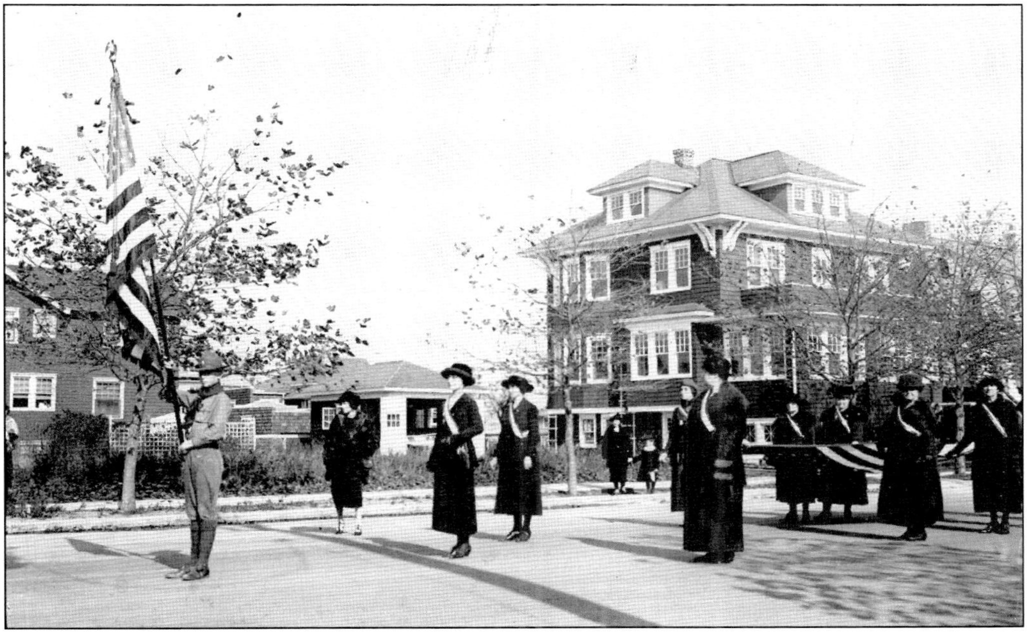

The women of the American Legion Auxiliary line up for a parade in 1921.

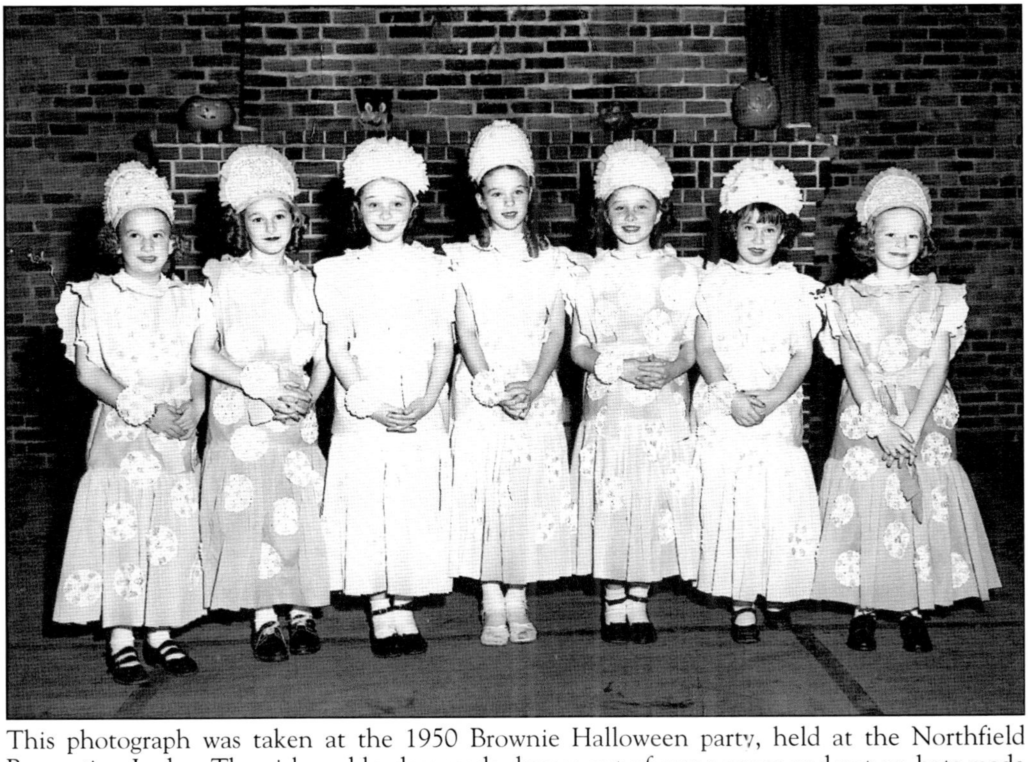

This photograph was taken at the 1950 Brownie Halloween party, held at the Northfield Recreation Lodge. The girls and leaders made dresses out of crepe paper and put on hats made of doilies. From left to right are Betty Lovett, Carolyn Petrie, Marian Horner, Jackie O'Donnell, Penny Horner, Nancy Dedera, and Patty Gillen.

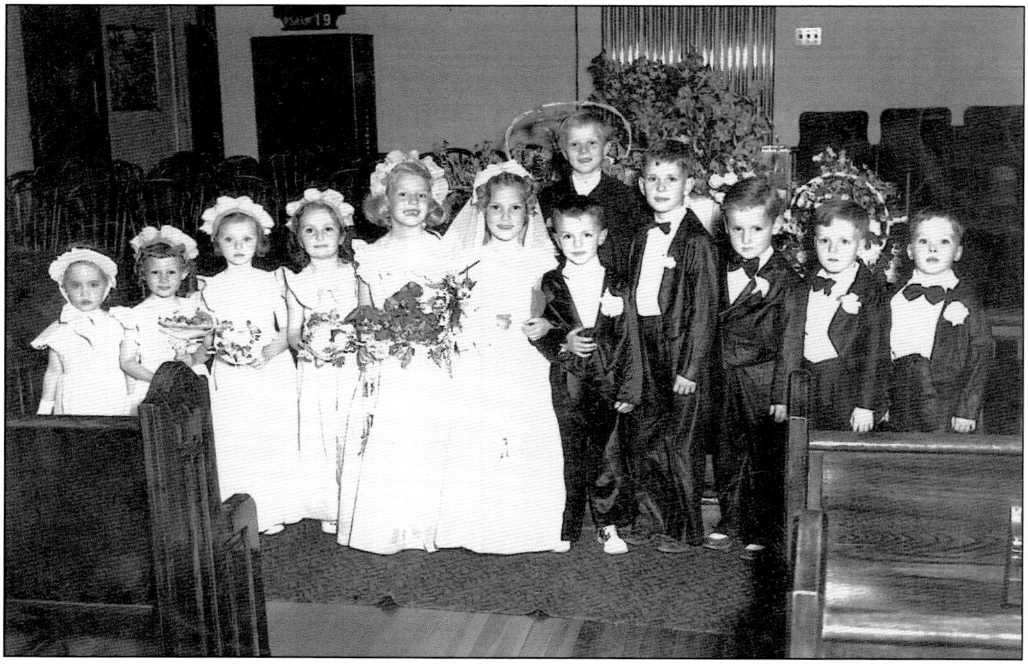

These photographs are of Tom Thumb weddings presented by the Northfield Methodist Church. These mock weddings, performed with young children, were often used as fund-raisers. In the 1939 wedding ceremony below are, from left to right, the following: (first row) Kenny or Donald Adams; (second row) two unidentified persons, ? Mullis, unidentified, Peggy Walton, Al Miller, three unidentified persons, ? Adams, Mary Lou Ake, Pauline Fuss, Richard Monroe, and Frank Wolcott; (third row) Billy Ake, Jim Stapleton, Katherine Davis, Eddie DeMille, unidentified, John Fuss, Barbara Burkhart, Lois DeMille, Barbara Siefried, and four unidentified persons; (fourth row) Ruth Naylor and four unidentified persons; (fifth row) Nancy Snyder (Truex), Maude Craig (Venute), and Willa Lovett (Cwik).

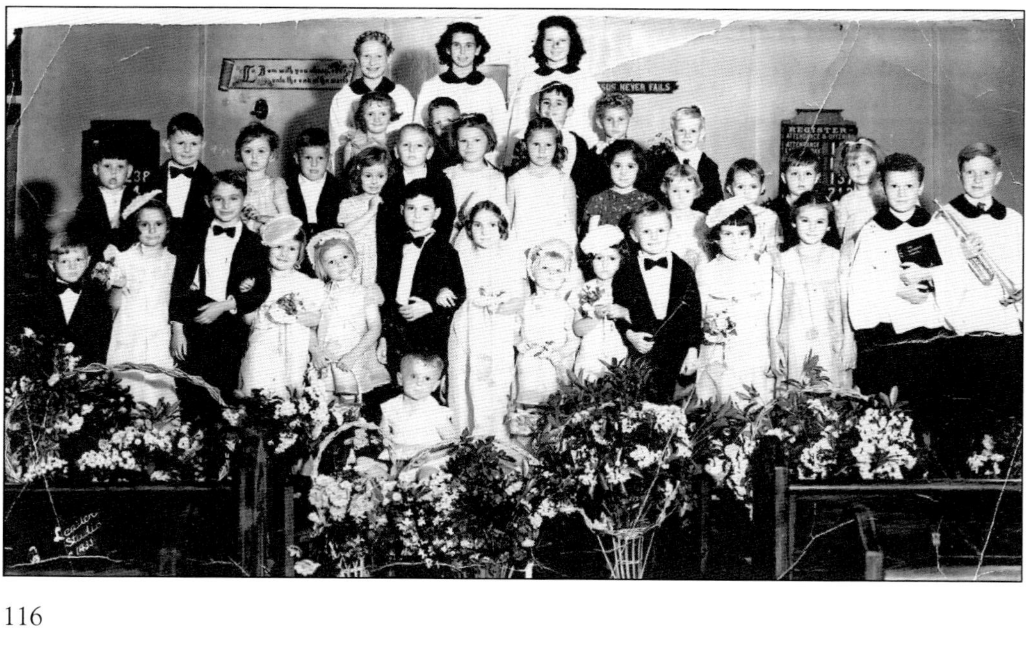

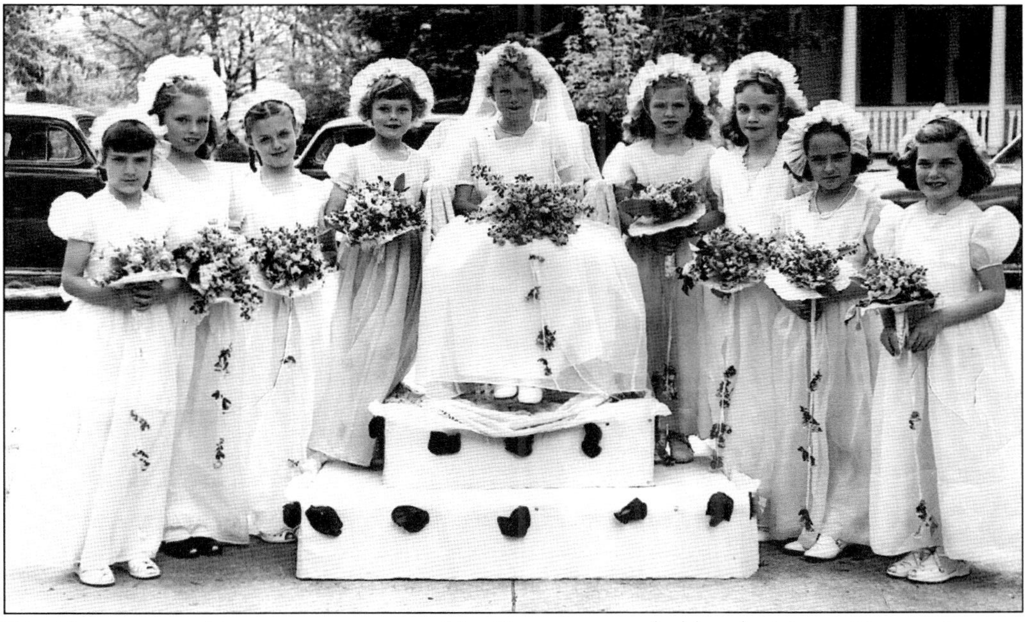

The May queen and her court appear at a May Day ceremony held at the Mount Vernon Avenue School. From left to right are Jane Collins, unidentified, Mary Ann Collins. Judy Downs, May Queen Lois Rockelman, Ruth Garrison, unidentified, Dottie English, and Mary Peter.

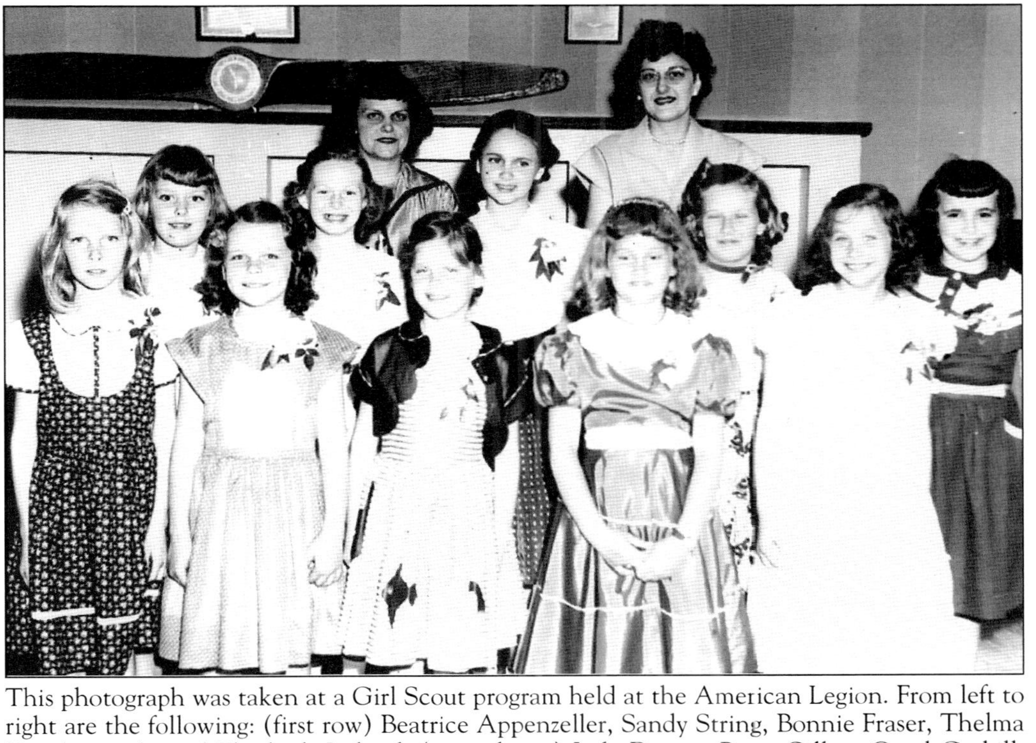

This photograph was taken at a Girl Scout program held at the American Legion. From left to right are the following: (first row) Beatrice Appenzeller, Sandy String, Bonnie Fraser, Thelma Hundertmark, and Elizabeth Ireland; (second row) Judy Downs, Patty Gillen, Carol Gaskill, Catherine Long, and Betsy Slaybaugh; (third row) Mrs. String and Mrs. Petrie (leaders).

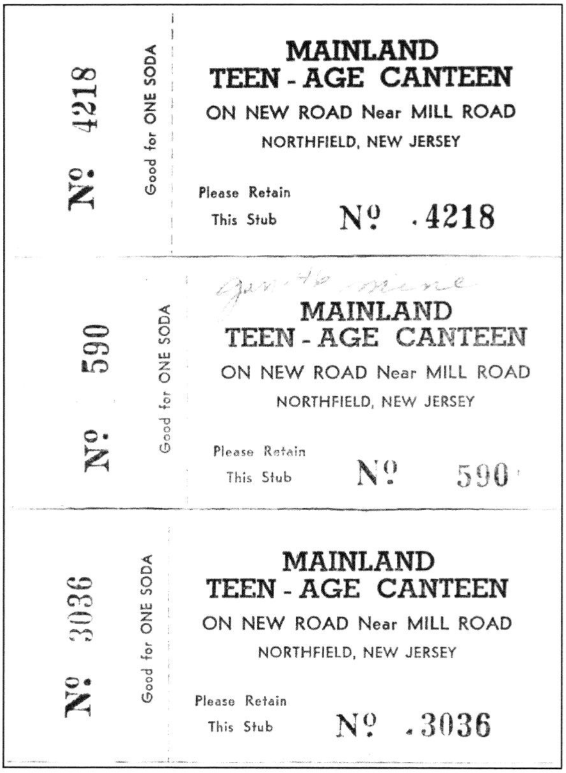

Canteen dances, which were popular in Northfield in the 1940s and 1950s, were held at the Northfield Recreation Lodge. The lodge, located behind Mill Road School, was built as a WPA project in the 1930s. Among the dancers in this photograph are Joyce Hampton, Rose Marie Bob, Norman Hilton, Shirley Paulin, Nancy Snyder, Marie Ordille, Bob Grubb, June Adams, Doris Bruckler, William Dixon, Ruth Reinholz, Mary Lou Ober, Bernadette Shutz, Peggy Morton, Doug "Cookie" Irwin, Millie Gommel, Katie McGrath, and Debbie Millar.

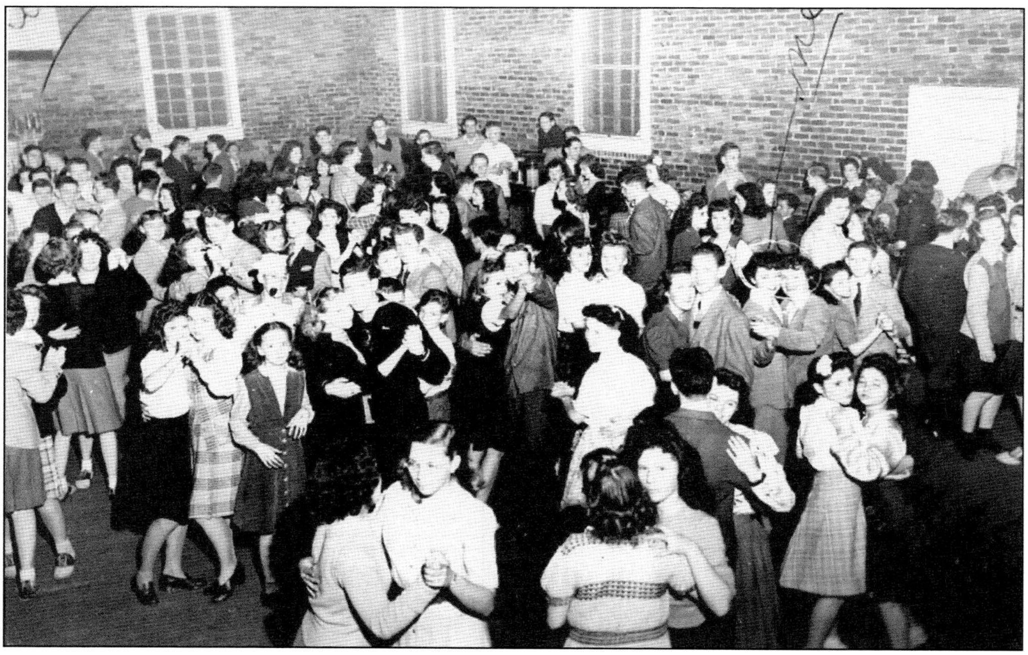

For the election held on May 16, 1944, these Republican candidates for county committee and city council promised lower taxes.

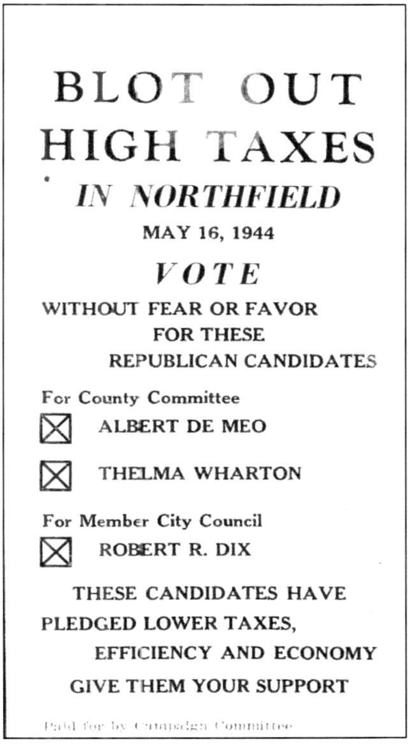

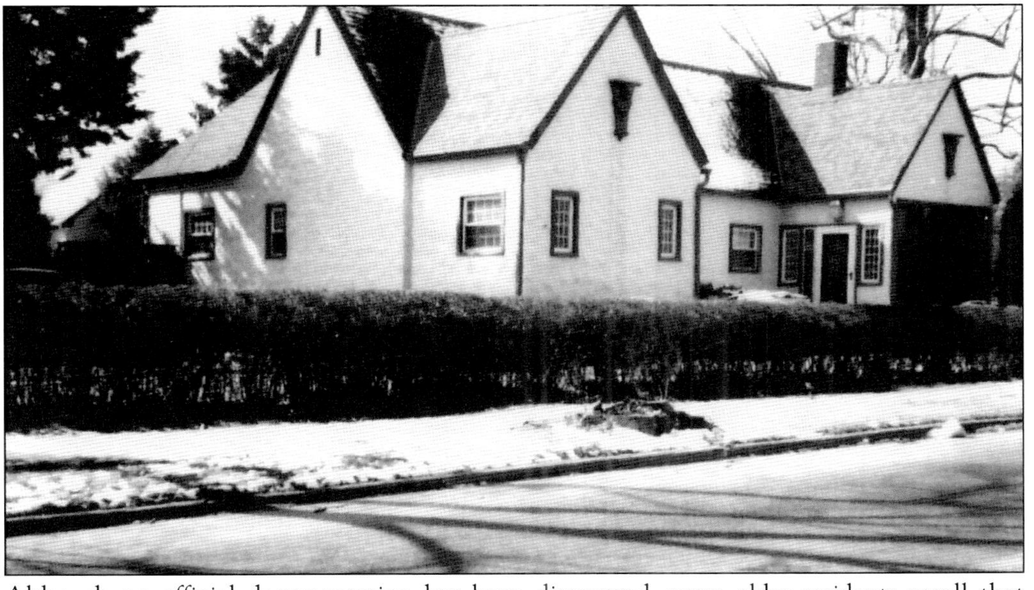

Although no official documentation has been discovered, some older residents recall that Evelyn Nesbit lived in this Northfield house for a time during the mid-1920s. Evelyn Nesbit was at the center of a notorious murder that happened on June 25, 1906, in New York City. Her insanely jealous millionaire husband, Harry Thaw, shot and killed the well-known architect Stanford White, with whom Nesbit had had an affair. A 1955 movie about the scandal, *The Girl in the Red Velvet Swing*, starred Joan Collins.

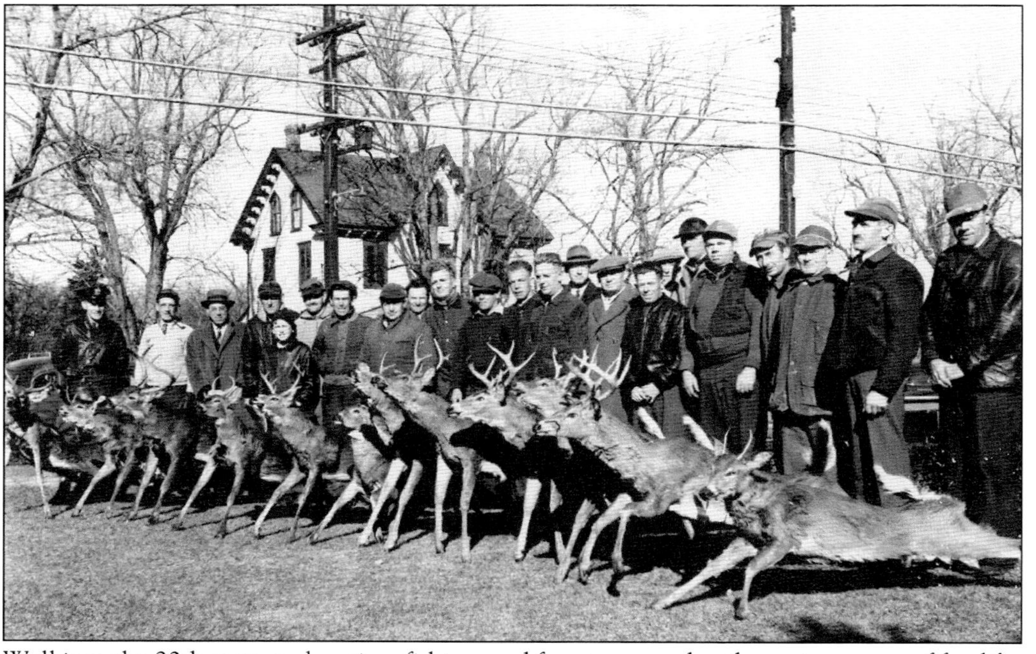

Well into the 20th century, hunting, fishing, and farming served as the main sources of food for many residents. This 1941 photograph shows successful Northfield hunters with their deer. A newspaper article dated 1933 gave notice that "gunning for game on the east side of New Road will not be permitted this season."

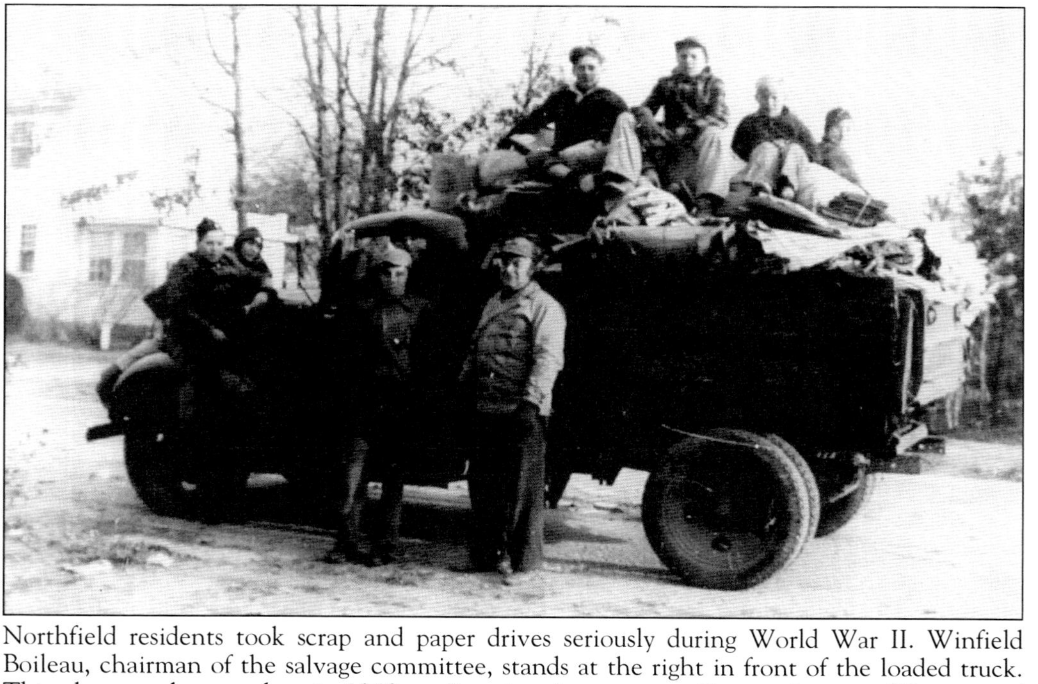

Northfield residents took scrap and paper drives seriously during World War II. Winfield Boileau, chairman of the salvage committee, stands at the right in front of the loaded truck. This photograph was taken in 1940 on Banning Avenue near Burton Avenue. (Courtesy of Mary Boileau, daughter-in-law of Winfield Boileau Sr.)

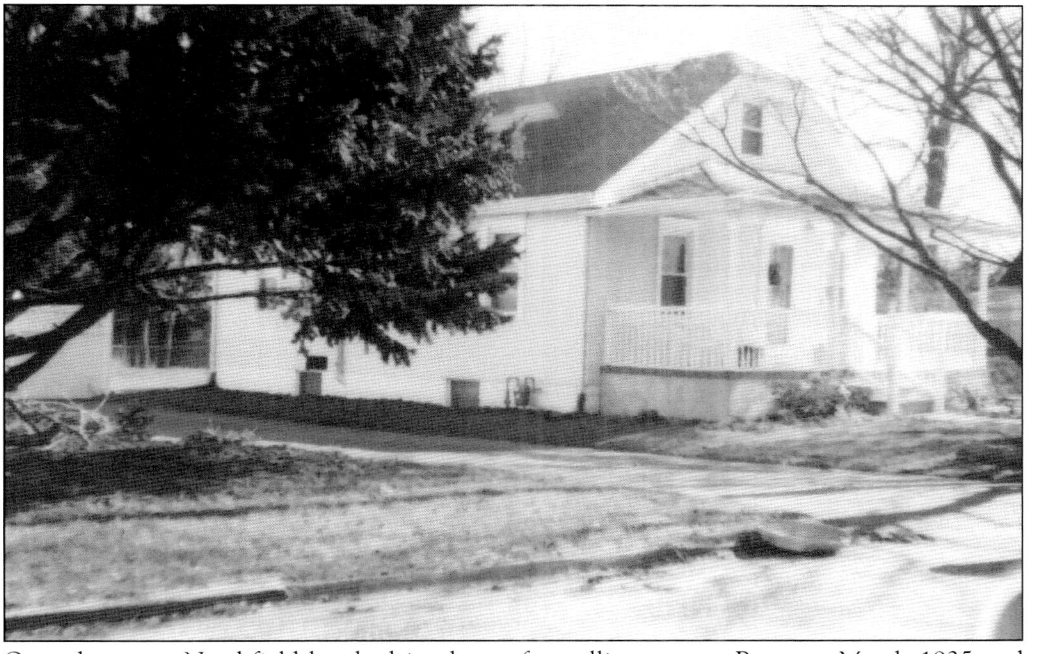

Over the years, Northfield has had its share of appalling events. Between March 1935 and March 1938, more than 13 fires in Northfield and the surrounding area were believed to have been works of arson. In 1938, a former member of the Northfield Volunteer Fire Company was arrested and admitted to setting six of these fires. In 1998, the current homeowner of this house, while doing renovations, discovered skeletal remains of two people who had been killed many years before by a previous homeowner.

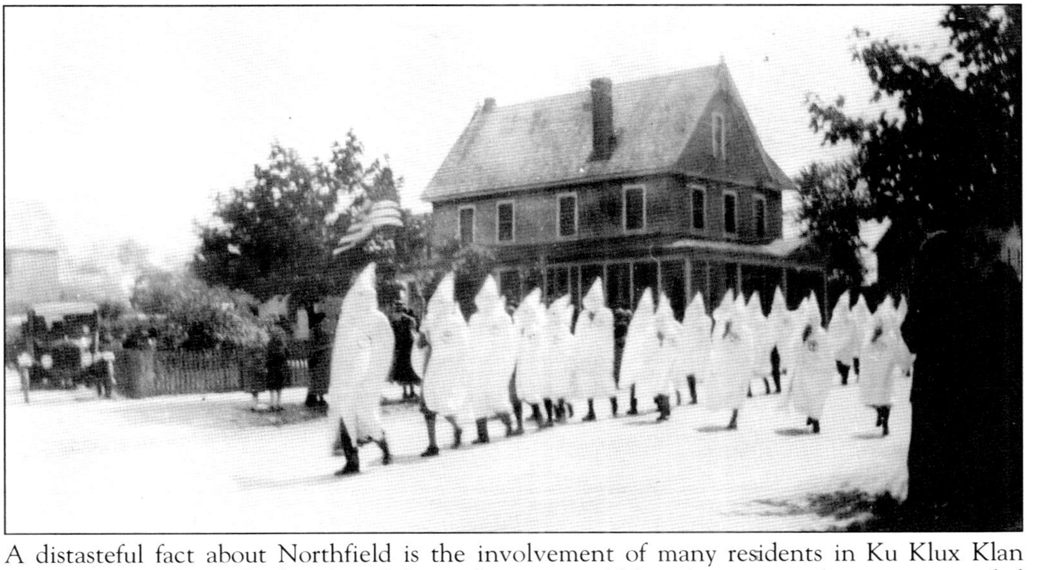

A distasteful fact about Northfield is the involvement of many residents in Ku Klux Klan activities into the early decades of the 20th century. Although some residents just attended Klan social activities, others participated in ugly activities such as cross burnings. One *c.* 1937 newspaper article reported that a large cross was burned at a house on Banning Avenue. This photograph shows Ku Klux Klan members participating in a local parade in the 1920s.

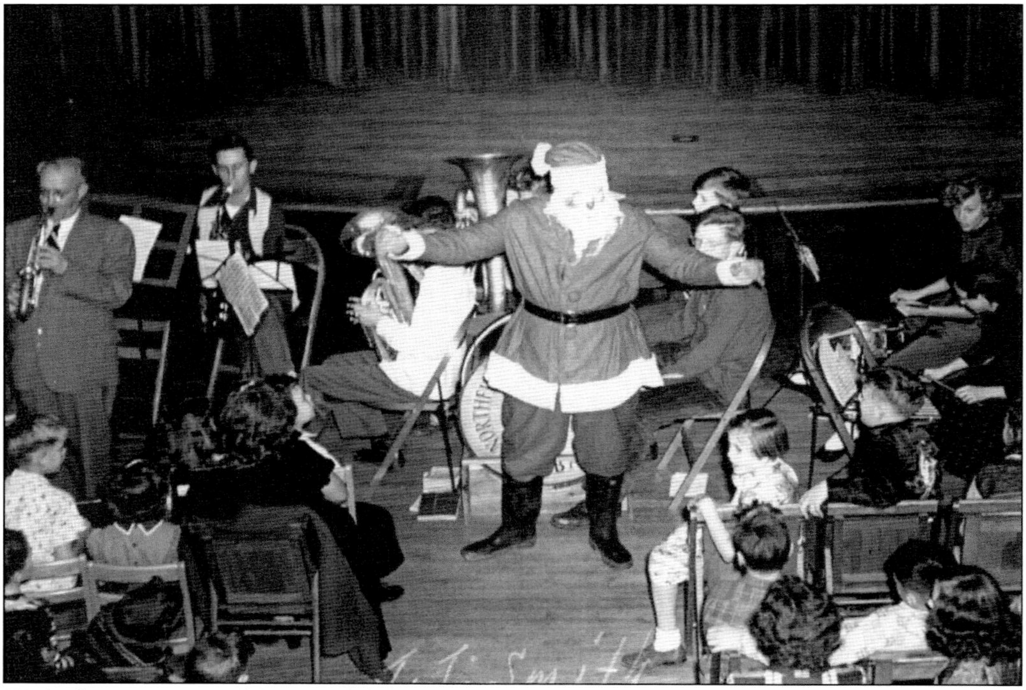

With the assistance of the Northfield Fire Department, Santa Claus made special trips to Mill Road School. In 1951, he distributed 750 stockings.

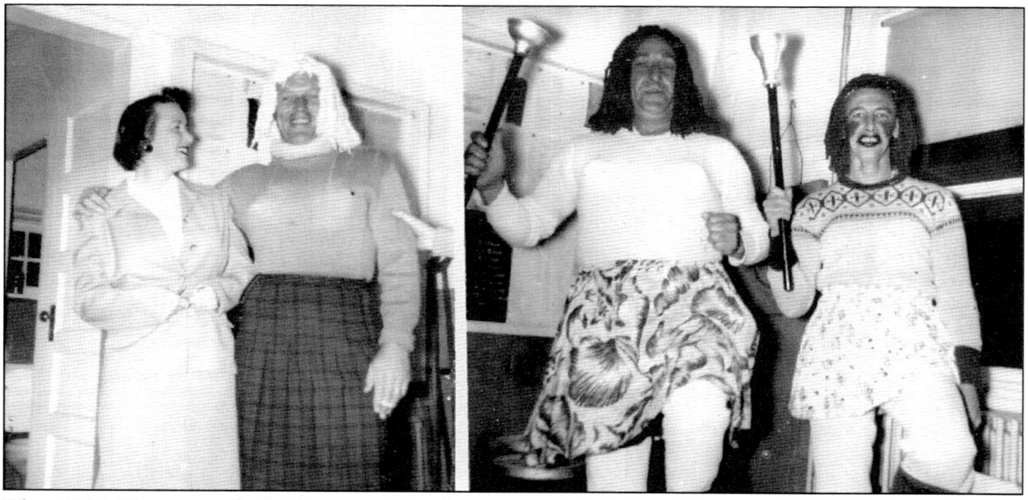

The 1954 Pleasantville Halloween Parade was one of the fire department's more lighthearted events. At post-parade festivities, a well-dressed Bill Casto (second from the left), the city clerk, socializes, and Tom Fuss (third from the left) and Bill Block entertain.

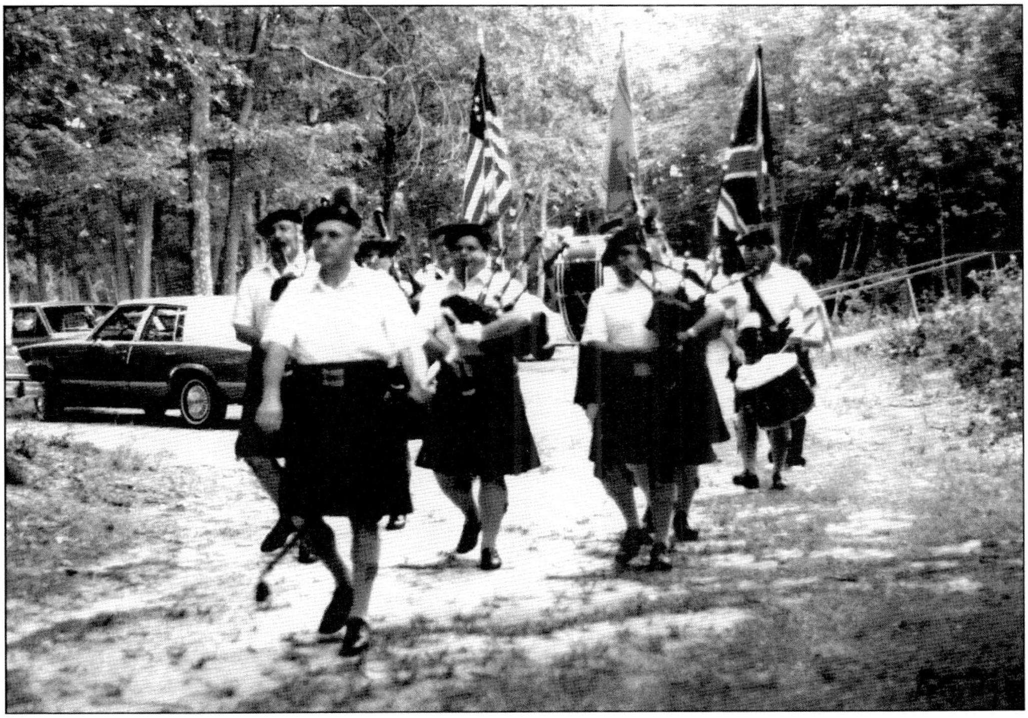

Bagpipers are seen heading toward the bandstand in Birch Grove Park to give a concert in 1984. On the right is the bridge that connected the baseball fields to the original bandstand drainage ditch area. It was later torn down because of safety concerns over its deteriorating condition.

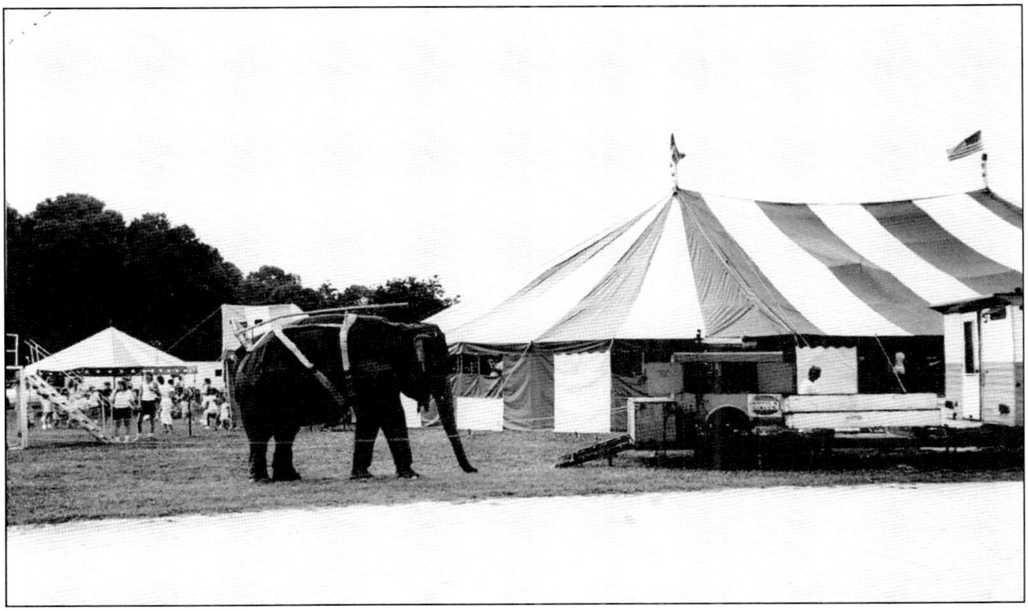

This elephants was a featured performer at one of the circuses and carnivals held at Birch Grove Park during the 1970s and 1980s.

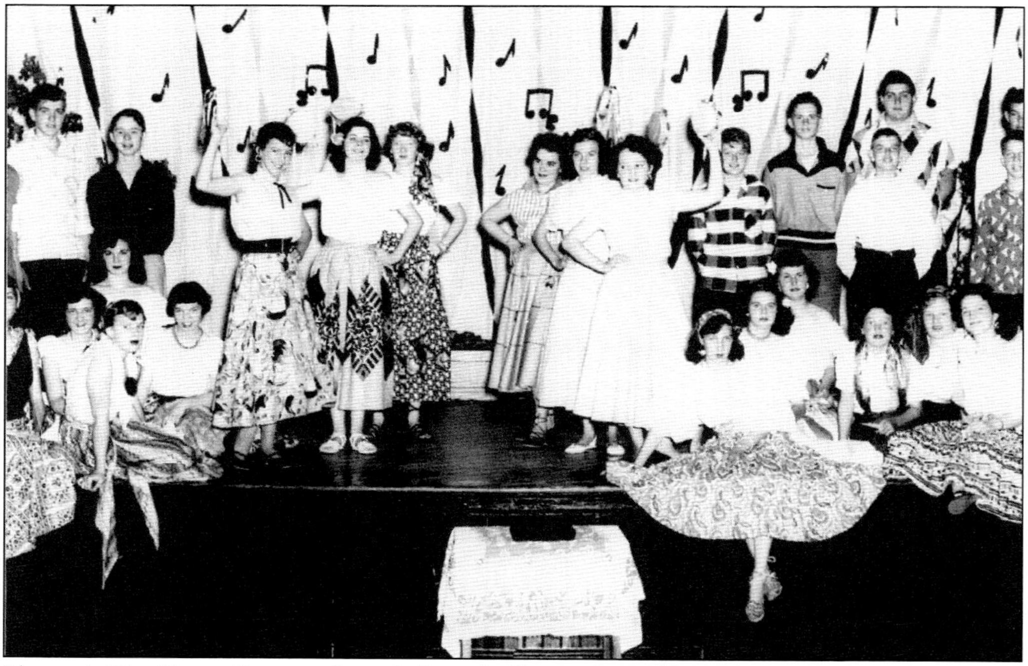

Shown is *The Gypsy Camp* at the eighth-grade Spring Assembly Program on June 5, 1953. The members of the Mill Road Class of 1953 are Charles Adams, William Ake, Muriel Booth, Sidney Bringhurst, Grace Burrell, Elizabeth Carty, Joanne Ceresna, Howard Clark, Donald Cook, Mary Cook, Virginia Cook, Marilyn Davis, Helen Dix, Ruth Ernst, Alberta Fries, Helen Garr, Martin Higbee, William Higgins, Nancy Hudson, Viola Ireland, Penelope Irelan, Eleanor Kamp, Ronald Lupton, Nancy Maholland, Lee Miller, Robert Miller, Beverly Norton, Nancy Pfirman, Gerald Thomas, Doris Vernon, April Wallen, and David Weber.

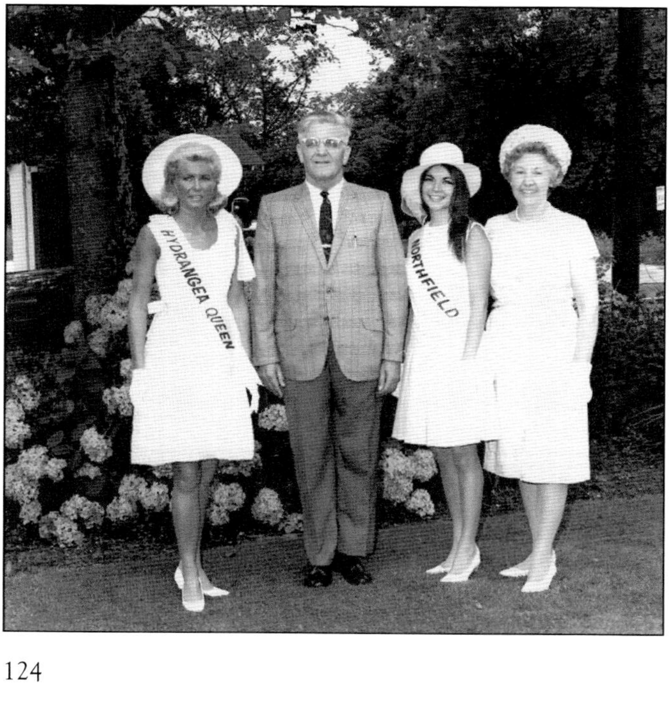

The Hydrangea queen and Miss Northfield pose with Mayor and Mrs. Otto Bruyns in 1968.

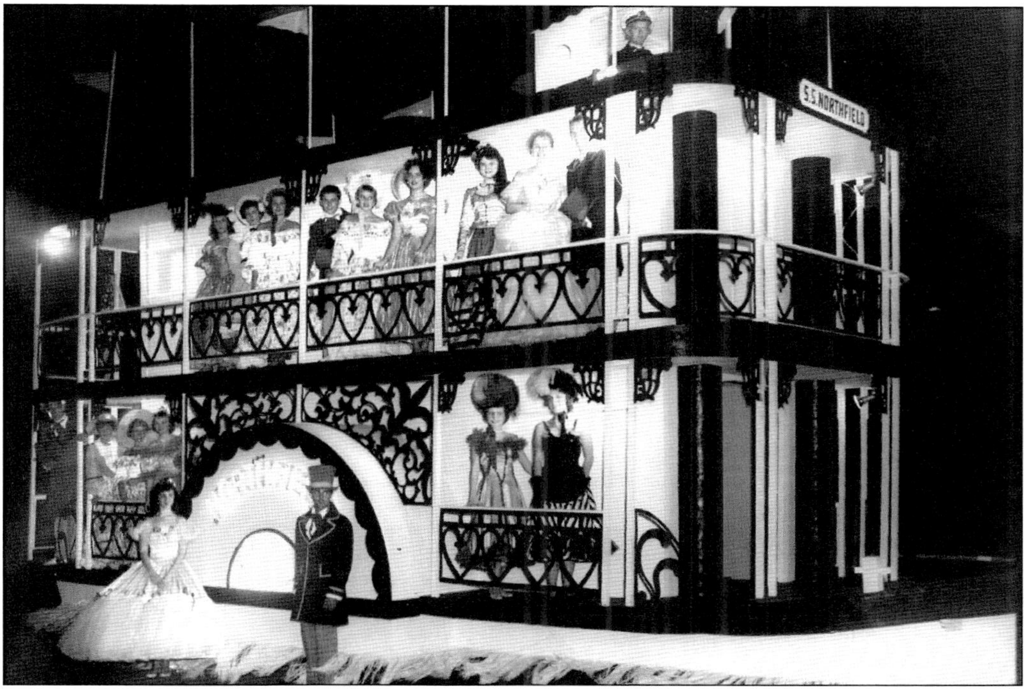

In September 1954, Northfield's float in the Miss America Parade won the Grand Sweepstakes Award. The above photograph was taken by Dan Cox, noted local professional photographer. Standing on the boardwalk are Betty Carty and Victor "Tuso" Plumbc. Also pictured are, from left to right, the following: (first row) Rich Kelleher, Pat Allen, Polly Clark, unidentified, Jeanine Woods, and Helen Garr; (second row) Jean Dixon, Helen Dix, Doris Vernon, Bill Schoenleber, Penny Ireland, Betty Lou Risley, Cass ?, April Wallen, and Ken Adams. On top of the float is Captain Bud Keller. The lower photograph shows Northfield residents on the M. E. Blatt float.

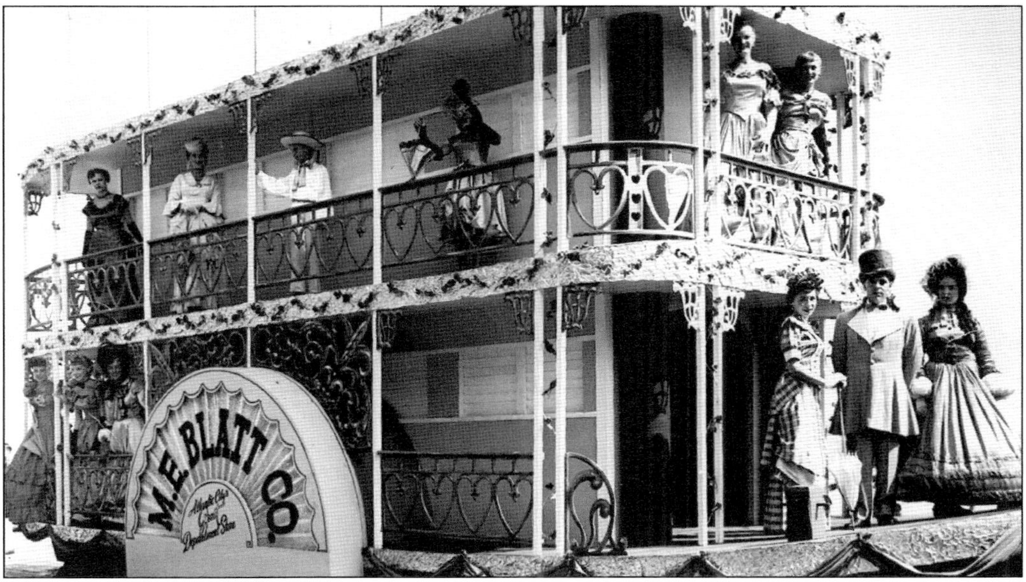

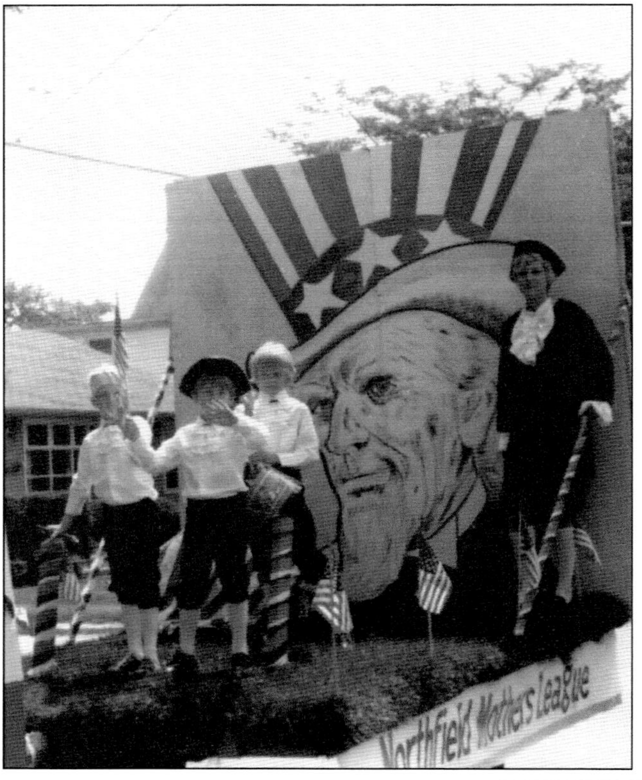

The Northfield Mothers League sponsored the Uncle Sam float in the July 4, 1976, parade, with the theme Spirit of '76. Seen as Betsy Ross is Terry Ellenberg; as the town crier, Janice Corneal; and as fife-and-drummer boys in the foreground, from left to right, Henry Martinelli, Billy McConville, and Steve Sundra.

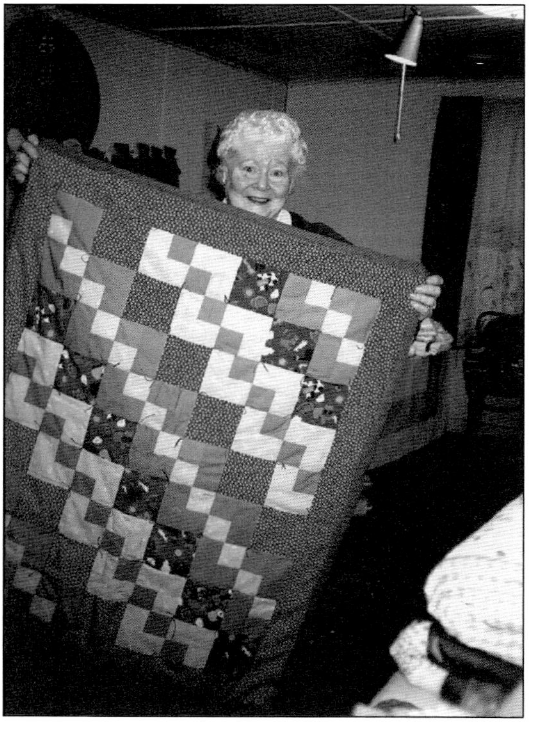

Marie Warren, president of the Northfield branch of NGA Inc. (formerly the Needlework Guild of America), holds up a handmade quilt and shows the branch's holiday donations. Every Christmas, members of this group donate two articles of each item (one to wear and one to wash). The NGA is a volunteer nonprofit organization whose mission is to improve the quality of life for needy individuals through gifts of new clothes, linens, and toiletries. The Northfield branch celebrated its 70th anniversary in 2000.

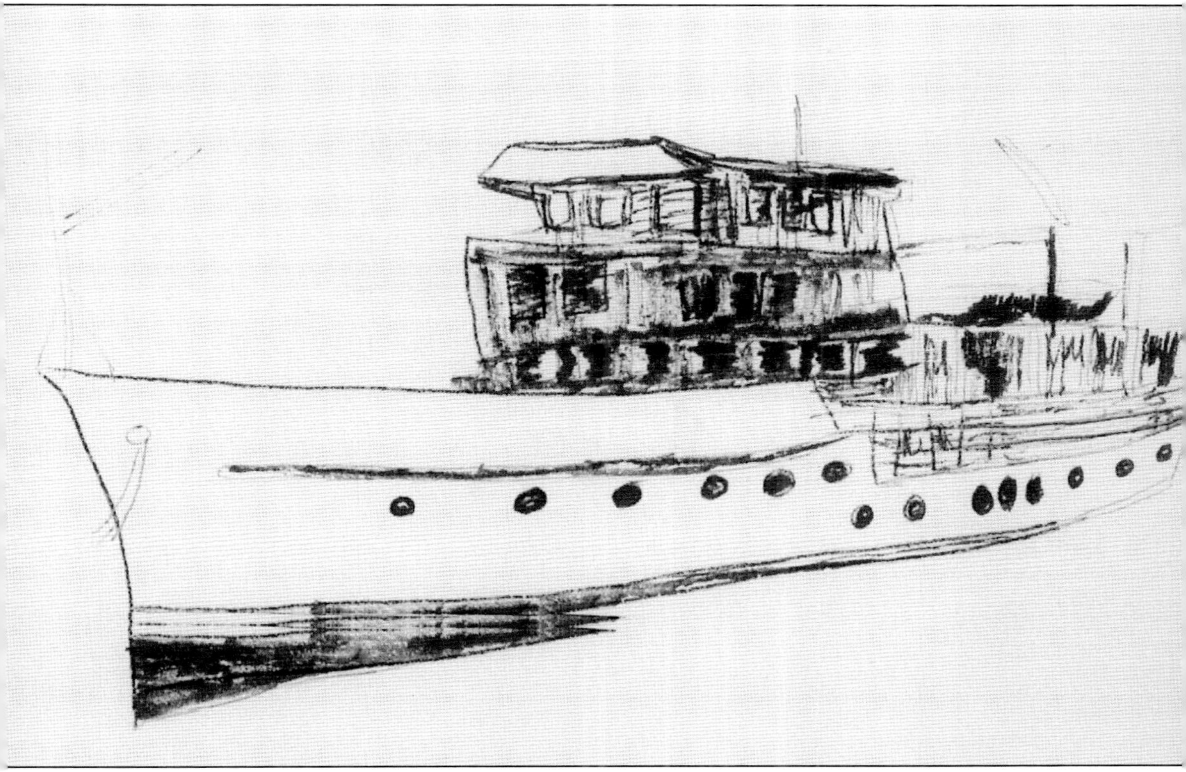

Just after 10:00 p.m. on June 11, 1925, the yacht *Crystal*, on a moonlit pleasure cruise chartered by the Social Independence Club of Northfield, exploded and burned eight miles off Atlantic City. Everyone on board was hurled into the ocean: five died and more than a dozen were injured. There was initial uncertainty about how many people were on the cruise: although 28 tickets, at $1 each, had been sold, it was believed that 24 passengers were aboard. The dead were identified as Warren Dilks of Linwood, John Hannum of Northfield, Deborah Knight and Martha Weist of Pleasantville, and Joseph Wilson of Northfield. Paul Ake and Estelle Banning, of Northfield, and Mildred Mack, of Pleasantville, were hospitalized with severe burns. Survivors identified as Northfield residents were Ralph English, Burt Lehman, Harry Lehman, Barbara Lehman, Jack Lindner, Curtis Lyle, William Krum, Richard McGlynn, Gertrude Mullet, Richard Myers, Lawrence Price, and Mary Toner. Other survivors were Anna Betterton and Catherine Arnold of Pleasantville and Capt. William Young and Vernon Tobey (seaman) of Atlantic City.

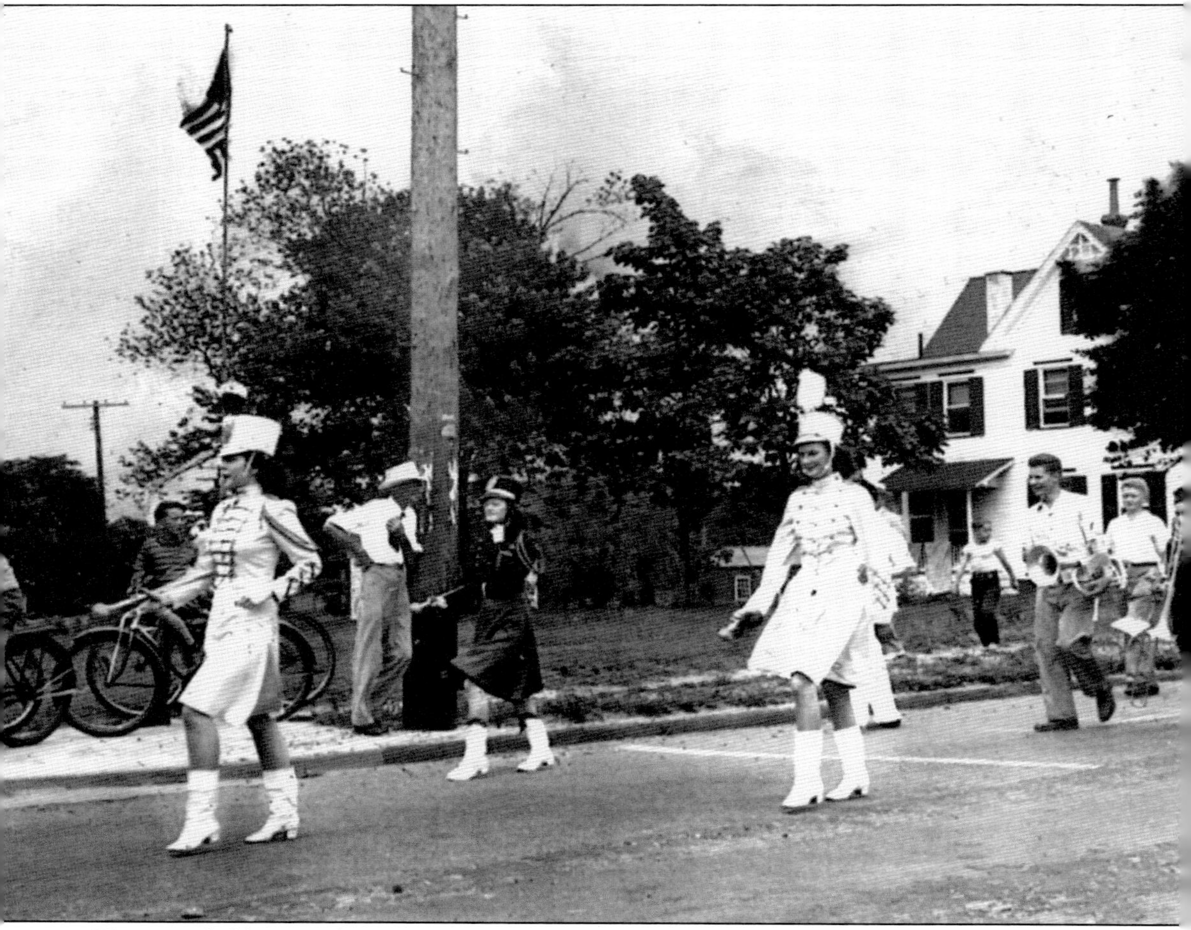

This is probably part of a Memorial Day Parade heading down Shore Road sometime during the 1940s. The marchers are, from left to right, Florence Probst, unidentified, Elaine Dericott, unidentified, Grant Kresge, Dwight Kresge, and unidentified.